The Ideology of Motherhood

Studies in Society

A series edited by Ronald Wild which sets out to cover the major topics in Australasian sociology. The books will not be 'readers', but original works—some will cover new ground and present original research, some will provide an overview and synthesis of source materials and existing research. All will be important reading for students of sociology.

Titles include:

Studies in Society: 21
Series editor: Ronald Wild

The Ideology of Motherhood

A Study of Sydney Suburban Mothers

BETSY WEARING

School of Social Work, University
of New South Wales

Sydney
George Allen & Unwin
London   Boston

First published in 1984 by
George Allen & Unwin Australia Pty Ltd
8 Napier Street, North Sydney, NSW 2060 Australia

George Allen & Unwin (Publishers) Ltd
Park Lane, Hemel Hempstead, Herts HP2 4TE,
England

Allen & Unwin Inc.
9 Winchester Terrace, Winchester, Mass 01890 USA

National Library of Australia
Cataloguing-in-Publication entry

Wearing, Betsy
  The Ideology of Motherhood
  Bibliography.
  Includes index.
  ISBN 0 86861 135 2
  ISBN 0 86861 143 3 (pb)
  1. Mothers—Social aspects—Australia.
  I. Title.
306.8'743'0994

Library of Congress Catalog Card Number: 83-071799

Set in 10/11 pt Times and printed by
Richard Clay (S.E. Asia) Pte Ltd, Singapore.

Contents

Tables

Figure   Appendix 3

Preface

I am indebted to many people for the help I have received in the preparation and execution of the research presented in this book.

The research was undertaken as part of my doctoral thesis. My supervisors Bettina Cass, Colin Bell and Lois Bryson encouraged me and extended my thinking in various ways suggesting relevant literature, asking searching questions and giving creative and constructive criticism. I would like to thank each of them for their individual contribution to my work. The faults in the finished product are mine, not theirs.

Thanks are also due to the members of the post-graduate seminars in the School of Sociology, University of New South Wales, 1977–79, who listened patiently and made helpful suggestions some of which have been incorporated in the work.

The research was made possible by a Commonwealth post-graduate research award administered by the University of New South Wales. I am grateful for the granting of this award.

Without the help and support of community workers in the Mt Druitt, Hornsby and Kuring-gai areas the task of obtaining research sample would have been extremely difficult. I would like to thank them for giving generously of their time and interest and for personally recommending me to potential respondents.

To the mothers themselves who also gave generously of their time, their interest and their own experiences, I am especially grateful.

My husband Leslie and my parents-in-law, Millie and Reg Wearing have given me both moral and practical support in very many ways during the period of planning, executing and writing up the research. Their help has been invaluable and I thank them.

Finally, I would like to thank my children, Jenny, Stephen, Susan, Michael and Chrissy for giving me my own cumulative and continuing 'lived experience' of motherhood.

1 Motherhood today

There is an ideal stemming from the tradition of our society that mothers of young children should care for those children themselves and not work; and that, if necessary, the Government should provide incentives to enable such mothers to care for their children themselves. (Report of the Commonwealth Inter-Departmental Committee Child Care, July 1970)

The word mother conjures up in our minds thoughts of propagation of life, self-sacrificing efforts spent in the interests of husband and children, long hours of work spent each day for which there is no monetary gain, examples of gentleness and advice freely and generously given.

In primitive and other societies womanhood is seen as being inferior to manhood and a woman tags along behind her husband and to her is given the menial tasks to perform. The Bible sanctifies womanhood by making women equal to men as the Bible says that God created both male and female . . . Because of this Mother in our way of life has great value and respect placed on her . . .

The idea of one day to honour her whose memory is so worthwhile recalling is to make some emphasis so that we will not forget her for the whole year.

The first "mother" according to Ancient Greek legends was the beautiful Artemus, better known as Diana by the Ancient Romans. She was the goddess of the morn, forests, animals and of women in childbirth and was known as the First Mother of the Gods. Artemus was the patroness of all women . . . At her temple on the Avantine Hill in Rome she was honoured as the Virgin Goddess.

(*Hornsby District Times*, Wednesday,
3 May 1978, printed as a prelude
to a special Mother's Day Supplement)

Both official and lay notions of motherhood in Australian society stress the responsibility of the biological mother for the rearing of her own children, especially during their early years. The above quotations demonstrate the mixture of myth and legend, sacred and secular ideas, sentiment and idealism, values of fertility and chastity and the moral worth of motherhood which provides a mystifying

9

aura surrounding motherhood in our society and which obscures the reality of the lived experience of mothering for women in an advanced, industrial, capitalist, society such as Australia in the 1970s. The purpose of this particular piece of research is to demystify motherhood by investigating exactly what mothers of young children believe about mothering, how they experience it, what effects the ideology has on their lives, what interests are being served by it and what challenges are being made to such an ideology in today's changing society.

My previous research conducted during 1975 and 1976 into the loss by women of the motherhood role in the middle-life period (Wearing, 1976)[1], alerted me to the fact that the problems of women at this stage of their lives have their origins in an earlier stage of the family life-cycle. My initial interest therefore in the lives of mothers with pre-school children, was centred on the effect that having children has on the roles a woman performs both within and without her family, thus shifting the emphasis of much previous research both psychological and sociological from the effect of the mother on the development of the child, to the effect of the child on the mother. However, my own previous research had also left me dissatisfied with structural-functional explanations of motherhood and women's positions in society (e.g., Parsons, 1955). The wealth of feminist literature which flowed from the women's movement of the late 1970s in the United Kingdom, the United States of America and in Australia, suggested that a power-conflict approach to women's position in society would provide a more useful framework for analysis of motherhood (e.g., Mitchell, 1971; Rowbotham, 1973: Firestone, 1970; Millet, 1971; Morgan, 1975; Curthoys, 1976). Few empirical studies concerned with the family have been carried out using such a framework, especially in Australia. It was anticipated therefore that the present research might contribute to a greater understanding of one aspect of family living by adopting a theoretical framework which challenges rather than accepts women's 'natural' propensity for rearing the children she bears and for performing associated household tasks.

In addition it was conjectured that investigation of the ideology of motherhood would reveal strongly-held beliefs which legitimate the subordinate, economically dependent and relatively powerless position of many women in contemporary society due to their responsibility for child care. In lengthy discussions of the economic functionalism of female responsibility for domestic labour (e.g., Gardiner, 1976; Harrison, 1973; Seccombe, 1974; Smith, 1978; Kuhn, 1978; Rushton, 1980), the domestic labour debate has overlooked the legitimation of women's responsibility for this labour through the motherhood ideology. Responsibility for parenting which devolves almost exclusively to mothers is seen in the present research to be a major factor in the subordination and oppression of women.

Ann Oakley's work (1947b: Chapters 7 and 8) has shown just how mythical are assumptions of a 'maternal instinct' and women's 'natural' propensity for child care. This research goes further by empirically investigating the use of such assumptions as legitimation for the division of labour along sex-lines within the family, with consequent restrictions on the ability of women to compete equally with men in the market and political arenas of society. Thus it is claimed that the ideology of motherhood obfuscates and perpetuates gender relationships of power which favour males in our society.

However, in our society certain changes are taking place which may alter the position of women, making them less dependent on men economically and politically. Women are bearing fewer children, achieving higher levels of education and remaining in, or returning to the work-force after the birth of children[2], so that some women may be in a position to challenge the existing ideology. In times of change when a subordinate group is in a position to challenge the status quo in favour of its own interests, utopian ideas are propagated which arise out of the existing order but transcend it and point the way to a new order which is as yet unrealisable (Mannheim, 1936:813−17). The present research examines utopian ideas of motherhood which are challenging the existing ideology and the changes which are indicated by these utopias. The theoretical framework of the research therefore attempts to account for changes in family life in a way that previous family theories have not.

In a recent discussion of 'New Directions in Family Research and Theory' D. H. J. Morgan (1980:4, 16) suggests that the institution of the family is in a unique position between the 'macro' and 'micro' levels of sociological enquiry, being 'both an institution in society, shaped by and partially shaping other institutions in that society and also a focus of some of the most intense and long lasting personal dependencies and positive and negative feelings'. For this reason he sees the family as an area in which future sociological investigation could profitably integrate the two levels of analysis and at the same time 'mediate between another popular sociological opposition, that between structure and process'.

This study attempts to place one aspect of intra-familial living, that is, women's subjective experiences of mothering and beliefs about motherhood and the division of labour in the home within macro-social structural explanations of gender relationships based on economic and institutional power in an advanced industrial capitalist society. It also attempts to integrate structure and process by incorporating Mannheim's concept of utopia to denote the process by which ideologies can become utopian forces for change when certain structural changes are occurring in the relationships between dominant and subordinate groups.

In this way the present research incorporates and attempts to integrate and go beyond previous insights into the sociology of the family provided by interactionist and developmental theories (e.g., Turner, 1970; Bell, 1963, 1975; Lopata, 1971) on the one hand and the macro-social theories of the Marxist feminists on the other (e.g., Mitchell, 1971; Rowbotham, 1973; Eisenstein, 1977; Molyneux, 1979).

This research suggests that it is not the presumed isolation of domestic labour which prevents women from realising their oppression (as the domestic labour theorists have suggested) but the ideology which obscures such oppression. In fact, the research demonstrates that the majority of mothers carry out their domestic labour with the strong support of networks of mothers, including kin, neighbours, friends and members of voluntary organisations. The ideas transmitted through these networks are crucial for reinforcing women's individual and privatised responsibility for parenting or, on the other hand, for challenging traditional ideologies and raising women's consciousness of oppression.

Besides being an empirical investigation carried out within a framework suggested by feminist ideas, this research examines the effects of feminist ideas on the subjective construction of variants of the ideology of motherhood or of utopias of motherhood, by including a sample of mothers actively associated with feminist groups. Theoretically and empirically therefore, it is expected that this research will contribute to feminist sociological literature.

Setting of the study

The empirical research was carried out in the Sydney Metropolitan area between March 1977 and May 1979 with 150 mothers with at least one pre-school child. Suburban mothers were chosen as this is the locale where a very high proportion of Australian mothers carry out their mothering.[3] Due to limited funds and the execution of the research by one person, the study is restricted to a small, non-random sample of mothers in one metropolitan area in Australia. There is no claim that the results can be extrapolated beyond the sample interviewed. Nevertheless, the in-depth interviews using open-ended questions have provided a richness of data concerning the lives and beliefs of these mothers which may not have been obtained in a larger, more statistically oriented survey.

The research looks at the 'mother's eye' view of her situation at one stage of the life-cycle. Had fathers or parents of older children been interviewed the results may have been different. This particular stage of the life-cycle was chosen as this is the stage for women when motherhood makes its greatest demands in terms of time and physical and emotional energy. It is also the stage which may otherwise have been crucial for these women in terms of career, job opportunities and experience, further full-time education or political involvement in some instances.

Limits of the study

The sample is restricted to mothers as it is their beliefs, their lived experience and the effects of the ideology on them which is the subject of the investigation. The study is also restricted to Australian-born mothers, or mothers who were born in New Zealand or the United Kingdom but who have lived the major part of their lives in Australia as it was felt that the ideology is probably culturally specific. Within the sample, groups of 25 mothers with specific characteristics such as employment/non-employment, working class/middle class, 'market capacity' (Giddens, 1973:103), one parent family/two parent family, mother's group/feminist group affiliation were interviewed. The sample was collected by the snowball method as this was found to be expedient, relatively cheap and with a low rate of refusal. An integral part of the research is an investigation of women's networks. This method also provided important data for this aspect of the study. Some use is made of quantitative data, but the focus of the research is on qualitative material which reveals the beliefs, attitudes, satisfactions, dissatisfactions, ideals and self-concepts of the mothers concerned.

Chapter 1 introduces the topic and its significance for family and feminist studies today. It also describes the setting of the study and its limitations. Chapter 2 outlines the theoretical conceptualisations of ideology and utopia and the operationalisation of these terms as applied within the research. Chapter 3 describes the research with regard to propositions, assumptions upon which the research is based and, the method of data collection and of analysis. Chapters 4 to 11 provide an analysis of the data which includes some tenets of the ideology and utopian ideas of motherhood; ideal types of mothers; the effects of social class, single motherhood and maternal employment on the ideologies and utopias of motherhood and sex roles as well as on the autonomy, self-concepts and life-satisfactions of the mothers interviewed. This section concludes with an analysis of the ideas propagated by caretakers of the ideology and agents of change. Chapter 12 discusses the findings of the research, the theoretical and empirical implications and suggestions for further research. Finally some conclusions are arrived at concerning the social determinants of the ideology of motherhood and its effects on the lives of contemporary suburban Australian mothers with pre-school children.

Notes

1 In this research I looked at two groups of mothers aged between 40 and 60, one with a professionally recognised problem such as clinical depression, attempted suicide, shop lifting and one with no such problem. In both groups the children of the respondents were no longer residing at home. The groups were compared for ease or difficulty of transition from the motherhood role and the availability of other roles, meaningful activities and group interaction, as well as other social factors. The problem group was characterised by lack of meaningful contact with husband and adult children and lack of alternative roles, activities and social interaction as well as lack of material resources. Women who had devoted themselves to their wife and mother roles from an early age, with few outside interests, experienced greatest difficulty of transition from the motherhood role, especially if the wife role was no longer satisfactory to them.

2 For statistics see Note 2, Chapter 2.

3 *N.S.W. Handbook of Local Statistics 1977*, Australian Bureau of Statistics, Sydney, shows that of the total N.S.W. population of 4 914 300, 3 093 500 live in the Sydney Statistical Division (Appendix A, p 38).

2 Motherhood: ideology or utopia?

In considering the nature and operationalisation of the concept of ideology as applied to motherhood, this chapter explores both class and gender as bases for the generation of ideology. The class nature of the relations of production in advanced industrial capitalist societies such as Australia is an important source of women's oppression and provides a material basis for the generation of ideologies which legitimate women's responsibility for domestic labour and in particular for the reproduction of labour power. However explanations of women's position in such a society cannot be subsumed entirely under the class nature of the relations of production. Some consideration of the power relationships based on gender rather than class and related to the patriarchal nature of Australian society and the benefits to individual men in families across classes is also necessary for a greater understanding of women's oppression.[1] In addition, Mannheim's (1936:183) concept of utopia indicating ideas and values which transcend the existing order while arising out of it, and representing the interests of a subordinate but ascendant group within it, is explicated. This concept provides a useful tool for examining challenges being made to existing ideologies of motherhood and sex roles by sections of contemporary society. The concept of ideology as it appears in sociological theory has generally been derived from Marxian thought and refers to a legitimating mechanism which distorts the true relationships of material production while forming a superstructure based on an infrastructure consisting of these relationships. The ideology itself is seen to represent the interests of the ruling class as the interests of all members of society. By virtue of their domination of the means of production, the ruling class can have their ideas accepted as the ruling ideas of society, thus legitimating their domination of those who do not own the means of production and serving their own interests in a number of ways (Marx and Engels, 1970:42–47). Or, following Weber (Gerth and Mills, 1948:62–63), ideology has been presented as a 'world view' which legitimates power relationships based on class, status and party position and incorporates traditional, rational-legal and/or charismatic authority. In this view when ideas which have already gained acceptance in a society are aligned with the material interests of a particular stratum, they can form a persistant and effective ideology which serves the interests of that stratum and legitimates their position of power. Each of these conceptualisations of ideology contributes to an understanding of women's oppression in capitalist, patriarchal society and has been applied by feminist writers to the legitimation of women's position of subordination (e.g., Gardiner, 1976; Rowbotham, 1973; Davidoff et al. 1976; Bell and Newby, 1976). But it must be pointed out that they are male-orientated paradigms initially devised by male theorists to explain the domination and subordination of males in industrial societies and their terms cannot wholly explain the complex nature of the oppression of women in such societies. Feminist theorists such as Kuhn and Mitchell have attempted to develop fresh insights into the concept of ideology. They include gender itself as a basis for the generation of ideology (Mitchell, 1971) or see the family as the privileged place for the constitution of subjects in ideology based, not on class categories, but on the property relations between husbands and wives within the family across classes (Kuhn, 1978). In this chapter both 'orthodox' and 'feminist' conceptualisations of ideology are drawn upon in order to operationalise the concept of ideology as it refers to motherhood and as it will be used in this research.

Ideology in Marxian and Weberian theory

Application of a Marxian view of ideology to women's domestic labour in capitalist society reveals an ideology which stresses women's supposedly 'natural' propensity for child care due to her biological ability to bear and suckle children. Such an ideology serves the interests of the capitalist in a number of ways. Some of these ways are, the provision of child care services at minimal cost to the capitalist state, concealment of high unemployment rates by legitimating the lack of employment opportunities for married women, the provision of a cheap labour force for those sections of capital and periods of accumulation which require it, as well as the reproduction and nurture of future labourers. At the same time such an ideology obscures and legitimates women's position of subordination in capitalist societies.

The characteristics of ideology which are basic to Marx's development of the concept as it works in capitalist society are delineated by Lefebvre (1968:59—88) as follows and are clearly applicable to the ideology being discussed here.

1   The starting point of ideologies is 'reality', but a fragmented, partial reality. They refract (rather than reflect) reality via pre-existing representations, selected by the dominant groups and acceptable to them. The 'reality' Marx speaks of consists of the relations of material production. Women's relationship to these relations of material production, that is, her lack of ownership of the means of such production, her responsibility for reproduction of labour power for this production and her economic dependency are obscured by an ideology which stresses women's 'natural' propensity for child care.

2   Ideological representations though distorted and distorting, not because of some mysterious fate, but as a result of the historical processes within which they become a factor, tend to constitute a self-sufficient whole and lay claim to be such. Consequently they have two aspects: they are general, speculative, abstract, yet they are representative of determinate, limited, special interest. The ideas that women's chief fulfilment in life comes from mothering, that all women should be mothers, that the biological mother is the best person to care for her own children and that there is a mystical bond between the mother and her child, constitute some of the general, speculative, abstract concepts of motherhood which represent the determinate, limited and special interests of the capitalist.

3   To the extent that they have a starting point in 'reality' (in praxis) they are not altogether false. Ideologies utilise the language of real life and hence are not vehicles of the coercive pressure society exerts on the individual. As instruments of persuasion they guide the individual and give him/her a sense of purpose. Viewed from outside, ideologies seem self-contained, rational systems; viewed from inside, they imply faith, conviction, adherence. It is the role of ideologies to secure the assent of the oppressed and exploited. They represent the latter to themselves in such a way as to wrest from them, in addition to material wealth, their 'spiritual' acceptance of this situation, even their support.

Ideologies can affect 'reality' by imposing rules and limitations on actual living men so that, although they reflect only a portion of human reality, they can be part of actual experience. They offer a way of seeing the world and living which is at once illusory and efficacious, fictitious and real.

It is important in the present context to emphasise that the ideology of motherhood as explored in this research does not equal falsity but looks at the norms, ideals, duties and rewards of motherhood and the status and prestige accorded to mothers. The ideology describes, not only the beliefs mothers hold about motherhood but also the lived experiences of the mothers who assent to the ideology, who support and give 'spiritual' acceptance to it, who live by the rules and limitations it imposes and whose lives are given a sense of purpose and direction by it. The falsity of the ideology of motherhood lies in its ability to mask the gender specific nature of parenting in our society, women and women only are illogically endowed with the qualities of nurturance, rendering them the sole providers of children's physical and emotional care.

4   Ideologies account for and justify a certain number of actions and situa-
     tions which need to be accounted for and justified. Thus the ideology of
     motherhood which masks the gender specific nature of parenting and
     places the responsibility for child care on the biological mother justifies
     the exemption of the male labourer and the male capitalist from this
     responsibility. The bourgeois male can then pursue his accumulation of
     capital in the market sector and the proletarian male is released for full-
     time labour in the processes of production while future labourers are
     produced and cared for in privatised situations at minimal cost to the
     capitalist state. Women's secondary position in the market sector, her
     confinement to low-paid, gender specific work and/or her exclusion
     from this sphere in times of economic recession are also justified by the
     ideology.

Ideology as outlined above has relative autonomy and can act on the infrastructure in a reciprocal reaction, but it is ultimately determined by the capitalist mode of production and reproduction and the power to have such ideologies accepted lies with the owners of the means of production. There are other conceptualisations of ideology however which do not rest entirely on the economic infrastructure of the capitalist relations of production and these conceptualisations also have something to contribute in the present context. Firstly, I will look at the ideas of Weber, then at the contribution feminist theorists have made to the concept of ideology especially as it applies to women.

Although Weber does not use the term 'ideology', like Marx he sees ideas as being dependent upon the structural position of differing groups in society and as legitimating the interests of a dominant group without coercion. Like Marx he sees that ideas are powerless in history unless they are fused with material interests. However, he does not view ideas as a reflection or refraction of those interests. To some extent differing spheres such as the intellectual, psychic, political, economic and religious follow developments of their own. Where Marx sees a correspondence between ideas and interests, Weber also sees possible tensions between ideas and interests between one sphere and another or between internal states or external demands. The conception by which Weber relates ideas and interests is that of 'elective affinity'. For Marx ideas express interests; for Weber there is hardly ever a close connection between the interests or the social origin of the speaker with the content of the idea at its inception.

> But in time, ideas are discredited in the face of history unless they point in the direction of conduct that various interests promote. Ideas selected and reinterpreted from the original doctrine do gain an affinity with the interests of certain members of special strata: if they do not gain such an affinity they are abandoned . . . Both the ideas and their publics are seen as independent; by a selective process elements in both find their affinities. (Gerth and Mills, 1948:62–63)

In the present context ideas emanating from post-war research into the development of children separated from their families during the war (e.g., Bowlby, 1958) which stress the importance of 'the child's tie to his mother' have been aligned with the interests of capital although not necessarily with the economic interests of the family and have become an important element in the ideology of motherhood.

For Weber, the power by which a dominant group can have its definition of the situation accepted by all is not exclusively derived from economic criteria. For him 'both political and military power are as historically significant as economic power and do not necessarily derive from it' (Giddens, 1971:214). He sees 'status groups' and 'parties' as phenomena of the distribution of power as well as economic 'classes' (Gerth and Mills, 1948:181). Elaborating on the means by which the support and compliance of the subordinate group is gained and maintained for those who hold power from whatever source and in whatever sphere, Weber employs the concept of legitimacy. As Giddens points out, the main prop upon which a stable system of domination is based is 'Belief by subordinates in the legitimacy of their subordination' (Giddens, 1971:156).

Weber distinguishes three ideal types of legitimacy upon which a relationship of domination may rest: traditional, legal and charismatic. Traditional authority is based on the belief in the 'sanctity of age old rules and powers'. In the pure type of legal authority those who are subject to authority obey their superordinate because of the acceptance of impersonal norms which are not the residue of tradition, but which have been consciously established within a context of either purposive or value rationality. The pure type of charismatic domination may be less permanent than traditional or legal domination and can arise in the most varied social and historical contexts. It depends on the belief of both leaders and followers in the authority of the leader's mission, such authenticity being achieved by the leader's supposed possession of specifically exceptional powers or qualities (Giddens, 171:156–60).

Weber's concept of ideology as a 'world view' or belief system or set of creeds which, without coercion, legitimates or justifies existing power relations between differing strata of society allows for an extension of the concept of the ideology of motherhood to the patriarchal nature of Australian society. In Australia, control of the party, the state, the church, and the legal system are sources of power for the male. In other words, in the intellectual, psychic, political, economic and religious spheres, the male is dominant and his domination is legitimated by a mixture of traditional, legal and charismatic authority. His market capacity, status, and party membership provide sources of potential power which exceed women's sources of power, thus giving him the right to have his definition of the situation accepted. It has been in the interests of all males, in whatever sphere, for women to assume responsibility for child care and household tasks. In the sphere of education, for example, the ideology of motherhood has been reinforced by the school system and women's motherhood responsibility has been invoked as the reason for separate and lower levels of education for girls (Summers, 1975:324–36). In the family sphere, post-feminist literature has emphasised the traditional authority which legitimates the husband's power in the marriage situation and structures the 'taken-for-granted' assumptions about social relationships within this sphere, allowing males to have their interests served at the expense of female subordination (Davidoff, L'Esperence and Newby, 1976; Bell and Newby, 1976). In this context the face-to-face, daily endorsement of the ideology of motherhood has legitimated male exclusion from the responsibility for parenting, thus allowing him relatively greater freedom to pursue his own interests within and outside the home.

The theorists discussed to date, that is, Marx and Weber, are themselves male theorists who developed theories to explain the relationship to the mode of production of the male labourer and the male capitalist, or the relationship of males to the dimensions of power in society. Although it has been shown that such theoretical conceptualisations of ideology, when applied to women's position and the ideology of motherhood in particular, provide some useful insights, they do not give a comprehensive picture. The ideas of feminist theorists, such as Mitchell (1971) and Kuhn (1979) need to be taken into consideration to show how such an ideology works more particularly in the spheres of society within which women live their lives.

Ideology in feminist theory

Juliet Mitchell (1971: Ch 5) criticises existing male orientated socialist theory for failing to take into account gender itself as a source of power and as a basis for the generation of ideology. She shows that being male has been historically a source of power enabling men to define women's position in society as 'natural' and 'inevitable' due to her physiological characteristics. Gender based ideology presents biology as destiny for women. Male orientated socialist theory, she claims, fails to differentiate women's condition into its separate structures which together form a complex, not a simple, unity. For Mitchell the relations of gender cannot be subsumed within class relations but must be seen as a specific structure which is a unity of different elements. She elaborates four elements of women's oppression, only one of which is determined by the relations of production and then it is the gender based relations of production of which she speaks, rather than the class relations. The four elements or 'structures' (to use Mitchell's own term) are, production, reproduction, sexuality and socialisation of children. Each of these structures may have reached a different 'moment' at any given historical time, says Mitchell, but they combine to determine the position of women at any one time. The ideology basic to the legitimation of women's oppression in each of these structures she suggests is the presentation of women's place as her 'natural' destiny not a cultural construction. Ideology in this view is then the presentation of a culturally constituted structure, institution or characteristic as 'natural'. Applied to women ideology presents certain characteristics as biologically determined and therefore 'inevitable'.

With regard to production Mitchell shows that the biological differentiation of the sexes into male and female and the division of labour that is based on this have seemed throughout history to be an interlocking necessity. The supposition is that women's physiology and her psycho-biological metabolism render her a less useful member of the work-force. But she sees that social coercion by powerful male groups has interacted with the straightforward division of labour based on biological capacity to a much greater extent than is generally admitted. She says (1971:105), 'Physical deficiency is not now, any more than in the past, a sufficient explanation of women's relegation to inferior status. Coercion has been ameliorated to an ideology, shared by both sexes.'

Secondly, with regard to the reproduction of children, Mitchell shows that the gender based ideology of maternity forms the core of women's natural vocation and is a definition of woman. 'But', she says (1971:109) 'it is only a physiological definition. Yet so long as it is allowed to remain a substitute for action and creativity, and the home an area of relaxation for men, women will remain confined to the species, to her universal and natural condition'. She also shows that the mode of reproduction, that is, women's responsibility for reproduction does not necessarily vary with the mode of production but can remain effectively the same through a number of different modes of production, as long as it is defined and presented as a natural phenomenon, and the perogative of women.

Thirdly, Mitchell claims that marriage and the view of sexuality contained within it are presented ideologically as an exclusive, permanent and natural bond which present conditions are revealing as illusory.

Fourthly, she reveals that socialisation of children remains woman's biological destiny as mother becomes a cultural vocation. In bringing up children woman achieves her main social definition. Her suitability for this task is ideologically linked to her ability to produce milk and her occasional relative inability to undertake strenuous work. Such ideology fails to indicate that other modes of socialisation are conceivable.

Mitchell's emphasis on gender as a basis for the generation of ideology which is independent of the material relations of production although 'ultimately and only ultimately determined by the economic factor', is an important contribution to understanding women's position across classes in present society. Nevertheless it is her elaboration of the concept of ideology as a mechanism by which that which is socially constructed in the interests of a dominant group in society is presented as 'natural' and therefore 'inevitable' which is perhaps more important in the present context. This is the core of the ideology of motherhood which serves the interests of the capitalist in class societies and the interests of all males in patriarchal societies.

Kuhn (1978) criticises previous analyses which have attempted to locate the effectivity of the family with regard to the structural subordination of women by positing the family as the transmitter or repository of social forces, including ideologies, whose real operation and generation lies outside itself. The family in these analyses, she says, becomes merely an 'empty signifier'. Instead she sees the family as (1971:53) 'property relations between men and women and the social relations of the family are those property relations in action'. Male property *per se* ceases to constitute the basis for male supremacy in class society, but the male wage earned by the labourer in the market sector becomes the 'property' of the majority of males, upon which the social relations of the family are predicated. Thus the male in the family, whether he actually owns property in the means of production or his wage, possesses the material basis for male supremacy within the family. On this basis Kuhn suggests that the family is in a unique position for the generation of ideology and the 'production of sexed and class subjects for representations of patriarchy and capital, that is for the constitution of subjects in ideology'.

Like Mitchell, Kuhn sees ideologies which act to legitimate and perpetuate relationships of domination and subordination not confined to the expression of class interests but extended to the interests of males across classes. Unlike Mitchell she sees such ideologies generated within the family on a material economic basis, that is, the male wage rather than on the basis of gender. What both of these feminist theorists have contributed to the concept of ideology is that in structures within which women live their lives across classes, male supremacy based both on material economic and gender relations, gives the male the right to have his interests met at the expense of the woman. In the present context then, through the ideology of motherhood, men are relieved of the obligation to take care of children and are in a position to perpetuate this ideology and the aspects of it which also legitimate their relative freedom from other domestic responsibilities.

Ideology as an analytic concept

From the above discussion it becomes apparent that ideology as an analytic concept in sociology is inextricably linked with power in all its aspects. The basis for the generation of ideology, whether it be capitalist relations of material production, institutional, status or party position, possession of the wage in the family or gender itself, is a source (or sources) of power. Its effects are to serve the interests of the more powerful group at the expense of the less powerful group and to call out subjects who are subjected to its demands while 'freely' choosing to put its precepts into action.

In a very real sense ideology, and especially the ideology of motherhood, acts as a mechanism of power in the meaning that Steven Lukes gives to the term in his third-dimensional view of power. Lukes (1974) posits a three-dimensional view of power which goes beyond previous one-dimensional views based on the probability of individuals and groups realising their wills despite the resistance of others and two-dimensional views based on the mobilisation of bias. In his third-dimensional view Lukes (1974:23–24) suggests that the exercise of power enables a dominant group or individual to influence, shape or determine the very wants of a subordinate group or individual. In this most effective and insidious use of power Lukes sees that people are prevented from having grievances, and obvious conflict is averted, by 'shaping their perceptions, cognitions and preferences in such a way that they accept their role in the existing order of things, either because they can see or imagine no alternative to it, or because they see it as natural and unchangeable, or because they value it as divinely ordained and beneficial'.

This view of power Lukes (1971:26) is useful for analysis of social relationships and of the interests being served and conflicts being averted and/or suppressed by such relationships. Such a view of power obviously has an extremely close alignment with the conceptualisation of ideology outlined above. Ideology is one mechanism by which such power is made effective. Ideology within the present research, as operationalised here, has been chosen as an analytic concept which will be used to attempt to unmask one important aspect of the gender and class relationships of power which keep women in a subordinate and dependent position, and limit their life-chances, life-options and autonomy. The core notion of the ideology under consideration is the supposedly 'natural' propensity of women for the nurture and care of children and the associated household tasks thus making parenting and domestic labour the specific responsibility of the female gender.

Mannheim's utopia

Although ideology is conservative and oriented to maintaining existing relationships of power and privilege, it is not static. If the interests and ideas of the dominant group change, this group has the power to change or adapt the ideology in keeping with such new interests and ideas. For example, when there has been a need for women as a reserve labour force to cut down on the infrastructural costs of migration, child care has become a political issue (Game and Pringle, unpublished paper, 1976:24), and the ideology subtly rephrased to allow women to leave their children with 'qualified' minders or other mothers with mothering experience in 'suitable' surroundings. Or, when an increase in tertiary industry which makes use of 'relational' rather than competive expertise has required managerial males to develop relational skills, these values have been incorporated into the male 'world view'. On the other hand, if the dominant group begins to question the goals of the system, this too could bring about changes in the ideology.

Lois Bryson (1974:297) following Weber, suggests that current intellectual technology incorporating the process of rationality, forms the basis of formal organisation in industrial society, and ideally requires an open minded or 'scientific' approach to all decision making which may lead 'ultimately to a questioning of goals as well as means'. The middle class male worker who uses these techniques may in fact utilise this intellectual rationality to question values such as the centrality of career orientation which was previously part of his world view. Bryson suggests that the effect of such questioning may be to create a re-emphasis on the family for these men, with consequences for the adult male and female roles within the family. It is conceivable that if the powerful middle class male redefines his situation to include more time and effort expended on the family and his involvement there accrues satisfaction for him and a lowering of the satisfaction he expects from his career, then ideology could be redefined to include men in family roles such as child care. These roles may, as a consequence, carry higher status. There is little indication that, in fact, there is any significant move in this direction by middle class males. Russell (1979) and Harper (1980) have shown some shifts by some males. But the theoretical point being made is important. That is, if it is in the interests of the dominant group to change or adapt an ideology, they have the power to redefine the beliefs and values incorporated in the ideology.

The main focus of this particular piece of research is not, however, on the official ideologies or ideology as propagated by the dominant male group or groups. The focus is on the subordinate group, the women who are the subjects of such ideology and their world view of motherhood, especially as it affects their life-options and autonomy. Challenges to the ideology can also come from this group.

For this research I will apply Mannheim's (1936:173, 183) distinction between ideology as a set of ideas representing dominant interests, and 'utopia' as a set of ideas representing the aspirations of a subordinate group.

For Mannheim (1936:173–90) the bearers of ideology represent the prevailing social and intellectual order and they experience that structure of relationships of which they are the bearers. But he sees that within any given society there are groups 'driven into opposition to the present order' who are oriented towards the first stirrings of the social order for which they are striving and which is being realised through them. These groups are bearers of utopian ideas which, unlike ideology, 'transcend the existing order' and attempt to 'break the bonds' of such an order 'while at the same time containing in condensed form the unrealised and unfulfilled tendencies which represent the needs of the age' and which 'become the explosive material for bursting the limits of the existing order'.

Mannheim's concept of utopia embodies four aspects which are important in the present context. First, utopia represents ideas which are 'transcendent' because their contents can never be realised in the societies in which they exist, and because one could not live and act according to them within the limits of the existing social order. That is, they are ideas which challenge existing structures and ideologies. Second, utopias exist in a dialectical relationship with the existing order. They grow out of the aspirations of particular strata or social groups and express tendencies already present within the existing order. Further to this point Mannheim points out that utopias are effective only when their aspirations are incorporated in utopias appropriate to the changing situation. Third, the social groups or strata which act as bearers of utopias are generally 'ascendant' according to Mannheim. In the terms of the present discussion this means that they are groups which are gaining access to sources of power in society. Fourth, whether a body of ideas is defined as ideology or utopia depends on 'the stage and degree of reality' to which one applies the terms. 'Utopias' says Mannheim (1936:183) 'are often only premature truths'...' It is always the dominant group which is in full accord with the existing order that determines what is to be regarded as utopian, while the ascendant group which is in conflict with things as they are is the one that determines what is regarded as ideological'. Thus ideology and utopia are seen to be *processes* inextricably linked to the relationships of power in any given society.

In times of political and economic instability an ideology is more forcefully articulated and reinforced. Nevertheless it is in such times that the climate allows the subordinate group to challenge the prevailing values and a utopia is propagated which emphasises the interests of this group and attempts to act as a force for change in existing power and social relations. Where the subordinate group succeeds in gaining power, over time this utopia can become the prevailing idea and the process continues. For example, the bourgeois utopia of individual freedom becomes the prevailing ideology when the bourgeoisie succeed in overthrowing the feudal system of power relations (Mannheim, 1936:183–84).

At the present time economic, political and technological changes have allowed an increasing number of women to enter the workforce, to achieve a higher level of education and to limit their child-bearing and some women have been able to question the ideology.[2] Feminist utopias are propagated which seek to challenge the existing power relations, to change social structure in favour of subordinate group interests. Presumably, if a women's revolution were successful, feminist utopian ideas would become the ideology of a powerful group of women.

The Women's Movement which began in the U.K., U.S.A. and Australia in the late 1960s and early 1970s can be seen in utopian terms as the expression of the aspirations of a particular group which is gaining a certain measure of ascendency in contemporary society due to certain technological, economic, legal and political changes. I refer to middle class professional women who have acted in this movement as bearers of utopian ideas which transcend the existing social order, challenge existing gender and class structures and relationships of power and reveal as ideological prevailing 'taken-for-granted' beliefs about gender relationships and roles. Aspects of these utopias are appropriate to the changing situation, such as the increasing entry of married women into the work-force, and are acting to partially transform some areas of women's oppression such as discrimination against the employment of women in certain sections of the work-force. Nevertheless feminist utopias are as yet unrealisable within the bounds of the present social order, while pointing the way to a future order in which women are 'more equal' to men than is possible under existing conditions. Thus Mannheim (1936:179) says: 'The existing order gives birth to utopias which in turn break the bonds of the existing order, leaving it free to develop in the direction of the next order of existence.'

It is this point of change and possibly new direction in the existing order of structures and relationships of gender which the present research seeks to explore. Mannheim's concept of utopia has been chosen therefore as a particularly useful tool for analysis of the possible impact of feminist utopias on the existing order, and particularly on the allocation of responsibility for parenting and domestic labour.

A variety of feminist utopias have been constructed according to the variety of political affiliations and value positions of feminist theorists. All of them attack in some way or another the question of women's responsibility for domestic labour and the majority reveal as illusory the core notion of the ideology of motherhood, that is, that women's 'natural' and 'inevitable' destiny is to bear and rear children and to take care of the associated household tasks. For example, some lesbian feminists construct a utopia in which men are eliminated from women's social context (e.g., Johnston quoted in Curthoys, 1976:4) and hence motherhood is eliminated.

Firestone's (1970) radical feminist utopia, on the other hand, involves a shift in emphasis from reproduction to contraception and the full development of artificial reproduction. In Mitchell's (1971:122) socialist feminist utopia all four structures in which women are oppressed (i.e., production, reproduction, sexuality and socialisation of children) must be transformed so that women are liberated from their ideological containment as physiologically inferior work-force participants and as natural reproducers and socialisers of children, so that they are free to transcend the limits of present sexual institutions. Liberal feminist utopias such as Rossi's (1972:353) include changes in employment conditions as well as in the family so that parenting replaces motherhood and women can participate equally and on their own terms, (as far as values and emphases are concerned), with men in production and in social and political life. In each of these utopias women's mothering and household responsibility has been seen to be an obstacle in the way of her liberation and some means of removing total responsibility for domestic labour with its gender specific ideological component, has been included.

Voluntary childlessness as utopia

That some middle class women have been able to challenge the aspect of the ideology which identifies woman's chief fulfilment in life as the bearing and rearing of children is evident from the increasing numbers of women who do not view having children as either a duty or a privilege. In a survey of Melbourne wives in 1971 carried out by the Department of Demography of the Australian National University (Ruzicka and Caldwell, 1977:348–55) 68 per cent of the sample agreed with the statement 'It is every wife's duty to have children if she can', but in the non-Catholic middle class, only half of all wives agreed with the statement and the proportion fell to four-ninths among those under 30.

In the semi-structured interviews of surveys carried out in Canberra, Sydney and Melbourne in 1975–76 by the same department, Ruzicka and Caldwell (1977:348) claim,

> The dramatic change was in the rise in self-confidence of those couples who felt they wanted no children or few children or none just yet, and in the fall in confidence of those who were inclined to advise young couples or young wives that it would be a good thing to have a baby or establish a family. Few any longer felt guilts about remaining childless for a while or indefinitely, while many who were tempted to have a third child, or were pregnant with a third, did wonder about the morality of the situation.

There had been a remarkable disappearance of guilts among childless couples even when talking to their parents.

They conclude (1977:354): 'Certainly decisions are being made to defer the first birth, but the order of subsequent events is complex and is likely to result in a greater proportion of childless and single-child families than was known in the 1950s and 1960s.'

In a seminal study of childless wives solicited through newspapers in London and Toronto J. E. Veevers (1973) found that most remained childless through a series of postponements of child-bearing during which time rewards from alternatives defined child-bearing as too costly an experience. The background of this admittedly non-random sample is interesting. Nearly all were middle class and many were upwardly mobile. Although educational level varied, the majority of the sample had some university experience. With one exception all were employed full-time or attending university. Most were either athiests or agnostics from Protestant backgrounds and of the minority who did express some religious preference, almost all were inactive.

A later sample study of a nationwide voluntary organisation, National Organisation for Non-parents in U.S.A. by Barnett and MacDonald (1976) revealed similar results. They found that the membership was disproportionately concentrated in the higher education and income brackets and not committed to religion. Like Veevers they also noted that these couples were able to withstand social pressures to have children from the media, friends and co-workers. In both of these samples the husbands as well as the wives agreed to the childless state, so that a dominant group as well as the subordinate group have challenged one facet of the existing ideology.

The Australian surveys and these studies suggest that it is those women who have access to male defined sources of power such as education, middle class job and high levels of income, (that is some middle class women), who are able to challenge existing male defined ideologies. In this case, that concerned with women's fulfilment through motherhood and the support given to this aspect of the ideology by religious institutions. These middle class women are bearers of a 'relative' utopia (Mannheim, 1936:184), that is, liberating ideas which are realisable within the emerging social order. Voluntary childlessness is the utopian answer to women's oppression adopted by some women, chiefly middle class professional women. For example, in a paper entitled 'Voluntary Childlessness—the Ultimate Liberation', Margaret Movius (1976:62) concludes,

In a world where alternate life styles are growing in number and acceptance, voluntary childlessness should be considered as the ultimate liberation. For a woman committed to a career, childlessness offers the freedom necessary for competing in today's world. Far from being a sign of immaturity or maladjustment, the child-free state indicates self-understanding and self-discipline. As an investment in the improved future status of women and in the increased flexibility and freedom of many career women, voluntary childlessness may be a viable life style alternative.

Voluntarily childless women may challenge women's fulfilment through motherhood and recognise the limitations motherhood would have placed on their life options and be liberated from motherhood, thus realising a 'relative' utopia. They may, however, still fully accept the idea that women's 'natural' propensity for nurturance makes the mother the logical person to care for her children, and make no attempt to change the structures which use this ideology to confine women to the domestic sphere. Mannheim points out that the 'utopias of ascendant classes are often to a large extent permeated with ideological elements' (Mannheim, 1936:183). The childless may have challenged one aspect of the ideology but they have avoided the lived experience of mothering which is one of the central concerns of the ideology under investigation. The research described in the following chapters concentrates therefore on women who *are* mothers. An attempt is made in the present study to discover what the subjects of the ideology are saying about motherhood and the effect that the ideology or challenges to it as well as the experience of motherhood have on women's life-options, family roles, self concepts and satisfactions with life.

Incorporating the concepts of ideology and utopia as developed in this chapter, the following chapter outlines the research.

Notes

1 For an excellent application of the concept of patriarchy to Australian society see Williams *Open Cut* (1981). 'Patriarchy' as Williams (1981:26) defines it and as I have used the term in this work, refers to the cultural and political interpretation of the biological differences between men and women so that female sex roles are accorded less power than those of the male.

2 In Australia in May 1965 the total civilian labour force was estimated at 4 668 500 of which females were 1 358 300 (or 29.1%). By May 1978 the labour force was estimated at 6 394 000 of which 2 321 400 (or 36.3%) were females. Over this period the number of married women in the labour force more than doubled, from 667 800 to 1 440 400. They accounted for a large proportion of the total increase in the number

of females in the labour force, rising from 49.2% of the female labour force to 62.0%. (Women's Bureau, Department of Employment and Youth Affairs, 1978:6).

That women are limiting their child-bearing is indicated by the following total fertility rates. In 1961 the total fertility rate for Australian women was 3.5, by 1971 it had dropped to 3.0 and by 1976 to 2.1, giving a percentage change between 1961 and 71 of −16% and between 1961 and 76 of −41% (Borrie, Smith and Dilulio, 1978:37). The authors of the supplementary report of the National Population Inquiry (Borrie, Smith and Dilulio, 1978:41) emphasise the basic fact that 'annual marital fertility rates, which have been declining since 1961, are now age for age, lower by a considerable margin than they have ever been'.

The increase in women participating in higher secondary school and tertiary education in recent years is evident when male and female participation rates between 1974 and 1976 are compared. Whereas male participation rates for 17 and 18 year olds in higher secondary education had remained constant at 32% and 10% respectively, female participation rates had increased from 28% to 31% for 17 year olds and from 6% to 7% for 18 year olds (Borrie, Smith and Dilulio, 1978:95). In tertiary education, the male participation rate had increased from 2.32% of the male population in 1974 to 2.47% in 1976 (+.15%) and the female participation rate had increased from 1.46% to 1.78% (+.32%) (Borrie, Smith and Dilulio, 1978:99).

3 The research

Key propositions

The previous chapter has pointed out that in advanced industrial capitalist patriarchal societies such as Australia, the ideology of motherhood attributes to woman and woman only, the qualities of nurturance necessary for the physical and emotional care of children due to her ability to give birth and suckle the young. Such an ideology legitimates women's responsibility for domestic labour and perpetuates existing gender and class relationships of power which keep women in a subordinate and dependent position. The lives of the subjects of the ideology, that is women in the child-rearing stage of the life-cycle, can be seen to be limited and constrained by it in a number of ways while also being given a sense of purpose and direction through it. The main proposition being investigated by the research may be stated thus:

Proposition 1

> The ideology of motherhood constrains the life-chances,[1] life-options[2] and autonomy[3] of women and maintains the gender based division of labour[4] in the home as well as concepts of self,[5] sense of identity and satisfactions with life[6] which are associated with the roles of mother, wife and housewife.

On the other hand, in times of political/economic change when there is a shift in the material and power position of some women, some challenge to the existing ideology may be possible. Thus, at the present time when women are achieving a higher level of education, bearing fewer children, and returning to the workforce after marriage in greater numbers, some women are gaining access to male defined sources of power. Under such conditions utopian ideas concerning motherhood and the position of women which challenge the status quo and transcend the existing order of society may have an effect on the ideology of motherhood. Utopias embodying the aspirations of ascendant middle class women which are adapted to changes within the present order may in fact challenge certain aspects of the ideology, increase women's autonomy, alter ideas concerning the division of labour in the home and extend women's self-concepts and life satisfactions beyond those based on the domestic sphere. A complementary proposition may be stated thus:

Proposition 2

When women are achieving a higher level of education, bearing fewer children and returning to the workforce after marriage in greater numbers, utopian ideas concerning women's position and motherhood may challenge the ideology of motherhood and may also affect ideas concerning the division of labour in the home, women's autonomy, self-concepts and life satisfactions.

Assumptions underlying research design

The assumptions underlying the research design are concerned with the empirical level of analysis which looks at the ideas of individual mothers towards motherhood and variations in these ideas at a particular stage of the life-cycle, that is when at least one child is of pre-school age. They are concerned with attitudes and experience rather than specific behaviour and are postulated within a power-conflict perspective which forms the theoretical framework of the research. Nevertheless within this overall framework ideas and concepts concerning self-concepts, identity and significant others are adapted from interactionist theory where applicable. They propose that variance of the ideology or utopia of motherhood may be associated with factors such as the respondent's social class position, level of education, participation in the work-force, single parenthood and membership of feminist groups or of formal mother's groups. In the following discussion some reasons for the possible association between these factors and reinforcement of the ideology or challenge to it are suggested. As well the concepts used are operationalised and some terms defined.

Social class position

Empirical sociological studies of the family have relied heavily on the social class position of the family measured according to the husband's occupation to show variance in socialisation of children, value orientation and husband/wife interaction. Such studies show that, compared with families of non-manual workers (termed 'middle class'), both men and women in families where the husband is in a manual occupation (termed 'working class') have limited life-options. For women it means a life centred around children, husband, home and kin, with the possibility of the extra chore of a low paid, repetitive job (Rainwater, 1959: Komarovsky, 1967; Gavron, 1966). The woman identifies herself as mother, wife and housewife, and within this triangle of husband, home and children many satisfactions are found, although many women feel tied down (Rainwater, 1959:40). Claire Williams (1976; 1981) in a study of an Australian mining town found that for the young mothers she interviewed satisfaction in life depended upon their wife/mother roles, that is, achieving a satisfactory relationship with husband, achieving healthy, well-behaved children and a perception that they were adequately fulfilling the mother role and seen by husband and significant others to be a good mother.

For the middle class wife there is more variety, less monotony, a greater number of personal and outside interests, in clubs, sports, meetings and outings with husband and friends and the possibility of a more interesting and more highly rewarded job (Rainwater, 1959:40). The life-satisfactions, sources of identity and contact with ideas are therefore wider for the middle class mother. In terms of material resources, status and power, she may have access to wealth and status through her husband and the possibility of greater community involvement than her working class sister. Her middle class husband may also have contact with changing ideas concerning both women and men and their home roles versus their roles in the market place.

In addition, studies of working class families such as Young and Wilmott (1957), Dennis et al. (1956) and Komarovsky (1962) suggest that the woman's world is separated from the man's world and that women are more closely associated with their own mothers, female relatives and friends and neighbours than they are with their husbands whose time and energy is spent both during working hours and outside it with other men. Although this could produce a high degree of solidarity amongst the women which could be used to challenge male domination, what it does, in fact, is to reinforce the tasks, values and orientations of wifehood and motherhood, or woman's culture as it has been defined by man. As Ann Battle-Sister (1971) points out it is in these contacts that women continually reinforce their identity as the counterparts of men, and, lacking an autonomous culture, use male culture as their reference for evaluation of themselves and each other.

Nevertheless few of the studies which look at the social class of the family (Gavron's study (1966) is an exception), take into account cross class similarities and differences for women. In fact, concentrating on social class operationalised as husband's occupation has obscured some of the cross class similarities in women's position in society and especially the position and life-style of mothers. As well it ignores the mother's own social class background, inherited wealth and market capacity through education and is inapplicable to the increasing number of mother-headed families (Acker, 1973:937). In the present study these factors will be considered, as well as differences associated with the social class of the family.

The empirical operationalisation of social class for the research follows Gidden's classification which adopts 'market capacity' as the basis of class in capitalist societies. Wild's (1978) application to Australian society is incorporated in the operationalisation of this concept for the research. For a detailed discussion of the views of Giddens and Wild on social class and their application to the present research see Appendix 1.

In the design of the research the assumption has been made that, privileged social class position of the respondent (that is middle class market capacity of the mother herself and her social class background as well as market capacity of her husband) may allow for some challenge to be made to the ideology of motherhood and ideas concerning the division of labour in the home, and extends the scope of the mother's autonomy, her self-concepts and her life-satisfactions.[7]

Level of education

Level of education can be viewed from several points of view:

1   As a source of status and power in itself.
2   As increasing a woman's market capacity and thus her power in the market sector and possibly in other aspects of the public sphere of society.
3   The content of the education (e.g., woman's study courses) may act as a source of ideas which challenge traditional ideology, sex roles, etc.
4   As a means of making contact with people with ideas which challenge the traditional ones.
5   As a source of identity and life-satisfactions other than those associated with wife/mother/housewife.

The last two would probably be dependent upon the mother's being engaged in an educational course at the present time, rather than education prior to marriage. Each of the above suggests that high educational level is more likely to be associated with challenges to traditional ideas and satisfactions than low educational level. For example, Komarovsky (1967:60) found differences in attitudes to child-rearing and sex roles along the dimension of high school graduation and less education. The less educated wife received less relief from her duties and less emotional support from her husband as well as less involvement in the home on his part. In their analysis of U.S.A. surveys 1964–74, Mason, Czajka and Arber (1976) found education to be a significant factor influencing change in attitudes to sex roles. R. R. Bell (1975) also found that the women in his Melbourne sample who were categorised as old with low educational levels saw their husbands as much more involved in segregated sex roles than those in his other categories. On the other hand those women with high education who were young, showed somewhat less involvement in the traditional dimensions of the marriage role as related to the mother and housekeeper role.

Nevertheless, education may also foster in its content and the types of contacts made, traditional ideas, such as those propounded by Bowlby.

Educational level is operationalised as the highest level of formal education achieved by a respondent. However, some tertiary (if incomplete) education is also expected to affect ideas and will be taken into consideration.

In the light of the above discussion an association between high educational level and challenge to the ideology and associated beliefs has been assumed in the design of the research. It is expected that a high level of education may allow some mothers to challenge and transcend the ideologies of motherhood and the gender division of labour in the home, to increase their autonomy and to extend their self-concepts and life-satisfactions beyond those of the domestic sphere.

Maternal employment

Empirical studies suggest that the husbands of employed mothers are more involved in household tasks and child care than the husbands of non-employed mothers. Mason, Czajka and Arber (1976) in their survey analysis also found recent employment of the woman to be a significant factor affecting sex role attitudes. Rapoport and Rapoport's dual career families (1972) showed relatively egalitarian attitudes towards sex roles. In a practical sense allocation of tasks at home may become more determined by time and personnel available to perform them than purely by gender once the woman enters the work-force. Rowbotham suggests also that male/female consciousness differs because of participation in different spheres of production. Entry into the capitalist mode of production may raise the woman's consciousness of the unpaid low status nature of her production in the home. At least work-force participation may give a woman an alternative frame of reference within which to view and perhaps question the inevitability of her roles.

The woman's wage, although in all probability lower than her husband's, may be sufficient to alter the economic basis of the marriage in the direction of greater equality between husband and wife.

Income from employment outside the home may give a woman the material means of transcending some of the limits of her domestic labour by enabling her to purchase help with some tasks and by providing the economic resources necessary to participate in many activities outside the home.

A job may also be an alternative source of identity and status for women, although the type of job, for example, middle class professional as against working class manual/clerical, may be the deciding factor. A job outside the home may put the woman in contact with non-traditional ideas, depending again on the type of job.

A repondent is considered to be employed if she is in paid employment outside the home at least three days per week. Non-employment refers to the position of the woman who is a full-time housewife; these mothers are also referred to as 'at home' mothers. Employment outside the home for at least part of the week has been selected as the criterion here instead of the usual full-time/part-time categories as it is felt that entry in to the capitalist mode of production physically as well as mentally for a reasonable part of the week is significant for the impact of paid employment on the mother's life experiences and attitudes.

Employment outside the home is expected then to enable some challenge to be made to the traditional ideologies, identities and life-satisfactions of women. The design of the research includes the assumption that, the employment of the mother outside the home for at least three days per week may enable some mothers to challenge some aspects of the ideologies of motherhood and sex roles, to increase their autonomy and to extend their self-concepts and life-satisfactions beyond those associated with wife/mother/housewife roles.

arenthood in the present context refers to mothers who have
een married or are separated, divorced or widowed and who
are ... t living in a de facto relationship. That is, they are bringing
up children in the absence of daily face-to-face contact with an adult
male in the home. It is conjectured that, in the absence of face-to-
face daily contact with a male authority figure, the woman in a
mother-headed family may be in a position to challenge an ideology
which is legitimated and stabilised by the traditional authority of
such a male. On the other hand, studies of one parent families
(Marsden, 1969; English et al. 1978) have documented the lack of
material resources available to mothers in this situation and this may
increase the time and energy that must be spent in the performance
of domestic labour by limiting the ability to purchase labour saving
devices, prepared food, ready made clothes, etc. It may also limit
participation in activities outside the home which require money.
Being a single parent may focus the mother's attention more directly
on her motherhood in the absence of the wife role and in the absence
of the emotional support of the father. In spite of these contrary
indications, this research proposes that single parenthood may
enable some challenges to be made to the traditional ideologies and
associated identities and life-satisfactions as well as increasing the
mother's autonomy. It is suggested that single parenthood in a
mother-headed family; that is in the absence of a male from the
daily interactions and from the structure of the family, may enable
single mothers to challenge the ideologies of motherhood and sex
roles, to increase their autonomy and to alter their self-concepts and
life-satisfactions.

Membership of feminist groups

Bott (1971) and Goldthorpe et al. (1971) have shown empirically
the importance of contact with networks for the propagation of
ideology. It is conjectured therefore, that regular contact with a
feminist group and consequently the ideas propagated by this group
and the network associated with it may enable some mothers to
challenge the traditional ideology of motherhood, in their own interests. Nevertheless, as Weber (quoted in Gerth and Mills, 1948:64)
suggests, ideas of themselves have little force for change unless
aligned with the material interests of certain members of the more
powerful strata of society. It is considered important therefore to
also investigate the class backgrounds of these women.
    Membership of a feminist group refers to regular association on
a weekly or monthly basis with a group which expounds feminist

ideas, for example, a consciousness raising group, a women's study group, a women's refuge or a political lobby group such as the Women's Electoral Lobby. It is expected that these mothers are those most likely to construct utopias of motherhood, to question the very basis of the division of labour in the home and woman's identity and life satisfactions associated with her home roles. The research design includes feminist mothers on the assumption that, mothers who are members of feminist groups are in a position to challenge the ideology of motherhood, the gender based division of labour in the home and self-concepts and life satisfactions associated with the roles of wife/mother/housewife and to exercise greater autonomy in the expenditure of their resources of time and energy.

Membership of formal mother's groups

Feminists such as Firestone (1970), Reed (1978), Rowbotham (1973) and Gardiner (1976) have suggested that theoretically it is the isolation of women in the nuclear family situation which prevents them from forming a common consciousness of their oppression. That is, although in the Marxian sense they may form a 'class in themselves', they have no opportunity to form a 'class for themselves'. Empirically, however, community studies such as Bryson and Thompson's (1972) and Oxley's (1978) have shown that women do meet and talk with other women frequently, on the phone, in kin, neighbourhood and women's groups. It is suggested here, that such women's groups far from raising consciousness, reinforce the traditional ideas concerning motherhood, sex roles etc. In fact, the ideology of motherhood individuates the concerns of women by propounding an 'ideal' of motherhood towards which each mother strives in competition with her sisters. Children and their achievements become the bench marks of good motherhood and rivalry between mothers in mother's groups could prevent any such consciousness raising. In mother's groups it is possible for the ideology to be regenerated and perpetuated in a form which is peculiarly adapted to the particular social milieu of mothers who make up the group.

Goffman (1963) gives some insights which help in understanding the mechanism of mother's groups although he does not perceive the importance of the power relationship between the 'normal' and 'stigmatised' group. He suggests that 'stigmatised' people tend to form groups in which they reaffirm the values, norms and attitudes which are peculiar to their category of persons as against those which predominate amongst the 'normal' whose definition of the situation is that generally accepted by society at large. Mothers form groups (designated 'formal' mothers' groups for the purposes of this research) such as play groups in which the norms and values associated with motherhood, such as nurturing, caring and supporting, are emphasised as against the competitive individualism of the market place. This emphasis has the effect of reinforcing the ideology and obscuring the subordinate position of the members of the group.

Informal neighbourhood, kin and friendship groups composed of mothers could also have the same effect. Membership of such groups both formal and informal is expected to reinforce the ideology of motherhood, the division of labour by gender in the home and self-concepts and life-satisfactions associated with the roles of wife/mother/housewife, as well as limiting the mother's autonomy.

The following chapter looks at some of the tenets of the ideology of motherhood as expressed by those who think within the ideology—those for whom it is 'their way of being in the world' (Rowse, 1978:15).

Notes

1   *Life-chances* are the chances an individual has of sharing in and making use of the socially created economic or cultural 'goods' which typically exist in any given society and includes wealth, income, education, as well as 'goods' in the conventional sense (Giddens, 1973:130).

2   *Life-options* refer to the choices an individual has concerning the way in which she will spend time, energy, talent and economic resources.

3   *Autonomy* refers to the individual's self-determined deciding and choosing and is related to life-options in that for autonomy to be exercised there should be real alternatives between which the individual makes a conscious choice. Nor should the alternatives be so loaded that she could not reasonably choose otherwise than she does. Autonomy is reduced to the extent that the individual is unaware of the determinants of her behaviour and to the extent that the alternatives before her are restricted (Lukes, 1973:127–28).

4   *Gender based division of labour* refers to wife/mother duties for the woman and husband/provider duties for the man. The terms 'ideology of sex roles' and 'sex role attitudes' are also used to refer to beliefs about the division of labour according to gender within and outside the family.

5   *Concepts of self* are the way in which the mother perceives herself, her primary identity, her sexual identity or 'feminity' and her ability/inability to influence her situation.

6   *Life-satisfactions* are the satisfactions that the individual expresses concerning the way she is using her resources, the rewards she perceives from such expenditure or the things in her situation which she perceives as providing some satisfactions in her life. Such perceptions are expected to be determined to some extent by the woman's class position, her gender and the spheres within which she lives her life e.g., the domestic

sphere only or a combination of the domestic and other spheres such as
the political and/or the sphere of commodity production.

7   Although it may have been interesting and desirable to include also
an upper class group, difficulties in acquiring such a sample and limitations placed on the research by finance, time and personnel precluded
inclusion.

4 Some tenets of the ideology of motherhood and some utopian ideas

This chapter is concerned with the questions 'What are some of the main tenets of the ideology of motherhood as held by suburban mothers with pre-school children?' and, 'Are any challenges being made to such an ideology?'

The mothers interviewed were more than willing to express their ideas and feelings on a topic which at this stage of their lives is of utmost importance to them. For these mothers the ideology expresses their way of being in the world at this point in their lives.

The core ideas of the tenets presented here were present in all groups interviewed and have been composed from the answers given to interview questions by the 150 mothers in the sample. Had other questions been asked no doubt other tenets would have been produced. This list is not presented as exhaustive, but it does give some idea of what these mothers believe are the principles of motherhood in their particular milieu. I do not mean to suggest that all mothers in the sample agreed in detail with all aspects of the tenets presented here. Variations between the groups interviewed have been taken into account and commented upon. Some mothers have challenged some aspects of some of the tenets or have presented alternative ideas; these too are noted and commented upon.

The tenets presented remain to a large extent as stated by the mothers themselves. This has been a deliberate attempt to keep the ideology as close as possible to the mother's view of their way of being in the world. Some generalisation and abstraction however has been necessary in order to analyse and interpret the ideas presented by respondents. Such abstractions have been guided by the theoretical perspective of the thesis.

Motherhood is an essential part of womanhood

In our society the norm in terms of expectations of adult women is that they have children, that they find fulfilment through them and that they love and care for them. This is a woman's privilege and duty.

42

Almost all mothers in the sample said that they were glad they had got married and had children. Although 63% of respondents commented on the discrepancy between what they thought motherhood would be like e.g., 'just a lovely baby to cuddle' and the reality of twenty-four hour a day responsibility for another human being, 84% said that they had always wanted to have children and implied in various ways that this is normal for women. Of the 16% who said that they had not always wanted children or that they had not really wanted them at the time they had them only one mother said that she was, in fact, sorry she had had children. In all other cases when motherhood was thrust upon the woman, she asserted that she would not be without her children now. Mothers who had not really wanted children felt that they were not quite normally female.

The following is a typical response of mothers who said that they wanted children and implied that this is the norm for women.

> Yes that was the biggest thing in my life, I think I've always wanted to have children. Even before I had a steady boyfriend I did, I wanted to have children. If you asked me why—I think it's probably bound into you subconsciously from the time you're old enough to realise—you always have dolls and things and it's just a natural progression I suppose. (Mt Druitt mother)

Some feminist mothers were fully aware before they had children of the restrictions having a child would place on their lives, but made a deliberate choice to have children and to try to rear their children as well as continuing with other activities which they also found fulfilling. Only 8% of feminist mothers said that they did not want to have children as against 16% for the total sample. Some challenge is made to this tenet of the ideology of motherhood by some feminist mothers, in that for them motherhood is not a necessary means of fulfilment for women, nor is it inevitable, nor does sole responsibility for child care automatically follow from motherhood. However these mothers, along with the majority of the sample, say that motherhood is fulfilling for women and a worthwhile part of their lives.

Kim Brandt[1] says,

> I did and I didn't (want children). I wasn't the sort of person who thought marriage meant children. I stayed out of marriage as long as I could because I realised it was a big commitment and I stayed out of having children as long as I thought I could for the same reason. I think it's a big commitment. And once you've decided there's no going back and we talked about it and said if I could combine a career with children then we'd do it . . .

Although women are limiting the number of children they have and some see child-bearing as a deliberate choice rather than an inevitable event, motherhood remains consciously a very important part of women's lives. To be an adult mature woman is to be a mother. One mother expressed it this way to me, 'After you've lost a baby you have this terrible feeling of inferiority—that you can't be a proper woman!' In this respect, following Lukes (1973:127–28) woman's autonomy has been reduced to the extent that she is unaware of the structural determinants of her behaviour, that the alternatives before her are restricted and such alternatives are generally so loaded that she cannot reasonably choose otherwise than she does. If she wishes to consider herself and be considered by others as a mature, adult female, motherhood is almost inevitable.

Some women (chiefly those associated with feminist groups) question the fact that woman's chief fulfilment in life comes from her mothering role and that the biological mother is inevitably the sole carer for her child, however almost all the mothers interviewed stressed that for them mothering is a worthwhile and rewarding experience, in spite of its interminable demands. This aspect of motherhood is further elaborated in the second tenet of the ideology.

Motherhood is hard but rewarding work

Although motherhood may be more difficult than expected—it is not all 'bliss' and 'joy', it is a hard job—the rewards are worth the effort. The 'bad' aspects of motherhood are balanced by the 'good'.

In answer to the question 'Is motherhood anything like you hoped or expected it to be? Is it worse or better?' 37% of the mothers interviewed said that motherhood was the same or better than they expected. These mothers had had experience with babies and children before marriage, they had looked after younger siblings or relatives or neighbours or friends' babies and had a reasonably realistic comprehension of the work that is involved. For them, the main difference is that now the child is their *own*, so they feel that the rewards are greater.

Colleen Renate was 23 when married and 25 when she had her first child. She feels motherhood is better than expected because it's her own baby. She says,

> Yes it's similar because when I was 15 I had a baby sister, I just fell into motherhood. It's better because she's *my* baby. (Mt Druitt mother)

For the majority of mothers interviewed a rosy glow had been cast over motherhood which obscured the reality of the situation until they were faced with a living, breathing baby for whom they were totally responsible 24 hours a day. For these mothers the first baby was a terrific shock, they were not prepared for the crying, the broken nights and consequent tiredness, the sheer demands and hard work involved. Yet the 63% of the sample who said that there was considerable discrepancy between their expectations and the reality of motherhood and in fact that motherhood was worse than they anticipated, also maintained that motherhood is worthwhile and has very definite rewards.

This sentiment was most clearly articulated by members of the Emerton (Mt Druitt), Friday Play Group for whom it had been emphasised by discussion. A typical response from this group of mothers is as follows,

> No it's not at all like I expected it to be. It's all made out to be so rosy. People say 'Oh you're going to have a baby. Oh that's lovely'. You think when you're in hospital—I know I did, that I could have got up—I thought I could and come home the minute he was born. It was all right for the first three weeks and then he got colic and that just finished me. And I thought once the colic was finished I'd be all right, but then it was teeth. I don't know what comes next . . .
> No, no I wouldn't be without him, there are times when I wish him to hell, but I just can't imagine life without him, it gives you purpose. I love him very much. (Mt Druitt mother)

Similar responses were given, however, in all the groups interviewed.

A feminist mother voices the lack of preparedness for the fact that children are a permanent commitment which was evident in many responses,

> Well, looking back I was so totally ignorant and totally unprepared. I'd never been with small children, I was the youngest of the family, I'd never had much contact with young children. I had no idea—it was a terrible shock. I wanted to have children and I married a man who made it clear that he wanted to have children and that was the basis that we went into marriage. It was understood that one day we would have children. But I was totally unprepared for the fact that they never go away. I mean 6 years later they are still here. (Feminist mother)

Different mothers emphasised different aspects of the discrepancy between expectations and reality. For some the amount of work was greater, for some it was the emotional tension and responsibility, for others the loss of personal freedom and continual demands and for others the fact that the commitment is long term, from babyhood, through toddlerhood to childhood and beyond. The rewards too vary from the love of the child to personal development of the mother herself through her experiences. In order to be more specific about the difficulties and rewards of motherhood two questions were asked: 'What are some of the "good" things about being a mother?' and 'What are some of the "bad" things, the things that "irk" you most?'

Except for the Mt Druitt mothers, the most frequently mentioned aspect was being tied down, being constantly in demand, lack of freedom and privacy and inability to plan ahead or complete tasks or even conversations. This aspect of motherhood was felt most by the feminist mothers and is expressed by one in the following terms,

> The worst thing is never being able to complete a task in one go, I think. I think now, I've been here five years now and I think I've basically resigned myself to the fact that I cannot complete a task. But there's nothing more infuriating in whatever you want to do, like—I'm talking to you now and there's a little voice on the left here saying 'Mum'. He wants something done, so I cannot even concentrate on this tape. Everything I do has the same thing, like 'Can I have a drink?', 'I want to go to the toilet', 'Help me do this'. Now you can understand that from the child's point of view I'm the only one here who can help them, so naturally they're going to turn to me. But when I try to do my work it's damned difficult.
> Excuse me, I'm now going to assist my youngster on the left. (Feminist mother)

On a wider level many mothers commented on their loss of independence and sense of being tied to the home and their inability to pursue former interests outside the home, or to participate in work or other activities to the extent that they would like to. These interests and activities varied from having a drink after work with colleagues to full-time studies, career, participation in politics and in women's movement activities to visiting, shopping or even going to a movie, or an art gallery. Feminist mothers saw this as a restriction on their own development as individuals, although many also saw it as character producing self-discipline.

The second most frequently mentioned 'irksome' aspect of motherhood was the child's disobedience, whinging, answering back, cheekiness, temper tantrums and the discipline involved. The ideology suggests that mothers should be in control of their children, in fact for many women this is the only sphere in which they are accorded power over another individual. When this authority is threatened the mother experiences distress. The emotional tension of constantly trying to maintain such control wears the mother down, however she dare not relinquish such control for any length of time, the responsibility is hers. This conflict of wills, for many mothers, destroys the rosy dream of the cuddly, compliant baby. A single mother who has no one to relieve her of this responsibility, even temporarily, puts it this way,

> I feel sort of—I didn't think I'd have as much trouble disciplining the child. Before I had Anna I always thought, "I'll never have kids". It wasn't by accident, nor by specific design I had the child and I started really thinking about the autonomy of people whilst I was pregnant and that was incredibly important to me. Just from feeling that they—I'd expected that she'd respect my needs as much as I'd try to respect her needs. The thing that I've found of course she doesn't, sort of total ego centred horror. Which is nice in some ways, but at the moment I'm fighting quite a big battle with her over it, everything's "me, me, me; my, my, my".

To balance such tensions mothers stress the love and appreciation that is occasionally shown and the evidence of the child's growth, development and achievement for which the mother can claim credit. The most frequent response concerning the 'good' aspects of motherhood in all groups was the child's growth, development and achievement and the second most frequently mentioned aspect in all groups, except the feminist group was the aspect of love and appreciation. Bearing a child and being able to mould another individual was also important to many mothers and was seen as an achievement peculiar to motherhood. For feminist mothers, some of whom consciously adopted a philosophy of children as people in their own right and who had formed a children's co-operative with this as a basic principle, the satisfying relationship with the child was important. The ideology of motherhood emphasises these means of achievement for women; these are the ways in which a woman should achieve in life, this is her identity, this is where her emotional and psychic investment lies, these are the rewards she can expect in lieu of economic and material rewards.

The belief that they are doing a demanding job which has emotional and character building rewards, appears to be an essential ideological support for the tasks and tensions involved in motherhood for these mothers. It is interesting to note that although many mothers mentioned the sheer physical exhaustion of the job and the long hours involved, that it was not this, but the emotional aspects which concerned them most when evaluating the positive and negative aspects of the role. The ideology of motherhood has stressed this aspect and, to a large extent, ignored motherhood as 'work' in the sense of labour.

In the mothers' own words the ideological support for what they express in no uncertain terms as a hard, demanding, physically and emotionally exhausting task is that it has intrinsic emotional and personal rewards which compensate for its difficulties and demands.

In spite of challenges to the concept of mothers as self-negating supporters of dependent sub-people by some feminist mothers, the mothers' own analysis of their situation varies little from group to group. Whether mothers are experiencing conflict from outside pressures or not, the dynamics of the role appear to be dependent upon a basic belief in the intrinsic worth and non-material rewards of a tough and demanding job.

Another ideological support for the difficult and demanding job of motherhood which the mothers in the sample volunteered, is the sense of autonomy that the mother at home experiences when she compares her present situation with that of her situation in the work-force. Fifty four per cent of the sample said that they would not want to be doing anything else rather than bringing up children at this stage of their lives, the majority of these were 'at home' mothers. The 46% who said that they would rather be doing something else, in most cases qualified this to mean in addition to their mothering. Mt Druitt mothers without a doubt prefer their 'at home' job, and employed and feminist mothers say they enjoy their work or other activities combined with motherhood, but still maintain that motherhood has its advantages. Factory, sales and clerical jobs are seen as more monotonous and boring with less freedom and control than mothering and housework, and professional jobs are seen as having more pressures with less freedom for personal interests.

Some typical responses illustrate these points.

I worked in a factory assembling drugs, but I'd rather be at home. (Mt Druitt mother)

I was a legal secretary before marriage. I'd rather be doing this. I loved it while I was doing it. I never thought to myself "I'm just filling in time", because it was a sort of involved job. There were lots of hours to put in the Children's Court, etc. I prefer staying at home and doing my own thing when I want to do it. (Nth Shore mother)

It's made a lot of difference to what I aim to do with my career. I can't take a full-time job which is annoying because in many ways I want to. I'm a doctor. But in other ways it's making me spend more time in the more personal aspects of my life than the career aspects. (Single feminist mother)

Ann Oakley (1974b:182) found autonomy to be one of the most highly valued dimensions of the housewife role. She writes, 'Being one's own boss—a phrase used by nearly half the sample—and exercising control over the pace of work is a facet of housewifery which contrasts favourably with employment work.'

Oakley however questions the nature of this autonomy and comments, (1974b:43), 'In the housewife's case autonomy is more theoretical than real. Being "your own boss" imposes the obligation to see that housework gets done. The responsibility for housework is a unilateral one, and the failure to do it may have serious consequences.'

In fact, this is even more true of mothering, which involves 24 hour a day availability. Nevertheless the sense of freedom and control in the job of mothering as against employment work acts as an ideological support for the commitment of women to this job and their sense of well-being within it.

A 'good' mother puts her children first

There is an ideal of the 'good' mother towards which all mothers should strive. A 'good' mother is one who is always available to her children; she gives time and attention to them, listens to their problems and questions and guides them where necessary. She cares for them, physically by keeping them neat and clean and providing them with adequate food and clothing, and emotionally by showing them love. She is calm and patient, does not scream or yell or continually smack her children. The cardinal sin of motherhood with its associated guilt is to lose one's temper with a child. Self-control should be exercised at all times. Even in extenuating circumstances such as when a baby screams with colic for days or when the mother has no emotional or physical support in her task, she must at all times be in complete control of her own emotions. Mothers will be especially patient with children who have behavioural problems—naughty children do not really exist, they are the product of a 'bad' mother. At this point in the life-cycle, a mother's main aim in life is to bring up her children to the very best of her ability, to be a 'good' mother to her children.

In order to build up a picture of the ideal mother several questions were asked, some concrete, some abstract, some suggesting presence of a characteristic, others the absence of a characteristic. The total responses to all of these questions have been content analysed and the results are given in Table 4.1.

The most frequently mentioned characteristic of a 'good' mother in all groups except the Feminist group was the availability of the mother to the child in the sense of giving time, being there when needed to listen, guide and comfort.

From Table 1 it can be seen that in all groups in fact, the needs of the child in terms of the ubiquitous availability of the mother, her affection, love and understanding, patience, consistent discipline and physical care are emphasised as important characteristics of

Table 4.1 Most frequent responses concerning the characteristics of a 'good' mother

Characteristic	Mt Druitt No. (%)[a]	Nth Shore No. (%)	Single No. (%)	Employed No. (%)	Feminist No. (%)	Total No. (%)
Always being available, giving time. Listening, guiding	91 (26.0)	42 (24.0)	44 (25.0)	39 (22.3)	18 (10.3)	234 (22.28)
Love, affection, understanding	35 (10.0)	33 (18.9)	38 (21.7)	29 (16.6)	35 (20.0)	170 (16.19)
Patience and self-control	62 (17.7)	15 (8.6)	22 (12.6)	28 (16.0)	12 (6.9)	138 (13.24)
Gives opportunity for development, doesn't smother, spoil, make overdependent	12 (3.4)	22 (12.6)	7 (4.0)	9 (5.1)	54 (30.9)	104 (9.90)
Caring for child physically, food, clothing, keeping clean	40 (11.4)	15 (8.6)	12 (6.9)	8 (4.6)	18 (10.3)	93 (8.86)
Discipline (consistent, neither too soft nor too strict)	23 (6.5)	18 (10.3)	23 (13.1)	16 (9.1)	10 (5.7)	90 (8.57)
Unselfishness	8 (2.2)	27 (15.4)	7 (4.0)	21 (12.0)	13 (7.4)	76 (7.24)
Mother a calm, stable person, happy in herself	1 (0.7)	11 (6.3)	1 (0.7)	11 (6.3)	27 (15.4)	51 (4.86)

Notes: [a] (%) number of times this response was given as a proportion of possible responses, i.e., 7×50 for Mt Druitt respondents and 7×25 for the other groups, e.g., $91/350 = 26.0\%$.

the 'good' mother. Feminist mothers modify this concept of the mother's availability to the child by stressing both the independence of the child and opportunity for the child's own development and that the mother herself needs to be a calm, stable person who is happy in herself. From these responses a core of ideas concerning the 'good' mother which is evident in all groups, emerges. A 'good' mother is one who is basically concerned with the needs of her children both physical and emotional, and who will make every endeavour to satisfy these needs. Mt Druitt mothers stressed more than the other mothers the physical aspects of child care. Feminist mothers on the other hand emphasised that the needs of the mother herself should be met before she can be adequate in her mothering role. In conjunction with this, they pointed out that a mother whose main interest in life is her children may smother her child and make it overdependent and not allow it to develop as an individual.

Around the basic core notion of a 'good' mother as being one who is there to supply adequately the needs of her children, two pictures of motherhood emerge from the interviews. One endorses the traditional ideology of motherhood, the other challenges some of the traditional ideas. The following excerpts from the interviews illustrate these views.

Rhoda Maclean, a North Shore mother exemplifies the traditional view,

> A good mother is a mother that's willing to give more than she probably thinks of any returns in terms of getting, it's giving but giving sensibly. Giving of *herself* really, of her time and her understanding and her love and communicating well. A mother that makes sure that she's home when her children are home, especially when they're young. Someone who has a routine that can be adhered to because I think that's important—that they get adequate rest, they get adequate nutrition and diet every day. (Nth Shore mother)

Kim Brandt, is a feminist mother who challenges the idea of motherhood as against parenthood and makes the point that children are individuals with their own rights to independence,

> I prefer the term a good parent because I think there's too much emphasis on mothering, it should be parenting. I think a good parent is one who really is involved with their children but wants to make them an independent person. They don't want to smother them and make them too dependent on themselves. I think you've got to be aware of the child as an individual with its own rights to be an individual as it grows into an adult. Someone who just watches, each step and is excited for the child and someone who doesn't let all the menial things get them down and that's very difficult.

My ideas of a good mother are coloured by my feminist views. Maybe I'm biased because I don't think a good mother is someone who stays home five days a week and puts all her energy into the children and lets herself just become a slave to the child and the house, I think a good mother is someone who is aware of her rights and wants to still be an individual and give as much time to the child as she can. I think once you've had a child you owe it the right of being with it and caring for it but making it aware that you're a person too and you've got rights and you're an individual. That's a very fine line to tread, so therefore a good mother to me is someone who is interested and concerned for her children but also is interested in her community and in social issues, but who wants to get out and do other things apart from just mothering the child. (Feminist mother)

That the concept of the 'good' mother is an ideal not attainable by mortal mothers became evident when mothers attempted to describe a 'good' mother they knew. Many mothers said that they could not think of a really good mother. 'No mother is perfect' they suggested, 'every mother I know has her faults, no one is a really good mother'. However, some feminist mothers such as Annette Erving were aware that the 'good' mother is an ideal and that there is more than one way of being a 'good' mother. She says,

You're asking me for an ideal and nobody ever fits an ideal. I know a lot of women who are trying in many different ways to cope as best they can and I'd say most of them are doing a good job within their ideas. But I know of some women around who are devoting all their life to their children and I think they're doing a good job—I know others who are going to work. I don't think I could pick out one person I really don't. (Feminist mother)

Even so, all the mothers in the sample implied that they had an ideal of the 'good' mother or 'good' parent towards which they were striving. Although this ideal varied somewhat between groups with some modifications and challenges being made by some employed and most feminist mothers, it still remained as a guiding principle in their lives, calling upon them to do their utmost to fulfil its requirements. Failure to live up to the ideal, whether on a grand or a small scale resulted in a sense of guilt. In mother's groups the traditional ideal tended to be reinforced and regenerated, in feminist groups it was challenged, with an alternative model being superimposed on the core ideas of the original ideal.

Chris O'Neil, a feminist mother tells of being caught between the two sets of ideals and the resultant guilt,

I feel guilty whatever I do, because I've got two sets of conditioning, I've got the culture's conditioning and I've got feminist conditioning. So that I find that if I'm doing what I intellectually consider to be O.K., like leaving her at day care, I feel guilty because I think I'm a mother I should be with my child. On the other hand if she was home with me, I'd feel equally guilty, because the feminist later conditioning part of me feels guilty about *me*.

Before turning to the mechanism of guilt which Chris O'Neil has described as an enforcer of the ideal, I wish to comment on an aspect of motherhood which was absent from the majority of respondent's descriptions of the 'good' mother. Only seven mothers in the sample mentioned liking or enjoying children as a character-istic of the 'good' mother. Many mothers told of difficulties in terms of personality clashes they had with one of their children and implied that they didn't really like this child although of course they still 'loved' all their children. The ideology assumes that all mothers like children and like their own children equally and indeed all the mothers in the sample were striving to be 'good' mothers to their children whether in fact they liked children or not.

That motherhood is believed to incorporate certain standards of action and the 'rightness' of such action is made plain by the inter-nalisation of guilt by the mothers interviewed. 90% of Mt Druitt mothers, 100% of Nth Shore, 88% of Single, and 92% of Employed and Feminist mothers said that they feel guilty as mothers. The most frequently given reason for guilt in Nth Shore, Mt Druitt and Single mothers groups was losing one's temper, being impatient, unneces-sarily smacking or verbally abusing a child. Such guilt emphasises the patience, and self-control of the 'good' mother, her understand-ing, tolerance and support of her children. Employed and Feminist mothers also felt guilty about these matters, but for them most guilt was associated with not spending enough time with their children or working outside the home. Although these mothers have adapted their ideal of the 'good' mother to include other activities for her than full-time mothering, they still feel guilty about not spending a large proportion of their time with their children. Other reasons for feeling guilty given by a few mothers in the sample were: having doubts about the way one is bringing up the child, putting oneself before one's children, children misbehaving in front of others, not being able to attend pre-school or school activities, not being home when the children come home from school, not coping, and having a sick child.

Mothers talk about their feelings of guilt in the following ways.

I feel guilty when I do my block. I haven't got a great deal of patience, often if I growl or I might hit her—out of—you know you just get your-self all worked up and you hit her and you feel relieved. I feel guilty then afterwards. Often I'll cuddle her, I'll get around it in that way. That's the only time I feel really guilty. (Mt Druitt mother)

One of the really big things that upsets me—I was thinking about this today—is this love/hate, not so much love/hate as love/discipline. I find that very difficult. You're patient and you love and then all of a sudden 'whack' and into the bedroom and then I feel guilty. You know the guilt feelings and it's very difficult and you need lots of reassurance if you're doing the right thing and you don't get it as a mother—you don't get it from anyone really. Not many people reassure you. Husbands don't know what goes on and they don't understand. They don't have the same sort of feelings that women do. (Nth Shore mother)

Some feminist mothers described their feelings of guilt at a 'gut' or emotional level, even when intellectually they had reasoned out their actions. The traditional ideas of the 'good' mother persist producing an emotional reaction of guilt when mothers disobey the rules of such 'good' motherhood. As can be seen from the reasons mothers give for such guilt feelings, the cardinal sin of motherhood appears to be losing one's temper with a child. In its extreme form this sin is baby-bashing.

Mothers in being given the sole responsibility for their children have been given an area of power and control which is almost exclusively theirs. The logical extension of such control is violence towards the powerless. But the ideology of motherhood prohibits this and emphasises the mother's self-control at all times. Yet the majority of mothers in the sample realise that baby-bashing is a possibility. The actual baby-bashing, however, can never be admitted as it constitutes the epitome of 'failed' motherhood.

In reponse to the question 'What do you think about baby-bashing?' mothers made the distinction between deliberately harming a child and hitting out in anger and frustration at the child. It is the latter form of baby-bashing that the respondents are talking about. Whereas 47% of the sample acknowledged that baby-bashing is a terrible thing, 85% said that they could sympathise. Sixty two per cent said that they themselves had come very close to bashing their child and gave an example and 52% said that self-control, breathing space or someone else stopped them. Sixty eight per cent of feminist mothers felt that it was the situation in which mothers in present society are placed and the pressures upon them that cause baby-bashing. Other mothers tended to say that it was up to the individual mother to control her emotions in whatever situation she was placed. Examples were given of mothers with colicky babies and 'hyperactive' children and of mothers who were bringing up children on their own without the support of a father or other family members who might be pressured into baby-bashing, but the implication was always that the mother must control her emotions.

The following are typical replies of mothers to the question 'What do you think of baby-bashing?'

> You could have asked me that say, even before Alan (4 years old) was born and I would have said it was disgusting, a depraved woman and that, but now I can honestly understand them. Even though I wouldn't bash the baby Neil—I wouldn't bash Alan either. But I know just a while ago Neil wasn't well and there was one day there he screamed and screamed, it went on non-stop for about half-an-hour and you couldn't do anything with him and you just got, so at first you cuddle and try to control it—but after a while it gets to some part of your mind and you can't help it, you feel like giving him a whack and you know you can't because it's a baby. But I think some women, they have these babies that don't let up 24 hours a day. I can understand them to a certain extent why they would. I know some people are cruel, they burn them or something, but you can get just an ordinary mother that would accidentally hit a child or something and they'd be so sorry afterward, that I really can feel sorry for them. (Mt Druitt mother)

> I think it's so understandable. After I had my daughter I could really understand it. I can remember having a talk with my sister about it, and she was saying she could understand it too. It wouldn't be just the result of a sick person necessarily. It's like some kind of torture having to go week after week, month after month, maybe even a year or more with no sleep. And that's even just with one child and if you have several others as well and if you're not getting any support from other people, and most people aren't very supportive. Mothers and mothers-in-law tend to see more what you're not doing than what you are doing. And husbands or fathers are so often absent or aren't quite as involved and everyone sees the child as your total responsibility, "Why can't you keep that child quiet?" And there aren't many places where people can go to when they feel perhaps like they're slapping too much to talk to someone. I don't think it's surprising at all. I think it's really tragic though. It's really part of the isolation of mothers and of fathers too I suppose, in today's society. (Feminist mother)

Even so, it is one thing to admit to being driven to the point of bashing a child and quite another to admit to actually harming the child one is supposed to love. The ideology of motherhood apparently does not allow the latter admission. One mother in the sample was strongly suspected by her two closest friends, who were also interviewed, of bashing her children and she herself said that her neighbours had accused her and she feared they had 'put her in'. This is what she says about baby-bashing,

I think it happens and I think it can happen so very easily. Funnily enough I have been accused of baby-bashing because I had a row with a few of my neighbours and someone rang my mother-in-law and told her I'd been bashing the children. The youngest was covered in bruises, but he keeps falling down the back stairs. He's always falling over his own feet, gets bruises on his legs and then he fights with this one.

I thought the Welfare were going to knock on the door and take my kids away. They don't look too badly treated, do they? But it can happen very easily. (Mt Druitt mother)

The ultimate sanction then, for mothers who fail to control their emotions where their children are concerned, is that society in the form of welfare agencies can step in and remove the child from the mother. Such a mother henceforth bears the stamp of 'failed motherhood'.

Of interest here, are the few mothers in the sample who said that they don't feel guilty as mothers. Such mothers are living in situations where they don't have 24 hours a day responsibility for their children and household tasks, e.g., with their own mother or, they allow that anger is a permissable human emotion, even for mothers and have found ways that are acceptable to them to diffuse such anger, without harming the child.

To give a more dynamic perspective to the characteristics of 'good' motherhood the question was asked 'Are you bringing up your children very differently from the way you were brought up?' The 33 per cent of respondents who said that they are bringing up their children very much in the same way that they were brought up imply a continuation of the same basic rules and values. North Shore mothers more than other mothers tended to say that they were bringing up their children similarly to the way that they were brought up (52% as against 33% for the whole sample). The 67% of mothers who said that they were bringing up their children differently are more concentrated in the Single (80%) Employed (72%) and Feminist (80%) groups. Deliberate changes which have been made which mothers see as 'good' aspects of mothering predominate in the reasons given for rearing their children differently. For example, mothers said that they are doing more things with their children, being more involved in their activities, giving children more freedom to express themselves and encouraging them to be independent and to develop their own individuality, not being as strict as their own parents were and substituting reward and encouragement for corporal punishment, being more honest about sex, showing more love and communicating better. Feminist mothers added that they were teaching less sex division of roles and encouraging children to relate to adults other than parents. Some typical responses are,

> We're not as strict, especially with food, lollies, biscuits and staying up. They're not as frightened of me as I was of my father. I was really frightened, if he said "jump", I jumped. But mine answer back and treat you like an equal. (Mt Druitt mother)

A more relaxed attitude to children and also a more child centred approach is suggested by the responses to this question. The labour involved in child care may have lessened, but emotional involvement and time spent with children as a principle of 'good' motherhood has become more salient. For some mothers this is offset by attempts to make the child more independent, that is to stand on his/her own feet and be less dependent on mother and by allowing the child to form close relationships with adults from an early age, other than the mother or mother and father. The responsibilities of 'good' motherhood have, if anything increased to include more stimulation, a more interesting mother, more communication and involvement, and a concern for the child's emotional as well as physical development.

Many mothers who initially claimed that they were bringing up their children differently from the way that they were brought up, as they talked on, came to the conclusion that in fact, they were repeating their own mother's formula for child rearing and so repeating the cycle. For example, a North Shore mother says,

> I think it's very hard to be any different, it's too ingrained, you can see yourself hating what you're doing but the tape plays over again, until you see a parent who is different. I guess for people who aren't the eldest in the family, if their older siblings treat children a different way that gives them a different approach. But apart from that you've only got Dr Spock and mother.

While women remain the chief child-carers it appears unlikely that attitudes to 'good' mothering will alter significantly and the need to mother will continue to be structurally and socially defined as part of womanhood. The ideology of motherhood will continue to produce acquiesence at the 'gut' level described by the mothers interviewed, and will continue to constrain the lives and behaviour of women.

That the 'good' mother should put her child first, at least at this stage of the life cycle, is exemplified by the fact that the majority of mothers in the sample said that their main aim in life at present is to bring up their children to the very best of their ability—to be a 'good' mother to their children. 86% of Mt Druitt mothers, 84% of North Shore and Employed mothers, 100% of Single mothers and 64% of Feminist mothers gave as their main aim in life to rear, educate or make their children happy. Typical of these responses is that of a Mt Druitt mother who says,

> It's most important to me to feel that I'm being a really good mother at home. I think I'm doing the best I can and the best for my children, and also to be a good wife.

Feminist mothers (68%) stressed as equally important their own self-fulfilment, growth and satisfaction. For example, Emma Neil says,

> To really make a stable, sound basis for the children to start their lives, because maybe it's so important. And to work out a really good relationship with Brian (husband). And to achieve personal satisfaction in other areas.

In keeping with their views of motherhood, feminist mothers superimpose on their concern for their children, a concern for their own needs and development. In terms of time, energy and emotional commitment, children are the main concern of these mothers especially at the pre-school stage even if, in addition, they have a concern for their own fulfilment as individuals. However, in Steven Lukes' terms feminist mothers come closer to his view of autonomy than other mothers. Lukes says (1973:133–34), that we deny a person's autonomy when we treat him/her as merely the player of a role rather than as a person capable of choice.

Feminist mothers do not see themselves merely as a mother playing a role, but as persons capable of choice within certain limits and with capacities for self-development. They refuse to be treated solely as child-rearers, although child-rearing is an important aspect of their social being. The distinction between role player and autonomous individual will be discussed in more detail when the self-concepts of mothers are examined. At this point it is, I think, important to note that some challenge to the constraints of the motherhood role has been attempted by feminist mothers. How this affects their daily lives is demonstrated when the activities of a typical day of the mothers interviewed is examined.

From Table 4.2, it is obvious that 'good' motherhood translated into daily activities means cleaning and other housework, feeding the family and caring for children physically. In all groups except the Feminist and Employed mothers groups where 100% of respondents mentioned employment and outside activities in which they, as distinct from their families were involved, these activities predominate, and even in these groups they are important. It is only in North Shore and Single mothers groups that more than half the respondents (56% and 60% respectively) mentioned spending time with

Table 4.2 Most frequently mentioned activities of a typical day

Activity	Mt Druitt No. (%)	Nth Shore No. (%)	Single No. (%)	Employed No. (%)	Feminist No. (%)	Total No. (%)
Feeding the family	32 (64)	23 (92)	23 (92)	21 (84)	23 (92)	122 (81.33)
Cleaning and other housework	36 (72)	23 (92)	23 (92)	17 (68)	13 (52)	112 (74.66)
Caring for children, bathing, dressing, etc.	14 (28)	20 (80)	20 (80)	18 (72)	23 (92)	95 (63.33)
Mother's own activity outside home, (employment, sport, visiting, meetings, classes etc).	12 (24)	16 (64)	6 (24)	25 (100)	25 (100)	84 (56.00)
Washing	27 (54)	13 (52)	15 (60)	8 (32)	8 (32)	71 (47.33)
Taking children to and from school sports, children's activities	4 (8)	13 (52)	19 (76)	16 (64)	16 (64)	68 (45.33)
Spending time with children, talking to, playing with, taking to park, swimming, etc.	8 (16)	14 (56)	15 (60)	8 (32)	8 (32)	55 (36.66)
Sewing, reading, hobby, music, studying, working at home	2 (4)	14 (56)	9 (36)	0 (0)	19 (76)	44 (29.33)
Shopping	7 (14)	16 (64)	10 (40)	6 (24)	5 (20)	44 (29.33)
Ironing	16 (32)	5 (20)	1 (4)	4 (16)	1 (4)	27 (18.00)
Watching T.V.	8 (16)	1 (4)	6 (24)	0 (0)	5 (20)	20 (13.33)
Spending time with husband	2 (4)	6 (24)	0 (0)	5 (20)	0 (0)	13 (8.66)
Relaxing, sleeping, resting	2 (4)	5 (20)	2 (8)	0 (0)	3 (12)	12 (8.00)
Gardening	6 (12)	2 (8)	1 (4)	1 (4)	1 (4)	11 (7.33)

children in child-centred activities. In spite of the extremely strong emphasis on spending time with children as an important aspect of 'good' motherhood, it is clear from these facts that 'good' motherhood in pragmatic terms in our society means 'good' house-keeping and the daily physical tasks associated with the care of children. The ideology ensures that these tasks are done by mothers as part of their responsibility for their children's well being. Feminist mothers mentioned housework less than other mothers and, in fact, observation revealed less emphasis in their homes on this aspect of their role, but they were equally as conscious as other mothers of their responsibility for feeding the family and physically caring for their children. In terms of daily activities feminist mothers more than other mothers mentioned activities both outside and inside the home which were self rather than child or house centred, revealing some challenge to the idea of the 'all-giving', 'selfless' player of a prescribed role. However the choice of such activities remains severely limited by the initial demands of the mother role.

Young children need their mothers in constant attendance

Until they go to school, children need their mothers with them constantly. Leaving one's own child with another person is all right for a short period of time, but the other person should be one's own mother, one's husband, or a female relative. The child is at all times the mother's own responsi-bility. The father or others may help, but the mother is primarily respon-sible for the child. Life would be made easier for mothers if they had more support in and relief from their motherhood duties. However, such support or relief must be acceptable within the above dimensions of the ideology, that is, the mother must remain the responsible person.

This tenet is highlighted by responses to the question, 'Do you think mothers of pre-school children should work or not? Why? Why not?' The majority of Mt Druitt (86%), Nth Shore (72%) and Single (68%) mothers think that mothers of pre-school children should not work unless it is financially necessary. The main reasons given are that pre-school children need their mothers and that the mother misses out on so much if she does. Almost all mothers who said that mothers of pre-school children should not work, made the proviso that it was acceptable if they needed to for financial reasons. There was no discussion of whether the child under these circum-stances suffered less, the emphasis in the responses was on the judg-ment of the mother and her duty and responsibility. For example, Jill Mark an employed mother says,

I think the responsibility for children is a very great one and I think you can only take time off that responsibility with great care and great restraints. Until the child can talk for itself and go to the toilet for itself and communicate how it can eat food, etc., I think it's really your responsibility.

The implication is always that the mother in paid employment who does not need the finance, is not fulfilling her duty as a responsible mother to her child. There is also an implicit recognition in these responses of the necessity in today's society for some families to have a double income, but as Anne Summers (1975:445) points out, although Australia is becoming a two-income society, it is still masked by a 'one-income ideology', where women are concerned.

Mothers who stressed that the young child needs its mother in constant attendance have incorporated into their ideology already existing ideas stemming from Bowlby (1971, 1972), Ainsworth (1973) and others. Burns and Goodnow (1979:89) point out that it is the simple form of an expert 'message' that influences public opinion and that in this case the simple form consists of the propositions that:

1   Nothing can replace a mother's love (or a child's love for its mother) as far as the child development process is concerned.
2   For the right kind of love to develop, mother and child should not be too much out of each other's sight during the first 3 and possibly 5 to 6 years of life.

Many mothers incorporated these ideas implicitly in their opinions on employment of mothers with pre-school children, some mothers who themselves belong with the 'experts' were more explicit. For example, Jan Carter who is a physiotherapist working with children, says,

It's wrong. I suppose in my work in this Association for the Welfare of Children in Hospital I've come into contact with people like James Robertson and the Bowlby people who've written books and I do not think that the pre-school child—those are the years that you've got to give up. I mean you've made your decisions before. And I think that the majority of girls today are intelligent enough and well educated enough to know, 'Right, if I have a child that means five years to get that child started in life'. Gee, it's a small price to pay and golly we're building a whole other generation and I think you can look at yourself and say, 'I'm not prepared to do this it's better not to have children' ...

I just think that you can't ask a mother substitute, unless she is in a constant one to one relationship that can have love, to look after a child. Because anyone that tells me that they can put their children into a creche of 4 or 5 children and whoever runs that child-minding centre, or creche

or kindergarten will be just as good as she is, is talking a load of rubbish . . .
   One can only love one's own children and you're the only person who
can give absolute love to your own children. You can't expect other people
to do the job for you. I think it's passing the buck of responsibility. I've
very strong views about that.

In exposing the myth that children need their mothers Ann Oakley
points out some of the fallacies of these arguments as well as the use
of the myth as a technique for the evasion of paternal responsibility.
Oakley (1974a:203–21) shows (and the mothers in my research confirm) that the mother at home does not necessarily devote all her
time to her children, perhaps being distracted by housework when
children need conversation, stimulating play or physical affection
and that there is no mystical tie between mother and child, ensuring
the quality of feelings a mother has for her child. A child in the one-
to-one relationship of the home is very vulnerable to the mother's
moods, and 'hang ups' apart from actual hatred or rejection or
personality clashes. She also queries the transfer of findings from
institutionalised child-rearing and hospitalisation to the family situation. In the latter instance the child experiences 'maternal deprivation' because it has become so dependent on the mother in the
one-to-one relationship. In the former instance the scarcity of any
form of warmth and affection due to the low numbers of carers produces an extreme situation of deprivation for the child, not just
'maternal deprivation'. Oakley goes on to comment on the use of
the term 'maternal deprivation' as a political statement tying women
more tightly to their children under the guise of exalting maternity
and thus absolving men from paternal responsibility.
   It is probably closer to the truth to say of some of the mothers in
the research sample that *they* need their children rather than that
their children need them, in the sense of giving them a purpose in
life and a feeling of being important to someone. For example, an
employed mother affirms the fear expressed by 52% of the North
Shore mothers that a mother drifts apart from her child if she works
outside the home. In answer to the question 'Do you think mothers
of pre-school children should work or not?' she says,

No, definitely not. No matter how much you love your child you still
slowly drift apart. I have a good friend, she looks after Melissa, she calls
this woman Aunty Lillian, but often she'll call her Mummy and I think
she's forgetting about me, she's slowly drifting apart. Some nights she
won't want to come home, she might be having a good time with the
other person's kiddies. No I could never recommend it, I don't think it's
right at all.

On the other hand, most Employed mothers (72%) and Feminist mothers (96%) were more likely to say that employment outside the home is permissable for mothers with pre-school children. These mothers take into consideration the needs of the mother herself, as well as the needs of the child and tend to stress the quality of child care rather than the quantity and the beneficial aspects for the child in relating to more than one adult. Incorporated in these responses are alternative attitudes to child care such as those expressed by Margaret Mead (1973). Mead points out that it is only in Western industrialised society that the total responsibility for child care is thrust upon the biological parents and more particularly on the mother, in other societies more people are generally involved in the rearing of a child. From Mead's point of view the mental health of both child and mother are more likely to be served by more inter-action with other supportive adults than by still more interaction with the mother.

These views are apparent in the following responses given by an employed and a feminist mother who are, in fact, challenging the belief that a pre-school child needs its mother in constant atten-dance. Concerning the employed mother, they comment,

> Looking back on Colin, it was the best thing for him. If I was going to spend my day being amused it wouldn't be with someone 31 years older than me. So therefore it's not unreasonable that he should feel the same way in his own little way. He's very well adjusted. When I go out with other mums with children the same age they're very clingy. Mine is off looking, exploring, doing, knocking himself over and helping himself. I think that's good because much as I'd like to bind him to me I still think it's better for him not to be. (Employed mother)

> I think it's a load of garbage that for the first five years you've got to stay at home with your kids. In fact I think a child that stays with a mother 24 hours a day, seven days a week is probably more neglected in a way than when a mother goes to work. Because I know when I go to work the time that I spend with my children I spend much more constructively. And I've spent a little time at home with pre-schoolers, 12 months I spent at home and it was terrible, I hated it and therefore they couldn't be happy. (Feminist mother)

While they have challenged the belief that young children need the exclusive and constant attention of their own mother, these mothers to a large extent leave unchallenged the corollory that the biological or social mother must at all times maintain primary responsibility for her children.

The mother's own responsibility for her child at all times is seen quite clearly in responses to the questions, 'If you want to have a break, go shopping, have your hair cut, go to the dentist, who do you leave your children with? If you want to have a night out with your husband who do you leave your children with? Are these arrangements satisfactory to you?'

Although the majority of mothers in all groups (Mt Druitt 62%, Nth Shore 80%, Single 68%, Employed 68%, Feminist 64%) said that they did have satisfactory arrangements for baby-sitters for brief periods, many mothers commented on the fact that they did not like leaving their children with other people especially for lengthy periods of time. Nine Mt Druitt mothers said that they never leave their children with anyone. 'I'm one of those people who don't believe in baby-sitters', said one. Many 'at home' mothers take their children with them wherever they go during the day, leave the child briefly with the father on Thursday evening or Saturday morning for shopping trips and travel miles to leave children with their own mother or mother-in-law for the occasional evening out with their husband. Middle-class mothers whose parents or parents-in-law do not live in Sydney and who go out fairly frequently with their husbands (e.g., once a month or more) tend to belong to baby-sitting clubs where baby-sitting exchanges are made with other couples with young children. In all cases the mother felt it was her own responsibility and not her husband's or anyone else's to arrange for baby-sitting. Mothers who 'dumped' their children on other people or who were not prompt in picking children up from pre-school or baby-sitters were frowned upon. Even feminist mothers associated with the Children's Co-operative where there was a deliberate attempt to get children to relate to a number of adults from an early age and to allow the mother to leave the child without warning and for any length of time during the day, were conscious that they should not overuse this facility.

In my sample no mother used a child care centre, three mothers who could not engage a relative, friend or neighbour preferred a mother approved as a home-minder by the council. To leave a child for any length of time with a stranger unless it is a council approved mother in her own home contravenes this tenet of the ideology, the child needs its mother and she must be the responsible person.

This sense of individual responsibility on the mother's part for her offspring is also evident when the responses to the question 'Can you suggest any ways in which life could be made easier for mothers with young children?' are examined.

'At home' Mt Druitt (52%) and Nth Shore (44%) mothers and some Employed mothers (24%) feel that their task would be made easier if some provision were made for relief from their responsibility for periods of time so that they can have a break. Such relief in most cases is specified as someone coming into the home to take over while the mother has a break. Some mothers (10% Mt Druitt, 12% Nth Shore, 8% Single) suggested that fathers should help more in this way and 20% of Feminist mothers suggested total role sharing.

In all cases the someone needed to be known and trusted by the respondent. There is an acknowledgement here of the tension and strain produced by 24 hour a day responsibility for a young child but the solution, except for the feminists' role sharing, is in temporary relief from, and support in, this responsibility. Woman's proper place is seen as in the home, caring for her children. It appears that perception of options for the majority of these mothers regarding the form of their child-rearing responsibility is severely limited and that the ideology of motherhood acts as a mechanism for such limitation.

The suggestion is made however by the majority of Feminist mothers (80%), some Employed (28%) and some Mt Druitt (16%) mothers, that the provision of more, cheaper and better child care facilities would ease the burden of the majority of mothers. These mothers see reliable long day-care, occasional day-care, after school care and child care in shopping centres as a solution to the burden of 24 hour a day responsibility for children, implicitly suggesting that it is permissable for mothers to leave their children with strangers. Feminist mothers (40%) further question the individual mother's sole responsibility for her child by suggesting community run co-operative child care, funded by the government, to alleviate the privatisation and isolation of the individual mother with her own child.

Some of the Feminist mothers interviewed had, in fact, set up a Children's Co-operative which, while not being government funded, had supplied them with an alternative to privatised, isolated motherhood and which they experienced as extremely worthwhile. Hiliary Chalmers says of this Co-operative,

> We have set up a Children's Co-operative where all the parents, male and female, do shifts, and occasionally we get volunteers doing shifts as well. Nerida's been going there for about 2 years in June, since she was 18 months. And over that period she's had a chance to build up good relations with these other people and she feels quite closely to them. And since we moved in here, she knows that there are other adults from the Co-op and she's become quite happy about going and talking to them about these things and even more if she's hurt she'll go to them. And that really comes out a lot in the Co-op. You get a chance to build up relationships with other children. Rather than just saying 'Mummy, Mummy',

they'll come running over and tell you about things. Just in the day to day care of the child, taking them to the toilet and cleaning them and giving them food you relate to them and they relate to you.

Having a lot of 'good carers' is important. And I think society has to take more responsibility for its children. It plans all the buildings, schools and things for the next 50–60–70 years counting on all these women to give birth and then when you do, they just don't want to know about it. They don't like you taking your baby into banks or buildings or on buses. They make it really inconvenient to go anywhere and do anything. And if your child cries, of course everyone turns against you. And I think society has to take more responsibility for children.

This mother goes on to describe a 'good carer' showing the realisation that the individual mother's complete responsibility for the child produces competitiveness between mothers, which is neither to their advantage nor to the advantage of the child. She emphasises the child as a person in its own right, which is also one of the basic assumptions of the Children's Co-operative. She says,

One of the most important things is to accept the child for what it is—to try to get rid of all your preconceived ideas like wanting your child to be popular, or wanting them to be extroverted when the child is perhaps an introvert who doesn't like talking and performing and I think we have to try to get away from the competitive thing. As soon as babies are born we start saying 'And they're racing'. They're all lined up and heading off and who will get the first tooth and all those different landmarks along the way. I think we really have to get away from that . . .
I think children are willing and keen to learn, you just have to give them a chance to develop at their own pace. I think they're the most important things because I think if you really try to practice these then you're really going to build up a caring relationship, you're really going to be taking the child's own characteristics and wants into consideration, then that brings in love and caring.

In this way some of the feminist mothers show an awareness of some of the effects of the ideology of motherhood on both the mother and the child which are not to the benefit of either. They have consequently made an attempt to replace some of the traditional beliefs about motherhood with some utopian ideas, especially concerning the individual mother's total responsibility for her own child.

In contrast to this many of the mothers in the sample felt that motherhood could only be improved if mothers themselves made an extra effort within their motherhood role to get out of the house and contact other mothers. For example a Mt Druitt mother says,

Up here everything possible is being done for mothers. The only thing that can make life easier for a young mother with pre-school children is if she uses her own initiative and her two little 'itty, bitty' legs and goes out that door and doesn't come back until the afternoon. There are a lot of women smouldering, they're sitting inside shut doors with pre-school children allowing these children to drive them around the bend and yet they don't do a thing to help themselves. I've gotten out.

A North Shore mother says,

It's really all up to you—I don't see that someone doing something is going to make it any easier . . .

Views such as these which emphasise the mother's own responsibility for her fate were expressed by 14% of Mt Druitt mothers, 28% of Nth Shore, 12% of Single and 4% of Employed mothers, but by none of the Feminist mothers. One of the functions of the ideology which has already been evident in the internalisation of guilt by these mothers, appears to be to individualise motherhood and its responsibilities, placing all the praise or blame for the consequences on individual mothers while obscuring the institution of motherhood which serves society's interests and ignores some of the needs of mothers and their children.

In all groups there was an awareness that the needs of mothers are ignored by the wider society. One Mt Druitt mother expressed the feeling this way, 'Don't you know there *are* no mothers in Australia?' Mothers felt that the general consensus of society is that mothers with young children should neither be seen nor heard outside their own homes. Consequently many mothers (22% of the sample) felt that their job would be made easier if there were more places such as play groups, or clubs, or restaurants, or art galleries or even shops or banks where they and their children are welcome and catered for.

Some mothers (11% of the sample) expressed the opinion that while ignoring the needs of mothers and children the community set very high standards for housework, child care and the public behaviour of children and that their job would be made easier if such expectations were more realistic.

The final tenet of the ideology of motherhood as presented here looks at the way the mothers interviewed felt that the wider society rates their job in terms of status and at how the mothers themselves assess their task.

Mothering is an important but low status job

Being a mother is an important job in our society, but it is generally not recognised today. Unless a person is part of the workforce, he or she is not considered important.

Only a very small number of mothers in each group (Mt Druitt, Nth Shore, Employed, 12%; Single, Feminist 4%) believe that without a doubt mothers are looked up to in society today. These mothers take an individualistic view, everyone has a mum and loves her, so that society in general must respect mums.

Within the high percentage in each group (Mt Druitt, Nth Shore, Employed, 88%; Single, Feminist, 96%) who do not think that mothers are looked up to in today's society, there are some interesting variations. Mt Druitt mothers tend to see themselves as a nuisance in shops, on buses, in public places and interpret this as a lack of recognition of the importance of mothers in society generally. For example a Mt Druitt mother says,

> People are very rude and think they (mothers) shouldn't be there and shouldn't exist and they've got no rights. Mothers are abused. I've even had it said to me 'You should be home with those children not out'. I mean what do they think they're supposed to do, stay at home 24 hours a day every day?

Feminist (40%), Nth Shore (36%), and Single (28%) mothers relate these ideas more directly to the low status of the roles of housewife and mother in a society which generally regards women and their concerns and jobs as inferior. For example, Jean Lang, a North Shore mother says,

> A lot of it depends on what you're doing and I think, I've found after—and I only started doing this Law course because we were living at Leichhardt and I had no friends around and no support in terms of anyone looking after him and I was starting to go up the wall because I was trapped in the house all the time. But I found—it was incredible—a lot of people are really status conscious and they introduce you to a friend and they say, 'This is Jean who's doing the Law course'. So that's got status. They never say, 'This is Jean who's the mother of two children'. So I think status is entirely in terms of what you're doing and that's wrong and I don't like that. I normally never tell anyone that I'm doing it myself and it doesn't worry me, I'm doing it because I needed an out, something for me to do. But I found that in terms of being a mother, I don't think you have any status whatsoever.

The dichotomy of status between those who are in paid employment and those who aren't, is emphasised by the 'at home' Mt Druitt (26%) and Nth Shore (20%) mothers who feel caught between the demands that a woman be in the work-force if she wants to be considered of worth and that she stay at home if she wants to be considered a 'good' mother. For example a Mt Druitt mother says,

> It's getting that way now that society expects all mothers to work, sometimes she thinks she should be at work because everyone's expecting her

to work. She's probably looked down on if she stays home and looks after her children. But the lady over the road went to work when the youngest was only 5 and everyone thought she was awful.

It is only those who belong to the sisterhood of motherhood who realise what is involved in the job, what a tough job it is and how worthwhile it is, say 26% of Mt Druitt mothers, 20% of Single and 12% of Feminist mothers. For example a Single mother comments,

> I don't think we're looked up to. I don't think a lot of people really realise what goes into being a mother because there's so many things that you've got to do, so many roles that you've got to play. It's only mothers who appreciate what is involved.

Some North Shore (20%) and Employed (4%) mothers feel that it is the mother's own fault if she is looked down on. They say that so many mothers present themselves as hassled, martyred and to be pitied or they neglect or over-indulge their children. So that even in the area of status it is possible to place the responsibility on the individual mother for the image she presents.

Many of the responses showed considerable ambivalence about the status of mothering in today's society. As can be seen from those quoted, some mothers feel that mothering has high status amongst mothers themselves but not in the wider society, that is, in the man's world. Others see that society has a hypocritical attitude to motherhood or a double standard, Annette Erving, a feminist mother says,

> Society is hypocritical, it has a double standard. There's this lovely 'we're up on a pedestal' in this sort of 'yukky', highly sentimentalised way—you know Mother's Day and all this goo, which I find absolutely revolting, but then, on the other hand, we are definitely looked down on because our opinion isn't sought and we are ignored, etc.

It is evident that, with a few exceptions, these mothers feel that their job is worthwhile and recognised as such amongst the sisterhood of mothers but in the wider man's world of big business, finance and world shattering decisions, that the job holds little status. The values of motherhood are at variance with the cash nexus society in which we live, but the ideology of motherhood puts the value of service, loving, caring above money value and status rewards. Although the job is a hard, dirty, demanding, exhausting one, with no status or money rewards, it is believed to be important and brings emotional rewards to those who persevere and dedicate themselves to it. The home as the 'private haven' in which the important tasks of creating and caring for future citizens are carried out as a labour of love and service, and in which a different and morally superior set of values operate from those of the wider world, becomes a part of the ideology accepted by the majority of mothers and reinforced by other mothers with a similar consciousness. The economic implications of such unpaid labour are thus obscured. As Sheila Rowbotham points out (1973:61), woman's consciousness is predicated upon the social relations of the home and man's upon the social relations of the market place. The fact that the domestic sphere is subordinate to and dependent upon the relations of production in the public sphere means that women as a group are subordinate to men as a group and this subordination is reflected in their consciousness.

Some of the mothers interviewed, such as Denise Watt, a single mother, express subjective feelings of inferiority which are part of the consciousness of the 'at home' mothers. She says,

> People do look down on the fact that you're a housewife bringing up your children, that you're not in the big outside world, that you can't communicate on things other than nappies and things. People do look down on that, so therefore a housewife becomes even less of a person in mind, so she rushes into work to build up her confidence. So I don't think that people really give housewives the credit they deserve.

In a society which is dependent upon the capitalist mode of production as the basis of commodity production and exchange and in which this sphere of production is both male orientated and male dominated, men have the power not only to define the identity of women in terms of their domestic roles, but also the power to define such an identity as inferior to their own which is based on the public sphere of production. The feelings of inferiority thus produced reinforce the structural inequalities between the sexes which already exist in society. In this way the powerful can, in their own interests, avert conflict and secure the acquiescence of a less powerful group even against the real interests of that group (Lukes, 1974:23–25). Although the powerless internalise such feelings of inferiority and identify with others who are in a similar position, as the above respondent indicates, they are not conscious of their conflict of interests with a more powerful group who both dominate and exploit them. Their inferiority is accepted as natural and legitimate.

Without endorsing the 'women as a class' thesis, it is useful here to apply Giddens (1973:112–16) differentiation between 'class awareness' or 'identity'; 'class or conflict consciousness' and 'revolutionary class consciousness' to mothers as a group. The mothers in the sample have some awareness of group identity with other mothers, they see that mothers as a group have low status in a market economy. It is only some of the feminist mothers, however, who have reached Giddens second level of class consciousness where perception of group unity is linked with a recognition of opposition of interest with another class or classes. Whereas mothers identify with other mothers and have a conception of their differentiation as a group, they do not see themselves as a group with a conflict of interests with men in general or with the capitalist male in particular. Even fewer mothers have reached Giddens third level of class consciousness where there is a recognition of the possibility of an overall reorganisation in the institutional mediation of power and a belief that such a reorganisation can be brought about by the action of women themselves, or of mothers themselves. The subjective feelings of inferiority associated with motherhood, felt by these mothers generally add to their individual feelings of powerlessness and so help to keep them in a subordinate position, rather than raising their consciousness of subordination and exploitation as a group in opposition to a more structurally powerful group.

Nevertheless, along with such feelings of inferiority goes a sense of the moral superiority of the values of nurturing, caring, etc. which are associated with motherhood as against the fierce competitiveness of the man's world outside the home. Rozaldo and Lamphere (1974:7–8) suggest that where the domestic and public orders are clearly distinguished and woman is defined largely in terms of a maternal and domestic role, she has limited access to the sorts of authority, prestige and cultural values which are the perogatives of men. Given such an imbalance in the exercise of power, the avenues by which women gain prestige and a sense of value are limited by their association with the domestic world and hence women's attempts to find meaning in their lives are in terms of the values associated with their housewife/mother roles. In this research it appears that the importance of their task and the positive evaluation of the values and rewards associated with motherhood are a necessary ideological support for an unpaid, low status, demanding job.

Conclusions

There is a core of ideas which form a normative framework for the mothers of young children in contemporary Australian suburban situations. These core notions, with some variations are held by a group of 'at home' mothers living in a two parent relationship in a working class area and a similar group in a middle class area, as well as by groups of single, employed and feminist mothers all with pre-school children. Superimposed on these basic ideas by some employed and most feminist mothers is another set of ideas which seeks to take into account the needs of the mother herself and to allow her to develop her own potentialities apart from those accentuated by her mothering, and to share the total responsibility for parenting with men as well as women and/or with other members of the community. The core beliefs of the ideology and some utopian ideas suggested by the mothers in the research sample are summarised below.

Table 4.3   Ideology and utopian ideas

Ideology		Utopian ideas
1	Motherhood and womanhood are intermeshed; to be considered a mature, balanced, fulfilled adult, a woman should be a mother.	1 Motherhood isn't necessary for women's fulfilment, nor is it inevitable, but it does 'build character'.
2	a A 'good' mother is always available to her children, she spends time with them, guides, supports, encourages and corrects as well as loving and caring for them physically. She is also responsible for the cleanliness of their home environment. b A 'good' mother is unselfish, she puts her children's needs before her own.	2 A good parent is all of (a) but is also attempting to fulfil his/her own needs by developing individual potentialities, apart from parenthood.
3	Children need their mothers in constant attendance at least for the first 3–5 years of their lives.	3 Children need to relate to a number of adults, both male and female. The quality of relationship with a carer is more important than quantity.
4	The individual mother should have total responsibility for her own children at all times.	4 The individual mother is primarily responsible for her children, but this responsibility should be shared with other adult carers, both male and female. The community and the state should take more responsibility for the rearing of children.
5	Mothering is a low status but important, worthwhile and intrinsically rewarding job in our society. The non-material rewards outweigh the lack of financial and status rewards.	5 Mothering is a low status, but important, worthwhile and intrinsically rewarding job in our male dominated society. If men participated more it's status would be raised. Changes in the employment structure are needed to enable men as well as women to participate in parenting and in the work force.

The ideology effectively bars men from the 'joys' of parenting but rewards them in terms of power in the wider society. The utopian ideas presented here challenge some aspects of the ideology of motherhood but do not attack in any systematic way, the structure of male power in our society which enables such an ideology to be perpetuated and so to retain the imbalance of gender relationships of power. The overall effect has not been to redefine motherhood so that the individual mother relinquishes her primary responsibility for her children, but to add another set of ideas to those already held. The total effect appears then to be the creation of an ideal of the superwoman which O'Leary and Depner (1976:315) term the 'superwoman syndrome'. Within this ideal, women attempt to respond simultaneously to the enactment of both male and female gender roles, to strive competitively for advancement outside the home while attempting to maintain the social and domestic responsibilities traditionally ascribed to their roles as housewives and mothers. Some evidence, say O'Leary and Depner (1976:315) indicates that college males in American society are now characterising their ideal woman along the lines of the superwoman profile. In fact, the mothers' descriptions of their way of being in the world which have formed the basis for the core ideas of the ideology and some utopian variations presented here, indicate that the individual mother's primary responsibility for her own children has in no way been diminished. In some cases it may have been relieved, but in most cases any advances in the area of development of personal abilities and potentialities and status achievement have been in addition to the responsibility of motherhood. One active feminist who had deliberately chosen to have a child at the age of 30, said that being a mother had not altered her career advancement or her participation in political and literary activities outside the home at all, but that she herself has become 'rattier and tireder'. 'I've proved that my life didn't *have* to change', she says, 'but in the process I've become angrier and tireder and more rushed and more tense'.

It appears that a sphere of interest and activity has been set aside for women in which they are given authority and an appearance of autonomy as well as considerable responsibility and a degree of individual ownership which the ideology presents as accruing rewards which are valued on a different dimension from those of the market place. An ideal of 'good' motherhood is presented which, if pursued, will keep the mother in the home while her children are young, caring for her family and pouring her psychic energy into this sphere of activity, leaving to the male the domains of power, authority, prestige and economic independence in the wider society. Feelings of guilt associated with breaking some of the more important rules of motherhood further act as an invisible control to keep the mother to her task and constantly striving after the ideal. If, for her, 'good' parenting also involves self actualisation in the male sphere of the wider society and the market place, these endeavours must be made in addition to the effort that is expended in mothering. Thus are existing male/female economic and power relations legitimated and perpetuated.

In the following chapter an accentuation of the 'essential tendencies' present in the points of view regarding the ideology of motherhood and those relating to utopias of motherhood are incorporated into abstract analytical constructs termed by Weber (1949:90–91) 'ideal types'. These ideal types are then used as tools for the analysis of the data presented by particular mothers.

Note

1   All names have been changed to preserve the anonymity of the respondents. Husband's and children's names have also been altered.

5 Ideal types of mothers

As has been evident in the previous chapter, the lived experience of motherhood as well as the views expressed concerning motherhood show variations within the research sample. In order to make comparisons between, and to develop explanations for these variations, in this chapter abstract analytical constructs termed 'ideal types' are formulated. An ideal type says Weber (1949:90),

> is formed by the one-sided *accentuation* of one or more points of view and by the synthesis of a great many diffuse, discrete, more or less present and occasionally absent *concrete individual* phenomena, which are arranged according to those one-sidedly emphasised viewpoints into a unified *analytical* construct (Gedankenbild). In its conceptual purity this mental construct (Gedankenbild) cannot be found anywhere in reality.

Such ideal types according to Weber (1949:92) are means not ends and are useful in analysis as they provide possible ideal limiting discrete cases with which one can compare empirical reality in order to determine the interdependence, causal conditions and significance of concrete cultural phenomena. In this chapter ideal types of mothers are constructed and the interview data and background information provided by respondents are compared with these ideal types in order to come to a greater understanding of causality, interdependence and significance of some of the variables of the research.

Four ideal types of mothers have been constructed, these are: the ideological traditionalist, ambivalent, ambivalent progressive, and radical utopian. In keeping with the concept of idealogy operationalised for the research, each ideal type includes both beliefs about motherhood and how such a mother perceives her way of being in the world, or her lived experience of motherhood. In actuality the lived experience of one type of mother may be associated with the beliefs of another type giving various combinations of these ideal types, but in their formulation, ideal types are treated as discrete abstract constructs.

Ideological traditional

The ideological traditional mother resembles Parsons' (Parsons and Bales, 1955) expressive carer. She is the mother who believes that 'woman's place is in the home', that women biologically and culturally are the best persons to care for children. The mature adult female in her view is a mother, one who adopts the expressive role in the home, by nurturing and caring for her children and her husband. Her role, she feels, is complementary to that of her husband, even if of lower status. If she is in the work-force she sees her job as secondary to her home role, or as an extension of her nurturing caring role at home. In terms of income and status it is therefore justifiably at a lower level than that of the husband and is in no way in competition with his role of provider and instrumental leader. She places great emphasis on the nuclear family as the best milieu for motherhood and child care.

If she is a single mother she would rather exist on the supporting mother's benefit than enter the work-force because she believes her place is in the home with her children. Her family she feels is incomplete without a man to be the instrumental leader, provider and male role model. She would very much like to get married again for the children's sake above all.

The ideological traditional mother endorses the tenets of the ideology. She believes that a 'good' mother is one who puts her children first at all times, one who is unselfishly available to them to listen, support, comfort, guide and correct them, one who never loses her temper, who consistently loves and cares for her children physically and emotionally and who provides a clean, healthy home environment for them. She believes that her children's mental and emotional health depend on her constant presence with them until they go to school, and on the very strong bond between herself and her children. At all times she, the mother, should be completely responsible for the welfare of her own children even if she has relief in this care for brief periods. Motherhood is women's work and although a tough and demanding job with few material or status rewards it is the most worthwhile and fulfilling job that a woman can do.

Such a mother sees herself primarily as a mother (or wife and mother) and feels that her satisfaction in life is through serving her children and her husband. She values femininity in terms of calm, loving, supportive behaviour, conventionally pretty appearance and generally being the complement of the male. She accepts the identity and role that has been traditionally prescribed for her, that is as a wife and a mother and makes every effort to adapt to these roles and their associated identity.

In terms of lived experience this mother is usually the mother at home who devotes her time and energy to her family, whose interests are those of the family. She has always wanted to be a mother and has no other real plan for her life. She married soon after leaving school and her first child was born soon after that. As the children grow older, her interests surround their school and sporting interests and her closest circle of friends are generally mothers of her children's friends. She may work outside the home part-time once her children go to school or pre-school, but she makes sure she is at home when they are at home, after school, during holidays and when they are sick. Or she may take full-time employment for short periods of time to supplement the family income for specific purposes. In this way she feels her family doesn't suffer. Her job is at all times secondary to her home commitments.

Although at times the ideological traditional mother may get harassed or 'fed up' with her situation, she expresses neither resentment nor rebellion, her place is in the home and it is up to her to adapt to or make the best of the frustrations as well as experience the joys of motherhood.

Ambivalent

The ambivalent mother endorses some of the core ideas of the ideology of motherhood in that she believes that her children need her in constant attendance at least until they go to school and that thereafter she should be at home when they come home from school, in school holidays and when they are sick. She differs however, from the Ideological Traditional in that she sees complete commitment to mothering as a stage in her life-cycle, a stage when her own progress in a job, or her development of her own interests and talents are arrested for the sake of her children.

In terms of perceptions of their lives and life-options, ambivalence for some of these mothers springs from the fact that they have had other options before children and have experienced identity and satisfaction from sources outside the traditional female areas. Like Hannah Gavron's middle class mothers they have combined thoughtful preparation and self-consciousness towards motherhood with a feeling that it is their right to be something more than 'just a mother' (Gavron, 1966:137). Consequently these mothers feel tied down by their present position. They feel that they are 'treading water' for the time being until their children become more independent, then they will pursue their own interests to a greater extent, but not at the expense of children and husband. The primary responsibility at this stage of the life-cycle is to husband and children.

For other ambivalent mothers there is a vaguer feeling of dissatisfaction with life at present. While energy and emotion are being invested in children, husband and the home, these mothers have not adjusted to their home roles and, like Betty Friedan's mothers (1963:32), they feel rather vaguely that life must have more to offer them, but they really cannot name what form that 'more' should take.

Ambivalent mothers see themselves primarily as individuals in their own right, with capacities, abilities and potentialities which make them different from other people and which can be developed independently of husband and children, but which, at the present time must take second place to their motherhood duties. Sources of self-esteem for Ambivalent mothers have come from options outside motherhood such as career or cultural interests, although at present . motherhood is absorbing most of their time and energy. If they are employed they feel guilty about the time they spend away from their children. They feel that the Women's Movement has helped women to stand up for themselves but reject any form of extremism which suggests a non-traditional feminine image.

They believe in some modifications of the traditional division of labour in the home but attach high value to the nuclear family as a milieu for child-rearing and tend to take full responsibility for child care and household tasks themselves. Their satisfactions in life come from their relationship with their husband (if in a two parent family) and their children, but also from career and cultural interests. Some resentment of their present position is felt although little action is taken.

Like the Crestwood Heights mothers of Seeley, Lim and Loosley's study (1956:180–81), they accept the culturally approved maternal role but reveal an underlying resentment. The more lively and interesting world of profession, office or travel or university before marriage has an appeal which is missing from the world of wife and mother. There is obviously not an unqualified acceptance of the cultural constraints placed upon them by the ideology. Also like the mothers in Crestwood Heights they are caught in the ambivalence of being prepared to become the object of their children's dependency, yet at the same time working towards the final dissolution of this dependency.

In terms of lived experience the ambivalent mother has probably married later and had her children later than the ideological traditionalist. Once she has had children she stays at home to care for them until they go to school or pre-school. Then she may take on part-time employment or increase her outside activities, but she will still be at home when her children are at home. In the meantime she attempts to keep up her reading and contacts with friends outside her immediate family. If employment is a necessity, home commitments come first.

Ambivalent progressive

In some ways these mothers have questioned the ideology. Motherhood they feel isn't necessary for women's fulfilment, nor is it inevitable, but it does build character and maturity. The biological mother need not be totally responsible for her child's care 24 hours a day, in fact several primary caretakers, both male and female are probably better for both the mother and the child. The quality of care is more important than quantity of time spent with one person, especially if that person also has full responsibility for household chores. A 'good' carer like a 'good' mother spends time with the child, listens, guides, supports, encourages, stimulates and corrects as well as loving and caring for the child physically. Such a carer should also attempt to fulfil his/her own needs by developing individual potentialities apart from parenthood. However, although others may share in this care, primary responsibility for child care and associated tasks remain with the biological mother. In fact, superimposed on the core ideas of the ideology of motherhood, is another set of ideas which leaves the mother with the bulk of the burden of child care and the additional responsibilities to develop her own potentialities and status outside the home. These mothers see the woman's world and the man's world as separate and feel they have a right and an obligation to be a part of both.

For ambivalent progressive mothers traditional sex roles can be reversed or redefined successfully but the mother retains a sense of guilt and loss of feminine identity if she relinquishes the major part of her home roles. Like the Rapoports' dual career families there is a tension line beyond which the mother is not prepared to go in experimenting with a new definition of sex roles as beyond this point her feminine identity is threatened (Rapoport and Rapoport, 1972:229). Nevertheless, they believe that they, as well as their husbands, or men in general, have a right to personal development and fulfilment outside the home. Feeling that they are respected for their individual worth, rather than as mothers, their self-esteem comes from a sense of their own abilities and characteristics rather than from their motherhood. Their life satisfactions are associated with the activities they pursue outside the home as well as those at home. The Women's Movement they believe has unequivocally helped women and they reject the traditional, fragile, pretty, passive image of the feminine woman.

For these mothers the nuclear family is not necessarily the ideal milieu for child-rearing. Families can vary in structure and culture, and parenting functions may be arranged differently according to whether there are one or two parents, whether one parent goes out to work or both or whether the family is an extended one or a co-operative commune. Different patterns of parenting are legitimate in different contexts without necessarily being irresponsible or deviant. Biological parents are not the only people who are involved in parenting functions, nor should they be. The community generally has a responsibility for its children and community participation in child care is encouraged (Rapoport and Rapoport, 1977:21–23).

In terms of lived experience these mothers have probably deliberately chosen to have children whether in a nuclear family situation or not and have had their children after some years of successful experience in the world beyond the home. Parenting is a part of their experience of life but not the overriding experience. Although in the allocation of everyday activities a large proportion of their time and energy is expended in the nurture and care of their children, they have in some way shown active rebellion against the traditional stereotype of motherhood in that they are also engaged in activities which are not child-centred but are regarded by them as personally fulfilling in terms of their own identity and development. Nevertheless, they retain primary responsibility for the care of their children.

Radical utopian

The radical utopian mother rejects the present structure of society and seeks instead a new breed of men and women, a new vision of the future, a future in which family, community and play are valued on a par with politics and paid employment for both sexes (Rossi, 1972:353). Such a mother believes that motherhood in its present form is neither necessary for woman's fulfilment, nor should it be inevitable, but one among a number of choices for women. To this end the radical utopian woman believes that women should be in complete control of their own bodies and should be able to make a deliberate choice without pressures from society to have or not to have a child (Bernard, 1976:90). The experience of parenthood is neither essential for, nor does it in itself achieve the goal of emotional maturity for women or for men. Depending on the circumstances, it may even be a deterrent to self-development (Committee of the Group for Advancement of Psychiatry, quoted in Rapoport and Rapoport, 1977:17).

Once having had a child, the radical utopian mother believes that responsibility for rearing that child and primary bonds with the child should be the perogative of both parents or of a number of caring adults of both sexes. This responsibility includes both the physical caring for and the emotional caring of the child, quality of the time spent with the child, as well as teaching, correcting, socialising, stimulating and watching over the safety of the child. The child, in fact, is not the private property of the parents but an individual in its own right and a future citizen of the community in which it lives. This community should therefore take some responsibility for the burden and cost of child care.

The radical utopian believes in the abolition of men's sphere and women's sphere by the inclusion of men in the total responsibility of child care and household tasks and of women in the total responsibility of the economic sphere and in the values associated with both spheres.

Some utopian radicals see the nuclear family in its present form as an institution for the repression of women and children, especially as it exists in capitalist society. For example members of women's groups in York, Leeds, Hull and Durham in a paper presented at the National Women's Liberation Conference in London 1972 (quoted in Allen, Sanders, Wallis, 1974:363), express beliefs about the nuclear family, children and the autonomy of women, which would be common to many utopian radicals. They see the nuclear family as a structure which denies women social, psychological, sexual and economic autonomy and represses children by defining them as possessions of their parents.

Consequently these mothers seek to bring up their children in a group situation rather than in the traditional nuclear family milieu.

Other utopian radicals seek the restructuring of both the nuclear family and the work-force so that men and women can share provider and domestic roles in a family situation where the man's career, ability and status does not have priority over the woman's but both are equally involved in child care, cooking, and other domestic tasks as well as in the work-force (Laudicina, 1973:284).

The utopian radical mother sees herself primarily as an individual with some control over her life-options. Parenting is one of her life interests and a source of satisfaction in her life, however it does not necessarily provide her with her main or primary identity, nor does it absorb the major part of her time. When she is away from her children she knows that someone else has assumed complete responsibility for them, leaving her mentally and emotionally free to pursue other activities wholeheartedly.

In terms of lived experience then, this mother may or may not live in a nuclear family situation. She may still give birth to children, but responsibility for caring for and rearing these children will be shared with others so that she is not defined primarily in terms of her mother role. Household tasks are also distributed amongst others or communalised so that the major proportion of her time and energy are not expended on child care and household tasks and she has time and energy for other pursuits which are important to her and bring her satisfaction. She feels neither inferior to men in terms of society wide status nor does she consider herself, her values or her gender as morally superior to those of men. Her spheres of activity encompass both the private and the public sphere and she and the significant others in her life, both male and female are equally 'at home' in either.

In the sample of mothers interviewed, no mother could be identified as a radical utopian. No mother had successfully been able to share the *primary responsibility* for the care of her child and the associated household tasks with another person or people. Apparently in present Australian society any shift in the power base between men and women has not been sufficient to challenge effectively the structures, institutions and ideology which allocates the responsibility for this sphere of activity to mothers. Any re-definition of motherhood so that the radical utopian ideal type of mother may be approximated in reality, would require a greater change in the balance of power between men and women in the wider society than now exists (Note 1 at end of chapter).

In a society where dominant males have the power, not only to define identity and appropriate tasks for women and to define these as inferior to their own, but also to define the sources of power as those accessible to men rather than to women, it is almost impossible for women to change the status quo in their own interests to any great extent. It appears that only as women gain access to male defined sources of power, i.e., power in the market place and political arena, will they be able to redefine power and male/female relationships and responsibilities in different terms. However, this is 'Catch 22', for, as Jessie Bernard points out, in order to do this women have to acquiesce to the male defined structures and dynamics of society. Male power must be wrestled from males on their own terms, in their own sphere, it will not be surrendered willingly. This means that by the time women have achieved positions of power on a par with or greater than those of men, they have also, of necessity, become part of the male defined system themselves and will probably be unwilling to relinquish such power or to redefine the sources of power to include those accessible to most women. Jessie Bernard (1975:25), sees the use of such power by women as, 'the most significant—and *deplorable*—evidence for the practical superiority of the macho values.' (my emphasis.)

No one mother exactly fits any of the other three ideal types, that is, ideological traditional, ambivalent and ambivalent progressive. However, each respondent does approach one of these types and approaches one more closely than the other two. Table 5.1 shows the distribution of the five groups of mothers interviewed in terms of the three ideal types. It is evident that the majority of Mt Druitt and Single mothers approach the ideological traditional ideal type: (88% and 56% respectively), Nth Shore and Employed mothers the ambivalent ideal type (56% and 64% respectively) and that Feminist mothers are most likely to be ambivalent progressives (92%). These trends do give an accurate but incomplete picture of what is happening.

The 'at home' mothers in two parent families living in a working class area tend to support the ideology and to have traditional sex role attitudes and self-concepts and life-satisfactions associated with these roles. On the other hand 'at home' mothers in two parent families living in a middle class area tend to have ambivalent attitudes towards the ideology and traditional sex roles, self-concepts and life-satisfactions, having experienced a less traditional life-style prior to marriage in many instances. Employed mothers in two parent families also tend to have ambivalent attitudes. Many have slightly modified the ideology and attitudes to sex roles to fit in with their own life-style, and employment for some provides self-concepts and life-satisfactions outside the wife/mother roles. Feminist mothers whether in a two parent family, single parent family or co-operative household tend to have challenged some of the aspects of the ideology and traditional attitudes to sex roles and to have self-concepts and life-satisfactions not entirely associated with wifehood and motherhood. These trends are those that were anticipated. In the case of the Single mothers however, this is not so. It was conjectured that single mothers may become more autonomous in the absence of the face-to-face situation with a male in the home and some mothers expressed a new awareness of themselves as people with freedom to develop in their own way once the husband had departed. However,

Table 5.1   Distribution of ideal types according to the five groups of
mothers interviewed

Groups	Ideological traditional No. (%)	Ambivalent No. (%)	Ambivalent progressive No. (%)	Total No. (%)
Mt Druitt	44 (88)	6 (12)	0 (0)	50 (100)
Nth Shore	10 (40)	14 (56)	1 (4)	25 (100)
Single	14 (56)	8 (32)	3 (12)	25 (100)
Employed	4 (16)	16 (64)	5 (20)	25 (100)
Feminist	0 (0)	2 (8)	23 (92)	25 (100)
Total	72 (48.00)	46 (30.67)	32 (21.33)	150 (100)

in many cases the desire for the approval of another male, or the continued awareness of the children's father's opinion of her motherhood performance reinforces the traditional pattern. A shift in emphasis from the wife to the mother role and complete responsibility with no 'help' serves to focus the mother's attention on her mothering. For many it becomes more important, it ties her to her mother role and reinforces for her the traditional ideology, self-concepts and satisfactions in life.

Nevertheless Table 5.1 does not tell the whole story. By examining the cases which do not comply with the trends, such as the Mt Druitt mothers who are not ideological traditionals and the Nth Shore mothers who *are*, a clearer picture may be obtained. In conjunction with this examination an investigation of the association between background factors such as age at birth of first child, respondent's educational level, husband's occupation, respondent's mother's occupation, etc. and the three ideal types gives more insight into underlying causal factors. Before proceeding to such an examination however, in order to make clearer some of the differences as well as some of the similarities between the ideal types, the answers of three representative mothers to some of the key questions of the interview are compared.

Three mothers: An ideological traditional, an ambivalent and an ambivalent progressive

Jeanne Carlisle represents the ideological traditional mother. She was born and brought up in an industrial-residential suburb where she attended a Catholic Girl's School and where she met her husband who was a neighbour. She moved to Mt Druitt when she married and they are buying their Housing Commission house. She left school at 15, worked as a clerk until she was married at 16, her first child was born just before she turned 17. Her elder son is now 4, the younger 6 months. Her father is a builder-carpenter, her mother worked in a factory before marriage and returned part-time when the three girls were at High School. Her husband is a mechanic having attended Technical College for four years after the School Certificate. Their income, before tax, is between $5000 and $10 000 per year. She can use the family car on some days of the week provided she drives her husband to the station and picks him up after work. Every Sunday they go home to her mother's for a baked dinner and the three girls and their mother are very close. She enjoys being a mother and never considered being anything else in life.

Concerning her involvement in motherhood Jeanne says,

> I've talked to a lot of mothers and they've had their kids and that, and they can't stand them, but I love every bit of it—I think that's what I was mean't to be. I mean, people say to me, 'What would you want to be?' and I say 'I'd just like to be a mother and a housewife'. It's just exactly what I want to be. If I hadn't got married and had children I'd probably be trudging along in the same old job, you know, a dead end-job, a clerk, doing accounts and that, the same everyday drudgery. I'd much rather be doing this.

She thinks that 'good' motherhood means,

> Patience, terribly loving—to be able to show it. Discipline the child, not to be slapping them all the time. Show them love and appreciation and let them know they're doing good.

Her main aim in life is,

> It mightn't be very exciting, but I think just to please my husband; to do everything he expects of me—and my children.

Although Jeanne finds being a mother rather trying at times, she is proud of her children and their achievements. She says,

> I think what most people say, they get the impression that mothers are—well housewives and mothers are—you know they don't go to work and that, they just stay at home, they don't realise the things you go through and how trying it is on the mother to have kids with her all day long.
>
> I know he (4 year old) gets on my nerves sometimes, but when he turns around and tells you that he loves you or tells you that he's glad about what you did for him. To sit down and teach him things, to be involved in the things he's doing, to play with him—not that I play with him that much, but if he comes and shows me something that I taught him and you look at him and think, that's mine and I had him and that, I taught him that. I love that.

She doesn't believe that mothers of pre-school children should work outside the home,

Well, it's up to them, but I wouldn't—I don't think they should. I suppose they can if they're still going to be there all the time—they should always be there for them, they could work part-time when they go to big school, not while they're at pre-school.

Nor does she believe in reverse sex roles,

No. It was on Mike Walsh one day—she had a salon. I think that's wrong.

Concerning Women's Liberation Jeanne comments,

I don't believe in it. As far as women shouldn't do the housework and that, well I think they should—why should men? It was the woman that did the housework and I love the old fashioned way of men opening doors for you and getting up and letting you sit down—that's what I love. I think to a certain extent it's been helpful in jobs. There are women bus drivers now and I think that women should be in politics. But I think it's dwindling out now.

Like 76% of the ideological traditional mothers (see Table 5.2) Jeanne sees herself primarily as a mother. She is really happy when the whole family is together enjoying themselves at home or on an outing such as a picnic. Sometimes she feels depressed by being in the house all the time, but soon gets over it by having a cry or by

Table 5.2 Primary identities included in respondent's perception of self

Identity	Ideological traditional No. (%) (n = 72)	Ambivalent No. (%) (n = 46)	Ambivalent progressive No. (%) (n = 32)	Total No. (%) (n = 150)
Mother	55 (76.38)	28 (60.87)	9 (28.13)	92 (61.33)
Person/individual in own right/me	18 (25.00)	25 (54.35)	27 (84.37)	70 (46.67)
Wife	30 (41.67)	11 (23.91)	5 (15.63)	46 (30.67)
Woman	17 (23.61)	10 (21.74)	9 (28.13)	36 (24.00)
Housewife	20 (27.78)	8 (17.39)	5 (15.62)	33 (22.00)
Servant/slave/maid	14 (19.44)	2 (4.35)	2 (6.25)	18 (12.00)
Sex object	8 (11.11)	1 (2.17)	3 (9.37)	12 (8.00)
Occupation (doctor, teacher, etc.)	0 (0)	1 (2.17)	4 (12.50)	5 (3.33)
Companion/friend	2 (2.78)	0 (0)	0 (0)	2 (1.33)

Note: % = number of respondents giving this identity as a proportion of the number of this ideal type; e.g., mother for ideological traditional ideal type = 55/72 = 76.38%. The total number of respondents giving mother as a primary identity is given as a proportion of the total number of respondents in the sample, i.e., 92/150 = 61.33%.

talking it over with her husband. She does not feel at all resentful of her present situation.

Rosalind MacArthur resembles the ambivalent ideal type. She was born in Hobart, brought up on the North Shore where she attended an Independent Protestant Girls' School. She has a Bachelor of Education degree from Sydney University and taught until her first child was born when she was 29 years—she was married at 24. She enjoyed teaching and would like to return when the children (two boys, 4 and 2) are at school, but for the present believes her place is at home. She would like to have a third child fairly soon. They have bought an older home which they have already paid for and are now renovating. She has her own car. Her husband was a neighbour. He attended an Independent Protestant Boys' School and he has a B.Sc. from Sydney University. He is a Systems Engineer and earns between $15 000 and $20 000 per year before tax. Her mother was a journalist who worked part-time after marriage and her father was a company secretary. Her mother is dead; her father and brothers live in adjacent suburbs. She sees her father frequently but not her brothers.

Rosalind enjoyed her work as a teacher before marriage and was looking forward to promotion. Nevertheless she would rather be at home. 'I'm glad I got married and had children' she says.

A 'good' mother for her is,

> someone who's genuinely concerned with bringing up their child in a way that's beneficial to the child, but that's probably a perfect mother and I don't think there are any of those around.

She feels her present situation is a stage in her life. Once through it she will pursue other activities, but, for her, there are tensions between being in full-time employment and mothering,

> I feel this is a stage, no matter how much I kick against it—this is a stage that I want to go through before returning to do something else. I would very much like to go back to teaching, but it depends very much on whether I could find a a suitable job. I don't think I could manage a full-time job with three children. Lots of people do it, in fact I know of lots of terrific mothers who do it, but I think their job must suffer to some extent. I know when I was teaching, it sounds good, 9 to 3, but I always worked at home and I always worked every weekend and you live that job in the same way that men live their jobs and you couldn't do that with children and I'd know I wasn't doing the right thing.

In her view pre-school children need their mothers and the mother would miss out on her child's development if she worked outside the home at this stage of their lives. The best aspects of motherhood for her are being able to watch her children develop and the love they give her. The worst aspect is the lack of time to pursue her own interests such as music.

Concerning Women's Liberation Rosalind says,

> I think that the basic ideas behind it are really good, but generally they're far too extreme and outlandish in what they are asking for and talking about, so much so that my husband for one is very anti the Women's Liberation Movement and yet he agrees with the principles behind it. I think it's had a bad effect in that a lot of people, women included, tend to think 'Oh, they're going too far, I wish they'd be quiet about that', and while people agree with the principles behind it, that women should be treated equally with men, some of the things they are asking for and talking about are too extreme, so that people are against what they want.

While she believes that men can parent as well as women, she thinks that, at the present time, the pressures of society prevent it from working out for most people. Happiness for Rosalind is when the family is all together. She gets depressed 'when I'm tired and when I've had to cope too long on my own'. Occasionally she feels trapped in her situation. At such times she tries to get out of the house and away for a while—even if it is only to drive in the car somewhere.

Like 61% (see Table 5.2) of ambivalents she sees her primary identity as that of a mother.

Felicity Martin expresses some ambivalent progressive ideas. Felicity was born in Melbourne, attended Melbourne Girls' Grammar School, matriculated and spent half a year at Melbourne University. She then dropped out to join a hippy commune in the country. Leaving the commune at 21 she was married and her son was born shortly afterwards. She is now divorced, her son is 4 years old and she is 25. Her father is a physicist, her mother a social worker. Felicity is studying a communications course at the New South Wales Institute of Technology where she has regular contact with a feminist group. Her income is less than $5000 per year, being derived from the Tertiary Education Assistance Scheme plus the Supporting Mothers' Benefit. She has no car. Felicity is the youngest of four children, with 2 brothers and a sister. She is close to one brother who lives in Sydney. Her mother lives in Victoria, she writes to her frequently and her mother visits when she can. She does not have contact with her father, her parents are divorced. Living in Glebe in a shared, rented house with another single mother and her son, evening child care is rostered between them and with a single father who lives across the road.

Felicity describes herself as,

> I was one of these hippy women—you know—"drop out and live in the

country and everything will be wonderful". So how far that would have taken me I don't know. Perhaps I would have just been living on the dole like everybody else and smoking dope (if I hadn't had a child). I'd rather be here.

She prefers the term parent to mother. She says,

I think anybody can be a good parent. I think men unfortunately for them have a bit further to go at present because they have to open themselves up to being considerate and being able to put themselves in the child's place, being warm and affectionate. A lot of men don't have that skill at all. The men I know who are involved in childcare have that part pretty well. Being a good parent to me involves being affectionate. I don't think the perfect parent exists in our society, but warmness, affection, flexibility, imagination, all the qualities we look for in partners for that matter.

Sometimes she would like to have a break from her 4 year old son,

I'd like to, without guilt, and knowing that he is being loved as he is with me and all these other provisos, I'd like to be free of him for 3 weeks at a time. Often there's a period when I'm only taking the wrong kind of notice of him.
I'd like to be able to get on with my own thing, studying etc., every once in a while.

Her main aim in life is,

Just to keep on doing what I'm doing and doing it well and just hope that there's enough stimulation and change and stuff that I feel reasonably interested in what I'm doing day to day. Apart from the aim of changing the world.

The best aspect of motherhood for Felicity is her relationship with her son. She says,

I suppose what I like is being interested in this little person more than I've ever been in any other person before. There's a part of romantic love where there's a particular kind of interest in another person, but I think in a sense that's a form of narcissism, it's a reflection of yourself. I suppose you could say the same thing about a baby, except that I don't feel that. I don't look at him and say 'In what way are you like me?' I find myself interested in *him* to an extent that I haven't been interested in anyone before. I like the strong emotions that I feel about him.

The worst aspect is,

The knowledge that he's going to be there for the rest of your life and the tremendous restrictions on your freedom in all sorts of ways.

Concerning mothers of pre-school children working outside the home she says,

> I don't have any opinions about it concerning the children. It depends on the woman. I can see that mothers of a number of young children have an incredibly difficult time in our society in present circumstances. If they *want* to work outside the home—(I don't see any reason why they should feel obliged to)—but if they *want* to they should be able to. I'm very resentful of the way women are regarded if they work outside and of the low regard in which child-rearing is held. Many women wouldn't need to, or wouldn't want to if they were highly paid for the work they do at home and if they were highly regarded for it. And also, I suppose, if they received more support for it, because it's such isolated work, so lonely. A lot of women work because it's a form of companionship—that's where they have friends—meet other people.

Felicity is in favour of Women's Liberation. It has had a positive effect on her life,

> In the house I lived in there was a young woman quite into socialist feminist politics, it was through her that I did the reading that I did and I did a lot of reading. I lived with some lesbian women for a while, in a shallowy way, I was more sort of observing, soaking it up than contributing in any way. Later I went on demos, and that sort of thing. At the Institute there's a fairly strong strand of feminism, it's connected with the Women's Study course. There's a women's group there. That involves me in going to conferences, etc. I did a short stint at the Rape Crisis Centre and ended up going home and feeling I needed counselling myself. I also belong to the Children's Co-op which has feminist ideas about child care and learning about roles, etc. For me personally it's been terrific.

She believes reverse sex-roles are quite legitimate, and can work today,

> Very legitimate. My brother does that—he gets housewive's blues. The kids are lovely—if that's the measure by which we judge—it does work. I have empathy with him, occasionally he is very blue, he has no productive work and all that stuff.

Like 84% (see Table 5.2) of ambivalent progressives, Felicity sees herself primarily as a person in her own right. Other people however, she says, tend sometimes to see her as a mother.

It can be seen from these extracts that the ideological traditional mother has had few options in life other than motherhood. Her vision of life and awareness of herself revolve around wifehood and motherhood and she is doing her best to adjust her life and outlook to its frustrations and limitations, as well as enjoying its rewards. She accepts life as it is and makes the best of it.

On the other hand, the ambivalent mother is aware of the limitations to her personal growth and freedom and her career or job, as a result of her motherhood. She adjusts to her role with some feeling of resentment by seeing full-time motherhood as a stage in her life. She is biding her time until she can pursue her own interests once more. In spite of her awareness of the conflict in herself, she does not question the ideology which places her in this position.

The ambivalent progressive mother gives more sense of being in control of her own situation, of having questioned the traditional ideology and of personal satisfaction gained from sources other than, or as well as, motherhood. Motherhood she sees as developing characteristics which are valuable in both men and women such as warmth, affection, consideration and sensitivity to the needs of others, but which are only valued in the woman's sphere of the home. In the wider man's sphere they bring neither status nor reward; other potentialities need to be realised to 'get on' in this sphere. Traditional motherhood limits the development of a wider range of abilities such as technical skills and professional experience which are recognised in a male dominated society, and in terms of time and energy, prevents involvement in self directed rather than child centred activities. The ambivalent progressive mother subscribes to certain aspects of the ideology and questions others and, although she is not happy with the situation, she still retains primary responsibility for child-care and household tasks.

Following Steven Lukes (1977:6–7) one of the central aspects of relationships of power is that the powerful (within certain structurally determined limits) have relatively more autonomy than those who lack such power. Lukes (1973:133–37) also links personhood with the capacity for autonomous choice and action, the capacity to engage in valued activities and relationships that require a private space, and the capacity for self-development. Where these are absent the person's freedom is endangered and she/he tends to be defined and to define herself/himself in terms of a role, thus failing to respect herself/himself as a person capable of choice, and of personal development. If Lukes is correct, women who see themselves primarily as mothers (the majority i.e., 76% of ideological traditionals, see Table 5.2) are being defined and defining themselves in terms of a role rather than as autonomous persons, entitled to the respect of others and to their own respect. Women who, on the other hand, define themselves primarily as persons (the majority i.e., 84% of ambivalent progressives, see Table 5.2) are asserting their right to choose within a certain socially limited range of options and to have some control over their life's course and the realisation of their individual potentialities. That is, they perceive their right *not* to have their choices and roles predetermined for them by the more powerful. This suggests that vis-a-vis the more powerful male group they have more autonomy than their sisters who see themselves primarily as mothers.

This is not to say that some of women's potentialities are not developed by a commitment to the motherhood role, as even ambivalent progressive mothers suggest that motherhood develops self-control and the capacity to be aware of and sensitive to the needs of others. But it is to say that unless women have a choice about this role as against other roles and see themselves as having a choice within the role, their freedom and autonomy is severely curtailed. In fact many ideological traditional mothers included in their primary identity, slave, servant or maid (19%, see Table 5.2) indicating some of the personal restrictions they see involved in the role for them.

It becomes evident, I think, over the range of responses of the three types of mothers represented here, that the ambivalent progressive mother has more sense of control over her life, its actions and her own potentialities than either the ideological traditional or the ambivalent. The former sees no other option than motherhood for her, and such motherhood is rigidly defined, the latter sees the development of her own interests as suspended for a certain period of her life.

When the social backgrounds of these ideal types of mothers are examined it becomes obvious that certain factors are associated with the ideological traditional ideal type as against both the ambivalent and ambivalent progessive ideal type and vice versa.

Background factors differentially associated with ideal types

By rearranging Table 5.1 it is possible to show how each ideal type is constituted in terms of proportions of the five groups of mothers interviewed. Table 5.3 thus formulated shows that, in varying degrees, each ideal type cuts across the five groups interviewed. Although the majority (61%) of ideological traditionals in the sample are from two parent working class families where the mother is at home, 14% come from similar middle class families, 19% from mother-headed families and 6% from families where the wife is in paid employment outside the home for at least part of the week. No feminist mother could be identified as an ideological traditional. The ambivalent mothers in the sample come mainly from middle class two parent families where the mother is at home (30%) or from families where the mother is in paid employment outside the home for part of the

Table 5.3 Distribution of the five groups of mothers according to
ideal type

Ideal type	Mt Druitt No. (%)	Nth Shore No. (%)	Single No. (%)	Employed No. (%)	Feminist No. (%)	Total No.(%)
Ideological traditional	44 (61.10)	10 (13.89)	14 (19.44)	4 (5.56)	0 (0.00)	72 (100)
Ambivalent	6 (13.04)	14 (30.43)	8 (17.39)	16 (34.78)	2 (4.35)	46 (100)
Ambivalent progressive	0 (0.00)	1 (3.12)	3 (9.38)	5 (15.63)	23 (71.88)	32 (100)
Total	50 (33.33)	25 (16.67)	25 (16.67)	25 (16.67)	25 (16.67)	150 (100)

week (34%). However, some also come from working class families
(13%), mother-headed families (17%) and a minority (4%) from
the Feminist group. The highest proportion (72%) of ambivalent
progressives come from the Feminist group, but some also come
from the Employed group (16%), a few from the Single group
(10%) one from the Nth Shore group (3%) and none from the Mt
Druitt group.

With regard to the composition of each ideal type the questions
are therefore raised, 'Is there anything that mothers who can be
categorised as approaching a particular ideal type have in common
which may cut across the original research grouping?' and consequently, 'Are there any underlying factors which are generic to
each ideal type?' An examination of the social backgrounds of the
mothers categorised in each ideal type provides some answers to
these questions.

Age, age at marriage and age at birth of first child

Although it could be conjectured that age of the mother may be
a contributing factor to beliefs about motherhood with younger
mothers being exposed to more progressive ideas[2] this is not borne
out by the research data. The age range of the sample is 16 to 40
years with 44% below 30 years at the time of the interview and
56% over 30 years (Table App. 4.1). In terms of ideal types (Table
App. 4.2) it is only for the ambivalent that age appears to be significant with 72% of these mothers being over 30 years. As some
of the ambivalence these mothers express stems from the varied
experiences of their lives prior to their present situation, this is not
surprising. In terms of experience of life however, age at marriage

and age at the birth of the first child are of greater importance. There is a slight tendency for ambivalents and ambivalent progressives to have married later (Table App. 4.4). Whereas 14% of the sample had married later than 25 years of age, 20% of ambivalents had and 21% of ambivalent progressives had. This tendency increases when attention is focussed upon the age at the birth of the first child (Table App. 4.6). Whereas 35% of the total sample had their first child later than 25 years, 57% of ambivalents had and 47% of ambivalent progressives had. On the other hand only 15% of ideological traditionals had their first child later than 25 years.

As the mothers have indicated in the interviews and other researchers have observed (e.g., Gavron, 1966:68) it is the birth of the first child which dramatically alters a woman's existence and the later in life that this event occurs for her the more experiences of life she is likely to have with which to compare her present situation. Social class plays an important part in determining the age at birth of the first child as well as the range of experiences available to a woman prior to the birth of her children and her subsequent perception of motherhood in terms of significant others and reference groups. It can be expected then, that the constellation of factors which go to make up social class, such as respondent's parent's occupations, husband's occupation and educational level and respondent's own occupation and educational level and family income will show a significant difference between ideological traditionalists and both ambivalents and ambivalent progressives. An examination of these factors (Tables App. 4.7–4.20) reveal that, for the sample of women interviewed, this is so.

Social class

Social class background, present social class and potential social class of respondents appear to be important underlying variables in the constitution of the three ideal types of mothers. Reasons for this association will be discussed after the evidence has been examined.

There is a tendency for ideological traditional mothers to have parents who are, or have been in skilled or unskilled manual occupations (Tables App. 4.8 and 4.10). Whereas 35% of the total sample have mothers who are or have been unskilled or skilled manual workers, 58% of ideological traditionals have. Whereas 43% of the total sample have fathers who are, or have been in these occupations, 71% of ideological traditionals have. On the other hand ambivalent and ambivalent progressive respondents have mothers or fathers who have been in managerial, professional or self-employed occupations. Ambivalent respondents tend to have mothers in these occupational categories (30% as against 14% for the total sample). Ambivalent progressives tend to have fathers in these categories (78% as against 44% for the total sample).

Ambivalent and ambivalent progressive mothers bring to their present situation attitudes and values as well as experiences of life made possible by the middle class market capacities of their parents. Ideological traditionals on the other hand bring attitudes and values and life experiences associated with the working class market capacities of their parents to their present situation.

It is interesting to note here that of the 10 ideological traditionals who were part of the Nth Shore group, 2 had fathers who were in skilled and unskilled manual occupations and two had fathers who were in clerical and sales occupations: nine had mothers in clerical occupations and the mother of one brought up her children on Social Services when the father died. These mothers tended to have lower educational levels (incomplete high school) and/or to have married and had children earlier than the rest of the Nth Shore group. Conversely, 3 of the 6 ambivalents in the Mt Druitt sample had mothers who were professionals and two had fathers who were self-employed. Four ambivalents had completed high school and pursued, if not completed, some tertiary studies before marriage and 2 had their first child after 25 years of age.

It appears then, that social class background is an important factor in determining the resources, experiences and attitudes which women bring to their family situation and consequently to their beliefs about and attitudes towards motherhood.

An indication of respondent's present social class position is given by husband's and respondent's own occupation and educational level (Tables App. 4.12, 4.14, 4.16 and 4.18). We find that ideological traditionals and their husbands tend to have market capacities which are working class, whereas ambivalents and ambivalent progressives and their husbands tend to have market capacities which are middle class. For example (Table App. 4.12), whereas 58% of the total sample have husbands who are in clerical, sales and skilled or unskilled manual occupations, 83% of ideological traditionals have. On the other hand only 32% and 35% of ambivalents and ambivalent progressives have husbands in these occupations. Similarly (Table App. 4.14), husbands of ideological traditionals tend not to have completed high school (19% as against 49% for the total sample) whereas husbands of ambivalents and ambivalent progressives tend to have some tertiary qualification (62% and 75% as against 43% for the whole sample).

The respondent's own occupation and educational level reveals a somewhat similar distribution. Only 25% of ideological traditionals are, or have been in, professional managerial or self-employed occupations (as against 34% for the whole sample) and 50% of ambivalents and 64% of ambivalent progressives have been in these occupations. Only 7% of ideological traditionals have some tertiary qualification (as against 29% for the whole sample) whereas 43% and 56% of ambivalents and ambivalent progressives have. In fact 81% of ideological traditionals have not completed high school (as against 54% for the whole sample).

High income level is also associated with ideal type. Whereas 19% of respondents have a family income per year before tax of over $20 000, only 3% of ideological traditionals have and 28% of ambivalents and 44% of ambivalent progressives have.

Potential market capacity also appears to be relevant to ideal type in that the ambivalent progressive mothers who are on very low incomes are mainly single mothers existing on Supporting Mothers Benefit plus a T.E.A.S. allowance which allows them to study at tertiary level thus increasing their potential market capacity.

It is clear from the data presented here that mothers from middle class backgrounds, in middle class family situations or with potential market capacity for professional or managerial occupations do not unreservedly accept the ideology of motherhood, women's place as in the home and all the restrictions on participation in the wider society which adherence to such an ideology generates. It is the middle class woman who has ambivalent or ambivalent progressive orientations towards motherhood. In their discussions of the origins of the Woman's Movement in the U.S.A. and U.K. Juliet Mitchell (1971:Ch 1) and Jo Freeman (1975:Ch 1) suggest some reasons why middle class women have become dissatisfied with their relegation to inferior positions in both the domestic and employment spheres and why some of these women have been able to challenge this situation.

Juliet Mitchell (1971:22) suggests that whereas the 'most economically and socially underprivileged woman is bound much tighter to her condition by a consensus which passes if off as natural', the middle class woman is in a position to realise the gap between the deprivation she suffers as a woman and the glory she is supposed to enjoy. She points out that it is never extreme deprivation alone that produces an awareness of deprivation, but the prospect of something better. Jo Freeman (1975:31) takes the argument further by showing that in the U.S.A. in the 1960s the expectations of college educated middle class women had been raised due to their higher levels of education, decision to have fewer children and partial acceptance as family providers, but that in comparison with their husbands, former class mates and professional male associates they suffered relative deprivation in terms of job opportunities, income and status. Working class women, on the other hand experienced little discrepancy between the rights they had and those they felt entitled to. The middle class woman then experienced strain and conflict between their expectations and reality. In the present sample it is the middle class women who realise the discrepancy between their income, status and job opportunities prior to motherhood and their relative deprivation now due to their motherhood responsibilities, who form the core of the ambivalents.

The middle class women in the U.K. and U.S.A. who rallied to the cause of Women's Liberation were those who, in addition to their middle classness and consequent sense of deprivation had contact with reference groups such as student radicals, civil rights groups and labour movements which challenged the prevailing ideologies and espoused the ideals of equality and individual liberty (Mitchell 1971:35-36; Freeman 1975:28). As Mitchell points out (1971:34) it is the combination of revolutionary ideas and a material base which enables oppressed groups to challenge the status quo, so that initially ideological challenges are likely to come from the economically and ideologically dominant class. In the present sample it is this combination of these factors, that is, a sense of relative deprivation, middle class market capacity and direct contact with significant reference groups which challenge the ideology of motherhood and endorse the ideals of equality and liberty for women, that are closely associated with the ambivalent progressive ideal type mother.

The high proportion (72%, Table 5.3) of ambivalent progressive mothers who are actively associated with feminist groups can account for the difference between middle class women who are ambivalents and those who are ambivalent progressives. This fact is endorsed when more closely examined the data reveal that *all* ambivalent progressive mothers in the sample have had some contact with a feminist group and feminist ideas, although they may not now be actively associated with such a group. Ambivalent progressives who are not part of the Feminist group interviewed are, with one exception, middle class mothers who have had contact with the ideas of the Women's Movement through Women's Electoral Lobby, a Women's Refuge, University Women's Study Courses and in two cases through a progressive Catholic church where these ideas are discussed in groups. The only working class mother who appears as an ambivalent progressive is a single mother who was helped to leave her husband through a Women's Refuge and who has maintained contact by helping there at weekends.

It appears that social class provides the necessary but insufficient material base for challenge to the traditional ideology of motherhood.

However, it is only when alternative ideas concerning motherhood and women's position become aligned with such a base that some challenge to the traditional ideology is possible. The mechanisms of reference groups and networks for the transmission of traditional ideas or alternative ideas concerning motherhood will be discussed in greater detail later in the book.

By constructing ideal types of mothers and comparing the data and background information provided by the research interviews with these abstract constructs it has been possible to establish the presence in the sample of three distinct ideal types and the absence of one. Some causal factors associated with these ideal types have also been suggested.

In terms of lived experience it appears, however, that in present Australian society, the fact of being a mother generates its own kind of experience, its own set of duties and obligations which most women who are mothers come to accept and endorse in some way. Although modifications are made to the ideology to accommodate such factors as the mother's employment outside the home and relief from the constancy of motherhood and its demands, the ideology itself is pervasive and tenacious in its fundamental prescriptions. Lefebvre (1969:80) makes the point about ideology, 'An ideology may encounter problems, but not of a kind to shake it fundamentally. Adjustments are made, details are altered, but the essentials are left intact.'

Greater changes in the material and power base than exist at present would evidently be necessary for any effective challenge to the ideology.

Further research would be needed to compare the life-options of these mothers with those of women who aren't mothers, or with those of men of similar backgrounds. This research shows that within the experience of mothering a woman's life-options are constrained by the ideology of motherhood.

In the following chapters the data is examined more particularly in relationship to the effect of social class, educational level, employment status, single parenthood and group affiliation (formal mothers' groups or feminist groups) on the ideology of motherhood, self-concepts, sex role attitudes and satisfactions with life.

Notes

1   In a study of 23 shared-role families Graeme Russell (1980:104) found that on average mothers were performing 53% of tasks such as feeding, dressing, changing nappies and fathers 47% (compared with 85% for

mothers and 15% for fathers in a traditional sample). However some mothers 'took over' all of the care/domestic chores when they returned from work and in one family the mother did not really relinquish any of the tasks when she went to work. Of the families which appeared to be strongly committed to sharing tasks, two reported that they shared everything except dirty nappies (mother's province) and responsibility for garbage (father's province).

Russell concludes that fathers are competent caregivers, but that for this shared-role pattern to become an accepted and viable alternative family life-style changes are necessary at both structural (for example, more job flexibility) and personal levels (for example, changes in beliefs about parental roles and the needs of children) (Russell, 1980:101).

2 For example, in a 1971 Melbourne Metropolitan survey (Ruzicka and Caldwell, 1977:350–51) of 2652 currently married women a significantly higher proportion of those under 30 disagreed with statements such as 'it is every wife's duty to have children' and agreed with statements such as 'husbands should help regularly with housework'.

6 Working class, middle class and feminist mothers

The social class (past and present) of mothers has been shown in the previous chapter to be a necessary condition for some questioning of the ideology of motherhood. Working class mothers tend to endorse the ideology of motherhood and to experience motherhood within the limits of such an ideology with no conception of alternative modes of mothering and little awareness of the conflicts of interests between women as mothers and men as providers which are legitimated by the ideology. Life as it is for them as mothers, is as it should be. Middle class mothers on the other hand have access to resources which have made possible experiences of life before the birth of their children and possibly present and future experiences which are not completely dominated by the demands of motherhood and domesticity. To varying extents they have therefore been able to transcend some of the limitations of the tenets of the ideology. For some middle class mothers consciousness of other options results in ambivalent attitudes to motherhood with consequent feelings of being trapped or of standing still in their own development and of resentment of a diffuse nature.

When certain factors combine, ambivalence towards motherhood becomes transformed into an active attempt to transcend some of the limits of mothering in an advanced capitalist society. That occurs, when middle class resources, experiences and expectations become aligned with utopian ideas of freedom and equality for women as expounded in feminist groups coupled with mothers becoming conscious of a conflict of interests between themselves as mothers and middle class men. Attempts to transcend the limitations of the traditional motherhood role take the form of sharing some of the responsibility for mothering with other adults (male and/or female), placing less emphasis on housework and pursuing activities which develop their individual potentialities in addition to those developed by their mothering activities. This chapter looks in more detail at the differences and similarities in the experience of mothering for working class, middle class and feminist mothers in a two parent family structure, where the husband is the breadwinner.[1]

Life experiences prior to motherhood

Working class and middle class women bring to their experience of mothering differences in life chances and expectations. The working class mothers in the sample have generally come from larger families with lower incomes than those of the middle class. For example, 14 of the Mt Druitt mothers came from families with six or more children whereas only one Nth Shore and one Feminist mother came from a family as large as this. Whereas 70% of Mt Druitt mothers came from families of 4 or more children, 28% of Nth Shore and 56% of Feminist mothers came from such families. Working class mothers in talking about their backgrounds often told of their own involvement in caring for younger brothers and sisters and their frequent absences from school or of the necessity for them to leave school at an early age. For example, Annette Garside says,

> My mother had 6 girls and 3 boys and I was left home to look after them. I was the eldest, half the time she didn't have a husband so I used to do the housework while she worked . . . I always tried to have it tidy before she came home, I had the tea on and everything. I was used to it. I was only nine and took my brother in my arms on the train from Auburn to Croydon . . . I was low educated, left school at 13 or 14 and minded my brothers and sisters while my mother went to work.

Other mothers tell of some of the material deprivations of their childhood. For example, Katie Beard whose father was a wharf labourer and whose mother was a cook, says,

> My mother went without everything all her life—she always has done . . . She owned one overcoat, it was dyed many, many colours over a period of winters and she always used to say, 'Next winter I'll get a new coat, next summer I'll get a new dress', but it never came. We didn't get a lot, but she had less, much less than we had.

Fathers of these respondents were in working class occupations. Eighteen were in low paid, unskilled manual jobs such as truck driver, wharf labourer or factory worker 21 were in skilled manual jobs such as baker, cabinetmaker, fitter and turner and 7 were in low skill clerical or sales jobs such as post office clerk or sales representative. In 4 cases the father had died or left when the respondent was very young, leaving the mother to bring up her children on wages she could earn or on Social Services Benefits. Like the fathers, the mothers also had low market capacity and although many had re-entered the workforce after marriage in order to make ends meet, their earnings were low and regarded as supplementary to those of the husband. Mothers of the working class respondents had been in occupations such as factory worker (19), cook, cleaner, nurses' aide, child-minder (8), shop assistant (6), low skill clerical (8), nurse (3). Some existed on social services (2) and in some households the mother had died or left home when the respondent was very young (4).

Middle class mothers on the other hand came from smaller families and had fathers and mothers with greater market capacity. Fathers of Nth Shore respondents were in professions such as engineering, medicine, law, politics, academia or science or in managerial positions (20). Mothers of these respondents also had greater market capacity than did the mothers of Mt Druitt mothers. Fifteen were in skilled secretarial positions and 4 were professionals, a nurse, teacher, physiotherapist and doctor. The higher income and greater resources of these parents have given these middle class respondents a wider experience of life prior to the birth of their children. A similar pattern is observed for the Feminist mothers with 21 fathers in professional or managerial positions, 19 mothers in trained clerical positions and 4 mothers in professions.

In describing their lives prior to marriage these mothers include experiences which are not so home centred as those of the working class mothers. For example, Sarah Trent whose father was an Air Force pilot and whose mother was never employed but did charity work tells of beginning a university course on leaving school, of learning typing and shorthand and working in several secretarial jobs, then as an air hostess, then in a travel agency, then in market research before getting married at 27 and having her first child at 28 years of age. Rita Karl, whose father is a politician and whose mother was never employed but did charity work says,

> I was really one of the those silver spoon girls who did nothing very much at all workwise, travelled a lot, an only child of well off parents who could virtually do whatever she wanted.

The combination of larger families and low incomes limited the experiences of life available to the working class mothers. Their activities generally centred around the home and some told of the expectations that they do the housework while their brothers played sport or got on with their education. What limited resources there were, were generally spent in educating the boys in the family rather than the girls. Two respondents have brothers who are teachers with university degrees whereas they did not go beyond the junior high school level themselves. Some respondents spoke of their brother's moving up in the world, said one 'now he's got a bit of money, you know, a swimming pool and a boat and they live at Oyster Bay instead of good old Punchbowl'. Several respondents resented their brother's freedom when they had to spend all their spare time doing housework or looking after children; when their work was finished it was too late for them to go out anyway. Their brothers were also given more pocket money, they said. Although in some cases, middle class brothers were also treated differently and given a higher level of education than the respondents themselves, generally speaking these mothers had a much broader range of experiences than the working class respondents. Their interests outside the home included music, sport, clubs and social activities generally of a mixed sex nature after the early teenage years.

Considering the backgrounds of the working class women, the number of children in their family of origin, the generally low income occupations of their fathers and their mothers and the preference given to the education of boys, it is not surprising that their own educational level is generally low (82% did not go beyond the junior high school level) or that the jobs they went into on leaving school were mainly in shops or factories or in untrained clerical positions (90% of the sample). The accepted pattern for the lives of these women prior to the birth of their first child was to leave school at fourteen or fifteen with no formal educational qualifications, or with minimal qualifications, to enter factory, sales or untrained clerical work for a year or two, to get married and have children almost immediately and thenceforth to devote time and energy to child care, husband care and household tasks.

Middle class mothers on the other hand continued on to a higher level of education and travelled or were employed for a number of years or both before marriage and expected to be able to continue their cultural interests after marriage and children. Smaller families and greater material resources as well as higher parental expectations enabled these women to achieve a higher level of education and hence a greater market capacity. In the Nth Shore sample only 36% had not completed high school and 40% had some tertiary qualification and in the Feminist group only 12% had not completed high school and 64% had some tertiary qualification. Consequently no Nth Shore respondents had been in skilled or unskilled manual occupations, 52% had been in clerical or sales and 45% in professional occupations. In the Feminist sample 70% had been or were when interviewed in professional occupations, 25% in clerical or sales and 5% in skilled or unskilled manual jobs. Before considering the effects of such class differences in life experiences prior to motherhood on the sex role attitudes and expectations of these women, some discussion of the effect of education in particular on the mother's attitudes to motherhood is necessary.

The findings of this research suggest that tertiary education is associated with ambivalent and ambivalent progressive ideas on motherhood (see Table App. 4.18). However in looking more closely at the data it appears that type of education or content of education can account for some of the difference between middle class ambivalent mothers and middle class ambivalent progressive mothers.

Ten Nth Shore mothers have tertiary qualifications and four are studying at the present time. All of these mothers except one have ambivalent attitudes to and experiences of motherhood; their study in the sciences or the humanities has given them a broader view of life with which to compare their motherhood experiences. However only one mother in this group may be described as an ambivalent progressive, and in her own words her previously ambivalent attitude to motherhood only became transformed into an active attempt to transcend some of the limitations of the sexual division of labour when she began studying law at Sydney University after the birth of her first baby. Through her fellow students she made contact with a women's consciousness raising group which heightened her awareness of alternative structures and provided a sympathetic group to support her endeavours to change her situation.

In the Feminist group 16 mothers have tertiary education qualifications and 4 mothers are pursuing tertiary studies at present. All of these mothers except two can be described as ambivalent progressives. The two who have ambivalent attitudes to and experiences of motherhood have been influenced in their thinking by Bowlby and associates, encountered in the course of their studies. This suggests that content of education could be important in influencing ideas. Nine of the ambivalent progressive mothers are either studying or lecturing or tutoring in tertiary courses which investigate women's position in contemporary society. The content of these courses includes questioning of women's position and consideration of alternative structuring of male/female relationships and provides some support from a significant reference group for active attempts to transcend some of the limitations of the traditional division of labour. The mechanism of networks for the transmission of ideas and support for alternative ways of mothering will be discussed in a later chapter. The point that is made here is that while a higher level of education made possible by the middle class background and position of respondents provides a basis for some questioning of rigid definitions of motherhood and the sexual division of labour, more specific ideas concerning liberty and equality for women, aligned with greater material resources, are necessary for the active transcendence of some of the limitations of the ideology of motherhood.

In the employed group of mothers the pattern is similar. Mothers with tertiary qualifications tend to be ambivalent except where such education has put them in touch with ideas which question women's position in contemporary society. The present research suggests that it is only when progressive ideas become aligned with material resources and the interests of a particular stratum of society that some challenge to the status quo is possible.

When a consciousness of their own interests as against those of middle class men becomes aligned with the material resources necessary to at least partially achieve those interests, middle class mothers are able to act to transcend some of the limitations placed upon them by the ideology of motherhood. On the other hand, working class mothers for the most part lack such material resources as well as the access to 'world images' which challenge the status quo. In the present sample, education in the form of women's study courses and the contacts made by women through tertiary courses have provided 'world images' which question women's position in contemporary society and a supportive group for some challenge to the traditional ideas and experiences associated with motherhood.

For the working class women in the sample it has been shown that as well as in the area of education, their life-chances and life-experiences prior to motherhood have been limited and to a large extent based on a rigid division between male and female oriented activities. Working class mothers therefore bring to their mothering, expectations of a rigid division of labour between the sexes. The ideology implicit in the term sex roles (Burton, 1979:65) is accepted as natural and just by these mothers. Middle class mothers have however been encouraged to pursue activities outside the home educationally, culturally and occupationally which have led to some expectations of equality within marriage. A more flexible division of labour between the sexes is expected although in practice for the majority of the present sample of Nth Shore mothers, if not for the Feminists, there appears to be little difference in the division of tasks between husband and wife from that in the working class sample.

Sex role expectations and attitudes

Interwoven with the ideology of motherhood in a milieu where there is a fairly rigid division of labour along sex lines is the ideology of equality between the sexes which constitutes the sexes as being 'different but equal'. For the majority of mothers in the sample who are living in a two parent relationship where the husband is the breadwinner and the wife is at home this is the ideology of sex roles which is used by the mothers in justification of the sexual division of labour. Middle class mothers both Nth Shore and Feminist have brought to marriage ideas on sex roles which do not totally agree with this model, and for the most part have expected more role sharing in the home. Feminist mothers do, in fact, receive more help with household tasks and child care from their husbands. Some of the ambivalence of Nth Shore mothers can be attributed to the discrepancy between what they expected and the pragmatic facts of their existence. The husbands of these women are for the most part in demanding, responsible positions which require long hours away from home and frequent or occasional trips interstate or overseas, so that the mother feels her part is to keep the home front running smoothly.

The father's part in child care and household tasks

In the sample under consideration 54% of working class mothers, 56% of middle class mothers and 80% of feminist mothers say that they are happy with the amount of time the husband spends with his children and the kinds of activities he does with them. For the working class and middle class Nth Shore mothers if the husband spends a reasonable amount of time before or after work and on weekends talking and playing with his children and taking an interest in their activities, especially their sporting activities, the mother expresses satisfaction. If, in addition he will change nappies and/or get up at night when they are babies, bath or put them to bed when they are toddlers and take them out with him or let them be with him in the garden or workshop and encourage their sport when they are older, she feels she is very fortunate. She also appreciates his support in disciplining them.

For example, Cathy Bates, a Mt Druitt mother says,

> He's very good, he bathes them, puts them to bed, plays with them—usually he's too rough with them and one ends up crying. He's really good with them. He spends most weekends at soccer with them.

A Nth Shore mother emphasises how busy her husband is during the week, but that he makes up for it at the weekend, she comments,

> He doesn't spend a great deal of time during the week, but he spends *all* his time at the weekends, nothing's too much trouble, he's a very placid, easy going fellow and very involved in what the children are doing. He's

prepared to drop what he's doing if one wants to play ball. He's marvellous really.

Feminist mothers expect more involvement on the father's part in child care and, for the most part, get more help and in some cases sharing of responsibility for part of the week. For example, a feminist mother comments on the father's part in child care,

> He helps a lot. Because he's an academic he's around a lot, he's not 9 to 5. Overall he's around as much as I am. The older one is at school all day and at the Play Centre at the Darlinghurst primary school from 3.30 to 5.30 p.m., so that by the time she gets home he's here and I'm here. He baths the children while I cook the dinner. That period of time when we're home he spends as much time as I do, unless he has a meeting or I have.

If the working class husband works seven days a week, is on shift work, has two jobs, or goes to technical college at night, the mother understands that he is doing the best that he can for them, but she really would like him to be able to spend more time with his children.

On the other hand, if the husband has a sport or hobby or interest which takes up most of his spare time during evenings and weekends and which excludes the family, or if he goes to the pub most evenings after work, or if he does not make an effort to take some interest in his children's activities, the mother is not satisfied with the father's part in child-rearing.

Kathy Fern's husband belongs to the Volunteer Bush Fire Brigade, plays squash with some of his own friends and used to own a motor bike which took up much of his spare time,

> He likes to be doing things on his own to occupy himself, rather than with his family . . . My husband does not spend enough time with the children. He usually has a rough and tumble with them and stirs the life out of them. At the weekend, he said himself he doesn't spend enough time with them. He's usually very busy and they're more a hindrance than a help and he just gets mad with them then.

Jill Dann is a middle class mother who is not satisfied with her husband's participation in child-rearing,

> I'm not happy with the amount of time he spends. No not at all. He does get home late and he's very, very tense when he gets home and he can't really bear the children shouting when he gets home and unfortunately the current affair type T.V. programmes are on about 7 to 7.30 and if T.V. happens to be on he has one eye on it. Anna's trying to tell him about her day and I get furious and turn it off and he'll turn it on and it's just a bad time. I suppose at the weekend he doesn't go out, he doesn't play

golf, he's bought a sailing boat but he doesn't have time to go out in it, he's got too much else to do.

Hannah Coral is a middle class Feminist mother who has remained in a marriage relationship which is very important to her, but whose husband has made few modifications to his own life-style to accord with her feminist ideals. In order to remain in the marriage she has modified her feminist ideas. Almost all the other Feminist mothers living in a two parent family had husbands who were sympathetic to Feminism and endeavouring to change along with their wives. Other Feminist mothers had withdrawn from marriage relationships. Hannah is not happy with her husband's part in child-rearing.

> No I'm not really happy with his part. I'm envious of my friends like Leanne whose husbands do work in the home, etc., or even whose husbands get home at 5 p.m. Paul's ambitious and part of that—I admire him for it and I bask in the glow of it—he has a very prestigious and responsible position, a very good job for a 34 year old man—but he is expected to work and socialise out of hours. He has to give up quite a lot of drinks after work and being a big man out of hours because I say he's got to come home. We have fights about it.

More Mt Druitt and Nth Shore mothers are unhappy with the amount of help fathers give with household tasks, than are unhappy with the father's part in child-rearing, although as Table 6.1 shows the two are interwoven in the minds of the mothers. Feminist mothers have higher expectations, but also receive more assistance. North Shore mothers have higher expectations than Mt Druitt mothers, but in fact, they do not receive much more help. 60% of Mt Druitt and Feminist mothers are dissatisfied with the father's part in household tasks and 80% of Nth Shore mothers are not satisfied in this respect. Table 6.1 demonstrates some of the differences between the Feminist mothers and other middle class mothers and the working class mothers in the sample. Whereas only 7% of Feminist husbands do little or no housework, 40% of Nth Shore and 32% of Mt Druitt fathers are in this category. Whereas 100% of Feminist fathers play with, bath, dress or take responsibility for children for a morning or a day, only 20% of Nth Shore and 8% of Mt Druitt fathers do. Whereas 53% of Feminist fathers cook for the family, no Mt Druitt or Nth Shore fathers do. Whereas 40% of Feminist fathers vacuum, 4% of Nth Shore and no Mt Druitt fathers do. Mt Druitt mothers included in their responses to this question comments such as 'my husband is not expected to help, it's the wife's place' (14%) and 'my husband is marvellous, he does more than his share' (18%), Feminist and Nth Shore mothers did not make such comments, middle class mothers do expect some help, whether it is forthcoming

Table 6.1 Husband's help with household tasks

Response	Mt Druitt No. %[a]	Nth Shore No. %[a]	Feminist No. %[a]	Total
None, very little	16 (32)	10 (40)	1 (6.7)	27
Play with, bath, dress or mind children	4 (8)	5 (20)	15 (100.0)	24
Everything if I'm ill	9 (18)	3 (12)	5 (33.3)	17
Anything I ask, but little otherwise	5 (10)	7 (28)	2 (13.3)	14
Washing Up	0 (0)	5 (20)	5 (33.3)	10
My husband is marvellous, he does more than his share	9 (18)	0 (0)	0 (0)	9
Cooking	0 (0)	0 (0)	8 (53.3)	8
I don't expect my husband to help it's the woman's place	7 (14)	0 (0)	0 (0)	7
Vacuuming	0 (0)	1 (4)	6 (40.0)	7
Anything when I'm pushed	2 (4)	2 (8)	0 (0)	4

Notes: [a] % = Number of respondents who included this comment as a proportion of the number in the group e.g., Mt Druitt 16/50 = 32%, Nth Shore 10/25 = 40%.
  For Feminist group, 10 mothers are single, so % is a proportion of 15 e.g., 1/15 = 6.7%

or not. For 28% of Nth Shore mothers and 20% of Feminist mothers in two parent families, at least some household tasks such as cleaning are done by paid agents. If the father pays for these services this is considered as part of his contribution to household tasks. For example Rita Karl, a Nth Shore mother says,

> He balks at certain things and still has ideas about the woman's capacity, but then he provides the extra income for me to have a girl come in and do the things that I don't like—so really it's on a financial level that he helps.

In all groups husbands will do almost anything in times of emergency, such as sickness, but in everyday terms the norm appears to be washing up and outside jobs for Mt Druitt and Nth Shore mothers. Where these expectations are not met the mother expresses discontent. For example, Jan Ferrier a Nth Shore mother says,

Literally nil. Outside he does. I'd love him to grab a tea-towel and help, but he's a spoilt only child and has been all his life and the phone is a 7 day a week company phone, and he's virtually rescued by the phone every time I talk him into taking a tea-towel. I'd love him to be more involved and understand what I do.

Feminist mothers expect more and express dissatisfaction if husbands don't make some effort to contribute to household chores. For example, in this feminist household the mother realised that once she was at home on maternity leave, her share of housework increased alarmingly,

I've become aware over the past week that I'm at home at the moment on maternity leave and I'm being paid for child-rearing. In my case that's quite explicit, that's what maternity leave is for. But I have become aware of the fact that I'm actually doing more of the housework now and I'm not being paid to do the housework.

In other feminist households and in the majority of both the middle class and working class families, once the mother stayed at home with her children she was automatically expected to assume the major responsibility for housework. This division of labour is seen as just and in this manner the ideology of motherhood comes to legitimate housework for most women.

The best life

Differences in expectations and attitudes to sex roles between working class, middle class and feminist mothers are further demonstrated by answers to the question. 'Who do you think has the best life the man or the woman, your husband or yourself?' 42% of Mt Druitt mothers, 24% of Nth Shore mothers and only 8% of Feminist mothers say that they think the wife has the best life. The reasons given include: 'I can please myself when I do things'; 'I have the baby all the time he doesn't'; 'I don't have the boss standing over me'; 'I don't have to get up early every morning and go off to work year after year'; 'He works very hard'; 'I can go out in the daytime if I want to'. The majority of Nth Shore mothers and 44% of Mt Druitt mothers say that neither or both has the best life and in these answers the rationalisation of the sexual division of labour in the home is evident, the division of labour is seen as fair with good and bad aspects for both. The 'different but equal' ideology is prevalent. For example,

I suppose the mother's life is harder in a way because it's a bit monotonous, but I wouldn't envy my husband's life, going to work for so many years. It's hard on men too, especially my husband has to travel. I suppose it's half and half. (Mt Druitt mother)

In our marriage I'd say neither of us has it better than the other, we have an equal life. I think he has more worries because he's making money that I can easily spend, so he has the greatest strain. I have the best social life. (Nth Shore mother)

Feminist mothers are more likely to say that the husband has the best life, at least in traditional marriages, or to see the limitations placed on both partners by rigid sex roles. For example,

The husband generally has the best life—even in a terrible job he has lunch breaks and tea breaks and set hours of work and a pay packet and independence and the fact that even if you're doing shit work it means something whereas wives don't have that. (Feminist mother)

Head of the house

Some questioning of the ideology of sex roles by Feminist mothers is also evident in answers to the question, 'Who do you think should be the head of the house, the man or the woman, your husband or yourself?' Whereas 52% of Mt Druitt mothers and 64% of Nth Shores mothers said that the husband should be the head of the house, no Feminist mother said this. Typical of their responses are,

I don't think it should be either, it should be consensus. I'm not too keen on the nuclear family set up—that's not supportive enough of people and obviously I don't think you should have a head of the house.

Typical of responses which said that the husband should be head of the house is,

The husband should be the head of the house, he is the strong one. I'd always ask him for the final decisions.

However in many responses which supported the husband's ultimate authority, as well as those which suggested the wife should be the head or that there should be equality, there is the assumption that the mother should be responsible for the children and decisions regarding their daily care and general welfare and that the father should be responsible for the welfare of the family as a whole. For example,

He is definitely, if I ask him something and he says "No", it's no good arguing. But as far as the children are concerned I've got the authority. (Mt Druitt mother)

Middle class wives do not dwell so much on their authority over the children, they are more likely to say that the husband should be the head of the house because of his prestigious job, or because he earns and controls the finances. For example,

> The husband should be the head of the household. He really makes the final decisions although we discuss it. Normally he looks after the finances, but just now he has his mind on his Ph.D. so I look after the accounts.

Control of the day to day finances and authority over the children tends to give the working class mother in the sample more authority in the home than her middle class sister, in spite of ideological differences in the opposite direction. The majority of Mt Druitt mothers control the finances (52% say that they do) and where responsibility for finances is shared (22%) it is the wife who takes care of the day to day household finances and the husband who looks after the mortgage, etc. In fact in all cases it is the wife who has to make ends meet as far as money for food, clothing, personal needs of the children and herself and household furnishings are concerned. Pride in their management of money is evidently one source of self-esteem for these mothers, and in money matters they are extremely shrewd. The Nth Shore mother on the other hand is more likely to use bank cards and credit cards and accounts to cover daily and weekly expenses, it is her husband who pays the bills at the end of the month and who has a very tight reign on the family finances, giving him a certain weight of authority in the day-to-day running of the family, in spite of his physical absence. Feminist mothers are more likely to share financial responsibility, to have joint bank accounts, etc.

Qualitative differences in the oppression of middle class women from that of working class women were evident with regard to access to economic resources. Working class women have few resources and must make them stretch over the needs of the family so that in most cases there is little or nothing left for personal expenditure, but this management of the husband's wage gives them a certain amount of authority in the family. The middle class wife is, in fact, more directly dependent on the goodwill of her husband for everyday access to his economic resources. In return for their large, well furnished homes, labour saving devices and reflected status provided by their husbands, many lived lives circumscribed by rearing children, keeping large houses clean and entertaining in support of their husband's business interests and participating in other status building activities associated with their husband's or their children's lives with no money they could call their own.

However, in spite of the working class mother's control of every day finance and skill in making a little go a long way, for all the 'at home' mothers in the sample whose husbands are the bread-winners there remains the fact of economic dependence on the male. The male breadwinner owns the wage which he has earnt in the market place (Kuhn, 1978:53) and holds the power to share or withdraw it. The mother is in the vulnerable position of being dependent on the goodwill of her husband to provide her with the economic base for her labour in the home and the fact that he owns and provides it gives him the right to appropriate her labour in child care and housework. The ideology of sex roles includes an aspect which extends beyond the child-rearing years of the life-cycle and which assumes that, in a male dominated society where males have the power to define themselves as the breadwinner, they also have the right to the labour of the wife in the home. The mothers in the sample have largely accepted this ideology, it is only some of the middle class mothers who have made any provision to support them-selves in the event of the husband deserting, or the like. Working class mothers especially were shocked by the question 'How would you support yourself if your husband left you suddenly?' Most said they had never thought about it.

Across classes the 'at home' mothers interviewed whose husbands are breadwinners, with one Nth Shore exception where inherited money was available, are in an economically dependent position which severely limits their autonomy and which ensures that their mothering and housework meets with their husband's approval. Such economic dependence is obscured both by the ideology of motherhood and by the concomitant ideology of sex roles which stresses sex roles as being 'equal but different'.

The feminine woman

The feminine stereotype or ideology which accompanies the 'equal-but-different' ideology of sex roles is of the pretty, well dressed, dainty, gentle, quiet, ladylike woman who needs the protection and guidance of the stronger, more capable male, and whose femininity is reinforced by a variety of such male attentions as opening doors, giving up seats on transport, etc. Although there is less emphasis amongst the Feminist mothers on appearance and more on charac-teristics such as gentleness and understanding, the most frequent responses to the question 'What do you think makes a "feminine" woman?' were similar in the three groups of mothers (Table 6.2).

Table 6.2   The feminine woman

Characteristic	Mt Druitt No. (%)	Nth Shore No. (%)	Feminist No. (%)	Total No.
Gentle, soft, warm, calm, not aggressive	11 (22)	19 (76)	11 (44)	41
Appearance, dress, make up, etc.	22 (44)	11 (44)	5 (20)	38
Loving, understanding, kind	7 (14)	9 (36)	10 (40)	26
Well-spoken, doesn't scream or yell	14 (28)	2 (8)	0 (0)	16

This suggests the pervasiveness of the ideology. However, a closer inspection of the Feminist responses shows that these mothers are more likely to recognise such stereotypes as ideological and to question the use of the word 'feminine'.

Whereas both Mt Druitt and Nth Shore mothers gave responses such as 'Feminine is little, petite, delicate, round, soft voice, never swearing, raising voice, running out and screaming at the children', Feminist mothers were more likely to give replies such as the following,

"Feminine" is a word dreamed up by men to keep women out of responsible positions.

or

I think it's such a value laden word, it's not difficult to use. I think what feminine implies is that the woman fits the female role very well or tries to fit it and succeeds. I mean there are small and petite women who need a lot of help because they're not very strong, but I don't think that all the attributes of feminity would be confined in one woman because in a society where women were encouraged to develop the aspects of themselves that they wanted to that women wouldn't feel the need to fit the feminine role so exactly—so I think it's society that makes feminine women. And it won't be until we have a society where human values are important, where there are enough jobs to go around that everyone will have the right to develop themselves fully.

The stereotype of the feminine woman whose appearance is always groomed and attractive may fit the single girl or the upper class woman who can employ people to do the sometimes messy and dirty jobs of motherhood and housewifery, but for the mothers in the sample it serves to obscure the hard and dirty labour involved for them. The majority of mothers interviewed, working class, middle class and feminist said they did not fit the feminine image. The stereotype of the feminine woman who is nurturant and caring, never loses her temper or raises her voice to her children, who is at all times calm and gentle and patient, reinforces the ideology of motherhood. Such women make 'good' mothers.

While the middle class and working class respondents in this study bring to their own experiences of motherhood expectations and attitudes to sex roles which are different in many respects, once at home caring for children while the husband fulfils the breadwinner role, the ideology that the sexes are 'equal but different' appears to take precedence, justifying the division of labour which they are living. Feminist mothers in similar situations however, have questioned such an ideology and, to varying extents have been able to challenge it's limitations.

The material conditions of mothering

The differences in husband's occupation and income between the working class mothers of the sample and that of the middle class mothers account for some of the material conditions under which these mothers carry out the day to day tasks of mothering. Husbands who are in managerial or professional jobs such as lawyers, doctors, architects, qualified accountants, lecturers, marketing managers, as are 84% of Nth Shore husbands and 73% of Feminist husbands (compared with 6% of Mt Druitt husbands, Table App. 4.11), are able to purchase housing which is large enough for the needs of the family, which is conveniently planned or is in the process of renovation and which is in a privileged area as far as public facilities such as transport, shopping, pre-schools and schools are concerned. In addition high incomes as indicated by 44% of Nth Shore and 40% of Feminist families in the category over $20 000 per year before tax (compared with no Mt Druitt families in this category, Table App. 4.19) can supply other conveniences which lighten the load of the middle class mother.

Two such conveniences are the motor car and technological or paid help for household chores. Whereas only 4 Mt Druitt mothers have their own car, 18 Nth Shore mothers have and 13 Feminist mothers have. Seventeen Mt Druitt mothers have access to the family car sometimes, 6 Nth Shore and 3 Feminist mothers have this access. On the days that they want to use the car these mothers drive their husbands to work or to the railway station or the husband makes other provisions to get to work. Average availability would be 1 or 2 days a week. The possession of their own car enables middle class mothers to shop more quickly, to visit more often in a wider area, to get to and from meetings and sporting activities more easily and to cope with the paraphenalia needed when taking out babies and young children. Lack of such a convenience or only occasional use of the family car ties the working class mother to her home or to her immediate neighbourhood. Mt Druitt mothers do not have any paid help in the house, although help with washing, ironing, cooking and child care is often given by the respondent's mother when she visits. Mt Druitt households do not have automatic washing machines or dishwashers or freezers which are common in Nth Shore homes. One Mt Druitt mother who was the only person in her street to have an automatic washing machine had comments from her neighbours when she bought it to the effect that she was getting above herself.

Whereas Nth Shore and Feminist mothers in two parent families are able to purchase clothing for their children, Mt Druitt mothers make their children's clothes or spend time hunting for bargains. Nth Shore mothers spoke of taking the family to a restaurant for a meal, of going out themselves with their husband for dinner and of holidays or trips where they were relieved of cooking and cleaning responsibilities. Mt Druitt mothers have no such relief from their responsibilities, family outings are barbecues or picnics where they are still responsible for the food, although the husband may cook the meat at a barbecue. Nights out with one's husband are confined to once or twice a year and holidays if they are possible consist of visiting relatives or caravanning where the mother still cooks, cleans and cares.

These differences are further exacerbated by the working class mother's emphasis on cleanliness and tidiness in the home and daily washing, ironing and cleaning. For middle class mothers, as other researchers have discovered (e.g., Rainwater et al. 1959:40), these activities are planned on a weekly basis and interspersed with weekly activities outside the home. Feminist mothers tend to put more emphasis on these other activities and to fit housework in when it can be accomplished. These emphases are illustrated in the following excerpts from the interviews concerning the activities of a typical day.

Sarah King, a Mt Druitt mother describes her typical day,

Up about 6.30, get my husband off to work. One wakes up at 7, the other at 8 o'clock, get their breakfast. Get her dressed for pre-school, take her to pre-school. Come back and do the housework. Sit down and watch T.V. in the afternoon and then start getting tea ready. And that's what I do practically every day. My husband gets home anywhere between 5 and 7 o'clock, if he works back it's 9 o'clock. I never know when he'll be in.

Rhoda Maclean is a middle class Nth Shore mother at home, she says,

I never have any set day to wash or clean or iron or whatever, I do it when it needs doing. I like my house to be tidy. I don't have help in the house and I hate to hoover and dust, etc., so I put it off. But then you've got to do it, so I get in and do it and then I feel good.

There's not often I have a day without going out at least once, if you've got a car you're inclined to get in it and go out. Sometimes I like to shop or to go visiting especially if Rob's bored and wants someone to play with—or I have a little friend over here.

Then I might have a day and cook, I like to do that and I put it in the freezer for a rainy day and I feel as if I've accomplished something there.

I go to a lot of school things, I'm on the ladies' auxiliary there, they have meetings once a month and a few money making things through the year.

I'm involved with the church too and occasionally teach scripture. Sometimes I play the piano and sing which I like to do. I usually have to remind myself that I should sit down and play with the children as well as that I should do something with them. I make an effort to do that because I think otherwise days fly by and you find you've been beside them but not interrelating.

Annette Erving, a Feminist mother describes her day,

It depends on what other projects I've got going. I've got myself on all sorts of committees and I'm very involved so that I tend to do housework in fits and cycles and I dust through and get it all done, then I spend 4 days where I don't do any housework at all, but I concentrate on other things.

But a typical housework day is where I get up, get the kids dressed, make the beds, wash the dishes, tidy around the house, do some washing and ironing, take the kids to school and bring them back again.

Another typical sort of day is where I do a quick whip around in the morning and sort of straighten the beds and wash the dishes and then proceed to spend the rest of the day doing other things. So I don't have a really typical day, every day is not the same.

My motto is if I can find something else to do instead of housework, I will do the other thing instead.

Although there is the illusion of 'freedom' in deciding what to do and when to do it, for the working class mother living in a suburb on the fringe of the metropolitan area where public transport facilities are limited to buses every hour to the main shopping centre and to the railway station and with no car available, her excursions beyond the home are limited. This limitation is compounded by the short spaces of time between her set daily routine, she cannot be out of the house for lengthy periods. For the middle class mother with her own transport or living in areas such as the Nth Shore or the inner city which are well served by public transport and without such a rigid daily schedule there is more variety, less monotony and a greater number of outside and personal interests in cultural, sporting and club activities as well as outings with husband and a vacation once a year or more frequent trips.

In addition within the Mt Druitt area there are few jobs available or suitable to the times the working class woman would be willing to spend away from her family and the women do not have the material resources needed to pursue many hobbies, crafts, sports or group activities. Their ideas of what they could do apart from child care, housework, shopping and visiting are also limited. 50% of Mt Druitt mothers do not want any more hours in the day, and if there were more hours in the day 32% say they would spend them in the same way as they do now, that is, in housework, washing, ironing, etc. On the other hand 76% of Nth Shore mothers and 92% of Feminist mothers would like more hours in the day and 28% of Nth Shore respondents and 76% of Feminist respondents would spend them in activities such as reading, studying, playing or listening to music, writing, painting or some other activity which gave them pleasure or a sense of personal achievement.

The number of children in a family also alters the material conditions of mothering. More children require extra expenditure of time and physical energy spent in child care and household tasks during their ‘pre-school years at least. The material resources that are available must be spread over a greater number of people in terms of food, clothing, etc. The tendency appears to be for Feminist mothers to have the smallest number of children and Mt Druitt mothers the most, thus showing a variation in this material condition of mothering which would be expected to tie Mt Druitt mothers more closely to domestic duties during this stage of the life-cycle than Nth Shore or Feminist mothers. Whereas 8 Mt Druitt mothers had four or more children (up to 7 in one instance), only one Nth Shore mother had four children and no Feminist mother had more than three children. On the other hand 96% of Feminist mothers had one or two children, 68% of Nth Shore mothers and 48% of Mt Druitt mothers had one or two children.

The material conditions of day to day mothering vary between middle class and working class mothers allowing middle class mothers relatively more scope to transcend some of the demands of mothering and household chores. Feminist mothers deliberately place less emphasis on the housework aspect of mothering and so are enabled to spend more time and energy in other activities. Nevertheless as Table 4.2, shows there is a core of daily activities which a mother with pre-school children performs for those children which does not vary across classes or with alternative ideas of mothering. In some respects the life styles of suburban mothers with pre-school children in a market economy where the husband is the provider and the mother is at home are very similar. The mother herself remains responsible for feeding the family, laundry, washing up, day-to-day tidying, the family's health and personal problems and child care and child safety. Across class these mothers themselves say that they have more in common with other families with young children than with childless friends. For example this Feminist mother tells of the difference now she is a mother.

> In a sense after you become a mother, you become more orientated to the pregnancies, family's people, people with babies and so on. And because your other friends don't know about all this there's a sort of gulf now and I'm much happier with people who've got children or who really care about children. My sister hasn't got a child of her own but she looks after lots of children and she understands what it's all about. So I feel closer to these sorts of people than those who don't know anything about babies and think their crying is a nuisance and stuff. I can't be bothered with these people. I mean you get to the stage where you think 'if they're not interested in the baby, I don't want to know them', because they're kind of mean minded and stupid, because they don't know what is involved on a day-to-day basis or how rewarding it can be.

In terms of time, interest and physical and emotional expenditure of energy, children have priority for all mothers in the sample, although activities and interests possible outside their child-rearing and household tasks vary between classes and with alternative ideas on mothering and housework.

Self-esteem

For working class mothers whose previous and present life experiences have been largely tied to the domestic sphere, except for the minimal number of years spent in an educational institution and a few years in a low status, low income job, it could be expected that any sense of self-esteem and satisfaction in life would be associated with the appropriate sex-typed roles of wife and mother. If significant others in their milieu such as husband, their own mother and friends see them as good mothers such self-esteem and satisfaction in their role is reinforced. Middle class mothers on the other hand who have a wider experience of life may have alternative sources of self-esteem and life-satisfactions.

Mt Druitt mothers are conscious of the fact that in the wider male sphere of the market place motherhood has low status, but that within the circle of mothers, motherhood is esteemed. In a milieu which is dominated during the day by women, the mother's contact with other mothers and her own mother is an important source of reinforcement for her identity as a mother and her self-esteem derived from this identity. Her husband's opinion of her mothering is also of vital importance to her and a valued source of self-esteem. The majority of these mothers feel that significant others in their social milieu such as their husbands (96%), mothers (74%) and friends and neighbours (62%) see them as good mothers. Their own self-esteem is closely associated with their mothering and this self-esteem is dependent on how they see themselves as mothers as well as how they feel others perceive them as mothers. Although a number of mothers feel that compared with the ideal 'good' mother they are not so good, these same mothers say that they consider themselves to be good mothers, most of the time at least, according to their own standards, considering the circumstances or compared with others they know. 76% of Mt Druitt mothers consider themselves to be good mothers and coping well with motherhood most of the time at least. Only one mother says that she is not a good mother and not coping with mothering.

A typical response is given by Cecily Derrick,

> I don't think I could do any better than I'm doing—apart from control-ling my temper at times. I don't physically abuse the children or any thing like that. No, I think I'm pretty good compared with others I know.

From the perspective of the male dominated public sphere, that is the market sector, politics, educational institutions, etc. the position of mother and the attributes associated with it have low status excluding mothers from some areas of social activity and keeping them in an inferior position. However, if a mother feels that she is exhibiting the virtues of her position and is living up to the expecta-tions of significant others for motherhood, that is, if she sees that others perceive her to be a 'good' mother and she sees herself as a 'good' mother, she will experience some sense of self-esteem and see herself as a worthwhile person in her immediate social milieu.

Clearly the identity of these working class women for the most part is as a married mother who is fulfilling the expectations of that society for its female members. In her world she is valued as a married woman and a mother and her confidence in herself comes largely from being recognised as an adult female who meets the expectations for her particular group of people. One mother said that people take more notice of her now than ever before because being a wife and mother is something she does really well. 'I can't remember being good at anything very much before' she says. Money and education are less important to the mother's sense of self-worth than are her roles of wife and mother. However she realises that the sphere of work and male identity could possibly give her more value as a person in the world of the wider male society. That these mothers have confidence and a sense of value within their own group is indicated by the fact that 41, that is 82% of Mt Druitt mothers say that in a group (provided it be a group of mothers) people pay attention to them and listen to their ideas and opinions.

Middle class Nth Shore and Feminist mothers are more likely to see their mothering as a part, rather than as the whole of their existence. For example, when asked whether other people respect them as a mother 40% of Nth Shore and 56% of Feminist mothers said that people respect them as a person rather than as a mother, for what they *are* rather than for their mothering. Only 8% of Mt Druitt mothers gave this response. Another 40% of Feminist mothers, as against 16% of Nth Shore mothers and 28% of Mt Druitt mothers, said that it was only other people such as the father or grandparents or other mothers who respect them as mothers, people they have contact with in the wider society aren't concerned with their motherhood. Some typical answers to this question are,

> Not really, partly because there's an unconscious, just acceptance of mothers, I don't think people think about it. I felt that as a professional I got more obvious respect. On the other hand that might have been a bit superficial. I think I'd have to say that I think people don't consciously respect mothers. (Nth Shore mother)

> No, I think they respect me because of who I am. (Feminist mother)

These mothers have high expectations of themselves as mothers and are conscious of the fact that they are striving towards an ideal which includes their children's emotional and intellectual development as well as their physical well-being. Some of them are less sure of their mothering than the working class mothers. Mothering for them is less rigidly defined and has wider ranging expectations. Whereas 48% of Mt Druitt mothers say quite confidently that they are good mothers and coping very well with motherhood, 28% of Nth Shore mothers and only 12% of Feminist mothers say this. 44% of Feminist mothers say that they could be better mothers according to their own expectations and 32% of Nth Shore mothers say this, as against 20% of Mt Druitt mothers. Typical of the middle class responses to the question 'How do *you* think you are coping with being a mother, do *you* think you are a good mother?' is the following,

> Yes I do at certain levels. Sometimes I think I could be a lot better. We're always striving to be the best we can and we're never really going to be perfect. But it's an ongoing process. (Nth Shore mother)

Feminist mothers apparently receive less reinforcement from their own mothers for the form that their mothering takes than do Nth Shore and Mt Druitt mothers. Whereas 74% of Mt Druitt and 62% of Nth Shore mothers perceive their own mothers as seeing them as good mothers only 28% of Feminist mothers do. Feminist mothers tend to have different ideas about mothering from their own mothers, so could not be sure of their mother's approval of their mothering. For example Betty Marr feels that she is not as neat or clean as her own mother and she has different ideas about discipline, she says,

> Only just now my parents are starting to treat my children the way I want them to. They really did have the old standards. With five children, it's hard to enforce silence, but they tried. However as I get closer to them, I think somehow—I sometimes think 'Mum keeps them awfully *clean*' and sometimes I feel guilty if I don't keep them that clean. As I get older and the sheer weight of having to wash nappies, etc. will impose more neatness on me, although it's an impossible task . . .
> I think my mother basically thinks I am a good mother, but I don't iron or care if they get dirty.

Like the Nth Shore and Mt Druitt mothers, Feminist mothers perceive that their husband, or the father of the child and friends and neighbours see them as good mothers, so that within their own milieu they have some reinforcement for their form of mothering and some self-esteem from this source. 96% of Mt Druitt mothers say that their husband sees them as a good mother, 92% of Nth Shore and 80% of Feminist mothers say this. 62% of Mt Druitt, 80% of Nth Shore and 76% of Feminist mothers say that their friends and neighbours see them as 'good' mothers.

The following response from a Feminist mother to the question of whether she considers herself to be a 'good' mother or not, illustrates that motherhood is not uppermost in the minds of this group of mothers.

> I don't think about it much. Joy seems happy. I feel I am. If she seems unhappy—as she was at day-care—she was bored and I felt terrible. But normally when she's happy I don't think about whether I'm a good mother or not. I don't think I'm a bad mother. I shout, I lose my temper a lot, but she understands that that's part of life.

Powerlessness

Four questions were asked in an attempt to assess the presence or absence of a subjective sense of powerlessness in the lives of the respondents. All mothers in the sample felt powerless on at least one of these dimensions, that is to say no mother felt that she was in absolute control of her own life situation. In any society, as Lukes (1977:6–7) points out, structural limits prohibit any person, even the most powerful, from absolute autonomy, but within these limits, relative autonomy varies between the powerful and the less powerful. Similarities and differences between Mt Druitt, Nth Shore and Feminist mothers in the answers to these questions give some idea of their autonomy, relative to one another, although they cannot be used to gauge the autonomy of these mothers relative to the more powerful male breadwinners in their families. Between 64% and 70% of mothers in the three groups say that they do feel people are 'using' them at least sometimes. Reasons given were similar in the three groups and included, husband's and family's constant demands, friends' demands when they have a car available and with regard to the minding of children. The situation of economic dependence as well as the ideology of motherhood which stresses selfless service to others has put these women in a situation which makes them vulnerable to the demands of others—husbands, children and other mothers. Those who say that they do not feel that people are using them, say that they now speak up and don't let people use them unless they want to be used. In effect they take control of the situation, instead of letting the situation take control of them.

Responses were also similar across class to the question, 'Does life ever get too much for you, so that you feel you can't cope?' Between 64% and 88% of these mothers say that life does get too much for them at least at times, so that they feel they can't cope. Although this question was included to test for a general sense of powerlessness, it has a particular application in motherhood. One of the common experiences of mothers is the sense that everything is piling up, the washing, ironing, cleaning, on top of the constant demands of children for attention to aches, pains, problems, their activities and productions and for food. Many mothers said that it was when they weren't feeling 100% fit that they felt they couldn't cope. The number of mothers who experienced this sense of powerlessness is higher for the Feminist group than for the other two groups (88% as against 72% for Mt Druitt mothers and 64% for Nth Shore mothers). This can probably be accounted for by the number of extra activities that these mothers attempt in addition to their mothering, so compounding the problem.

Nevertheless none of the middle class Nth Shore or Feminist mothers expressed themselves with the note of desperation evident in this Mt Druitt mother's reply to this question,

> Yes, I think it has got too much for me. It has got to the stage where sometimes I feel I could well and truly do away with myself. Being with this baby, I wish sometimes I wasn't having this baby (4th child). Some days I just feel I can't cope and he has come home and taken the brunt of it. Especially when the kiddies up the road come down and run through my house. They're not allowed to do it up there, why should they be able to do it here? I shouldn't have to rely on drugs, I should just rely on my own self-esteem to calm me down.

Middle class people with greater resources at their disposal generally have a greater sense of their ability to act upon the world and many working class people through their experiences at school and in the work place have come to doubt their own worth. For Mt Druitt inhabitants there is a stigma attached to living in that area which adds to a subjective sense of having failed in life. Observations made by the Community Social Worker in the area included in a later chapter confirm the sense of inferiority felt by Mt Druitt people in general and women in particular.

The difference in this subjective sense of powerlessness between classes is further demonstrated by responses to the questions concerning the future and being a 'cog in the machinery of life'. Whereas 30% of Mt Druitt mothers have a pessimistic attitude to the future, no Feminist mother has and only one (4%) Nth Shore mother has. Differences in responses between the working class and middle class mothers on this question are evident in the following replies,

> I'm scared of the future, for the children's sake really—wars, drugs, and the things that happen, you wonder what sort of world you're bringing them into. (Mt Druitt mother)

> I really look forward to the future, I always think it's going to be good soon. (Nth Shore mother)

> Rosy, I feel quite comfortable and optimistic about it. (Feminist mother)

Whereas Mt Druitt mothers are more likely to feel that they are a 'cog in the machinery of life' (50%) than Nth Shore mothers (36%), Feminist mothers are less likely to feel like this (24%). The following responses show the sense of powerlessness felt by 50% of Mt Druitt mothers, the ambivalence of some Nth Shore mothers and the feeling of the majority of Feminist mothers that it is up to them to bring about changes that are necessary both in their own lives and in the conditions of society. This is not to ignore the fact, however, that 50% of Mt Druitt mothers also gave replies such as the following,

> That's a rather unpleasant thought—I think largely you make your own happiness or whatever, mostly it's up to yourself.

Typical responses to this question are as follows,

> Yes, I feel it's just the same thing every day and I feel as though—I feel we're here for a purpose, but what for—we're going to end up all dying anyway. I'm going to die someday. The one's that don't want to live go on, the ones that really want to live go quicker. I feel that I'm going to live forever, I dread it. (Mt Druitt mother)

> Yes, at the moment I do. I don't know how long that's going to last, but certainly while the children are little, I don't know any woman, no matter what her qualifications or any other aspect who can get out of that uncontrollable cycle. I can see myself having a little more control and power later—especially when I'm qualified and I'm more financially independent. (Nth Shore mother)

> Society is very complex and you can let yourself be swept along. That's one of the reasons why I've become very involved in the political process. I am determined not to be a cog in the machine. (Feminist mother)

The inevitability of motherhood with it's constant demands, the limited range of other options, the concentration on home and family once children are born and the poorer material conditions of mothering of the working class mothers in this research put them in a position which exacerbates both the powerlessness experienced by all mothers and the peculiar sense of powerlessness associated with their class position. The way is therefore left open for the acceptance without question of an ideology which emphasises motherhood as natural and the satisfactions in life and self-fulfilment which are associated with motherhood. The following section looks at the life satisfactions of these mothers and compares and contrasts them with those of the middle class, Nth Shore and Feminist mothers.

Satisfactions with life

As has already been suggested life-options and life chances of mothers at Mt Druitt are severely limited by their social class position and by the ideology of motherhood which suggests that to be a fully adult female in our society a woman should be a mother and should continuously care for her own children until they are at school. At the same time the ideology emphasises the importance of motherhood and the tasks and values it incorporates and the rewards it offers. In addition an ideal of the 'good' mother is presented towards which all mothers should strive. If then a woman defines herself primarily as a mother and her image of herself as a 'good' mother is reflected back to her from her own mother, her friends, neighbours and her husband, she will experience a sense of self-worth in her present life situation. In spite of feeling powerless, encapsulated as she is both physically and ideologically, she will express general satisfaction with her lot with little awareness of other possibilities.

When asked the question 'when you feel really happy these days, what kinds of things make you feel happy?' 80% of Mt Druitt mothers said 'when the family is happy' or 'when husband and children show love and appreciate you'; 18% that it was their children's achievements; 12% being with friends or going out and 8% that they don't ever feel really happy these days. With the important addition of the money factor and housework a similar pattern in reverse is seen when feelings of depression are analysed. 42% gave as the main reason for feeling down or depressed children's misbehaviour; 18% housework piling up; 26% husband being out or away a lot or arguments with him or being taken for granted by him; 8% finances, 6% boredom and drudgery; 6% worries about their own mother/sister and 4% bad relationships with neighbours.

Middle class mothers who, by reason of their class have greater options than working class mothers can also be constrained by the ideology of motherhood, but are more likely to have an awareness that life could be otherwise for them and to include outside activities in their satisfactions with life. When asked the question 'When you feel really happy these days, what kinds of things make you feel happy?' like Mt Druitt mothers, Nth Shore and Feminist mothers emphasised relationships and activities associated with the family, husband and children and their health and well-being. These mothers added however, satisfactions achieved from their own interests such as a hobby, study, music, art and work for some of the Feminist mothers who were employed outside the home. 68% of Feminist mothers mentioned these activities and 28% of Nth Shore mothers. They also placed more emphasis on contact with people outside the family, going out, having friends in, etc. (44% of Feminist mothers, 24% of Nth Shore mothers, compared with 12% of Mt Druitt mothers.)

Similarly when asked 'When you feel really down or depressed these days what makes you feel that way?' these mothers gave relationships with husband and children priority, but gave a wider variety of responses than Mt Druitt mothers. For example, whereas no Mt Druitt mother said it was the pressure of all her activities that got her down sometimes, or the fact that she didn't have enough time to do all that she wanted to, or was committed to, 16% of Nth Shore and 20% of Feminist mothers gave this response.

It is of interest to note here that whereas housework was given as a reason for feeling down or depressed by 18% of Mt Druitt and 20% of Nth Shore mothers, nowhere did it appear as a reason for providing satisfaction. In a very real sense for the traditional and ambivalent mothers in the sample the satisfactions associated with motherhood, especially the relationship between the mother and her children emphasised by the ideology, obscure the dirty, demanding, repetitious nature of housework which brings no satisfaction in its own right. For the Feminist mothers who have questioned the ideology, satisfactions are still associated with their relationship with their children but housework is relegated to a position of minor importance, it does not appear in the reasons they give for being depressed.

In the minds of these mothers there is no doubt that the family and/or children bring a great deal of satisfaction as well as many frustrations to their lives. For Mt Druitt mothers it is almost the only source of satisfaction, for middle class mothers there are other sources as well.

Within the context of an interview on motherhood, although mothers have expressed throughout the interviews frustrations, anxieties and exasperations as well as joys associated with the tasks of motherhood, only 4% of Mt Druitt and 12% of Nth Shore and Feminist mothers say that they are generally not satisfied with their lives at present.

However when asked about being resentful or rebellious in their present situation more mothers were prepared to admit some dissatisfaction. 44% of Mt Druitt mothers, 48% of Nth Shore and 80% of Feminist mothers say they are resentful at least sometimes. 38% of Mt Druitt, 64% of Nth Shore and 76% of Feminist mothers say that they are rebellious at times. Typical responses are as follows,

> Sometimes I feel quite rebellious. I feel the need to get out of the house, being trapped, the confinements of mothering and housework and the fact that my husband has more freedom. (Nth Shore mother)

> Yes I feel rebellious when I think I put a lot of effort and energy into mothering and men don't appreciate this or have to do it or don't do it any way. I would like to use my time and energy in other ways. (Feminist mother)

Although some of the responses referred to the husband, the majority, as in the examples above, implied the restrictions and demands of children, child care and or household tasks associated with child care. As Hannah Gavron (1966:68) found in her study of London mothers, it is the restrictions and ambivalence of the motherhood role, not the wife role that presents a situation of conflict for mothers. The greater the awareness of other options and of the restrictions of motherhood, apparently the greater the sense of resentment and rebellion.

Some of the resentment and rebellion has, for Feminist mothers been channelled into attempts to change their own situation of mothering, for example the formation of a Children's Co-operative; some into the experience of co-operative households; some into political activity such as Women's Electoral Lobby or feminist drama groups or journalism and some into Rape Crisis Centres and Abortion Clinics. Nth Shore mothers tend to express their rebellion by driving away from the house and city for a number of hours, visiting friends, or having a good cry. Mt Druitt mothers don't even have all of these options and tend to see such thoughts as outside the realm of 'good' motherhood. The expression of their revolt against their oppression may be summed up in the words of Nora Hart,

> Sometimes I think you do feel rebellious, I sometimes I feel as though I could just rebel and get out of the house and not come back for a full day. I feel as though I can rebel and say, 'Right I'll go out and spend a full day doing something that I would particularly like to do without my kids and that'. Then again you don't do it though, you just stay around and stick it out.

It seems that resources associated with middle class position are a necessary but not sufficient base for some questioning of the ideology of motherhood. However it is only when the material resources available to middle class mothers are aligned with utopian ideas concerning gender oppression and motherhood that some challenge to the ideology is possible and there is a corresponding challenge to sex role ideology and traditional self-concepts. Satisfactions with life for these mothers remains closely associated with children and family, but also includes activities outside this area which are of particular interest to the individual mother herself.

The following chapter looks at the effects across class of women's employment outside the home on women's ideas and experience of mothering.

Note

1 Not all the Feminist group of mothers were in two parent families where the husband was the breadwinner, 10 of the 25 were single parents, and 5 of the mothers in two parent families were employed outside the home on at least 3 days a week so could be included in the 'employed' category. Most of the data presented in this chapter refers to the 'at home' mothers in two parent families in the Feminist group. However, Tables App. 4.12 to 4.17 were prepared for the whole group and refer to the 25 Feminist mothers interviewed. Data specifically relevant to employed mothers and single mothers is included in the following chapters.

7 Employed mothers

In this chapter the data of the research is examined with regard to the question, 'Does being employed outside the home affect mothers' beliefs about motherhood, their lived experience of motherhood and/or their sex role ideology, self-concepts and satisfactions with life?'

Within the sample of mothers who are employed outside the home on at least three days per week there are variations which can be accounted for chiefly by the social class of the respondent and there are cross class similarities which can be accounted for by the fact that these women have participated in the market sector of the economy.

Social class differences

Variations within the group of employed mothers who were interviewed for the research are revealed by examining the ideal types of mothers in this group. The four (16%) ideological traditional mothers in this group are working class mothers who hold very strongly to the traditional ideology but who must work for financial reasons. The combined incomes of both husband and wife in these families is below $12 000 per year and unless the wife were employed the family would have difficulty in meeting financial commitments because husbands' incomes are extremely low. These mothers would prefer to be at home and believe that that is where they should be. Financial pressure has forced them to find full-time factory or cleaning jobs which can be fitted in with their husband's work so that they can still be at home with their children during the day. Although the husbands of the four ideological traditional employed mothers in my sample give the children their evening meal and put them to bed, the wife still feels that this should be her responsibility and takes full responsibility for all other household tasks. Her material resources are low and the physical labour of home and job takes all her time and energy. These mothers look forward to the day when they can relinquish their outside jobs.

Typical of these mothers is Julie Carpenter whose husband is a garbage collector. His work is intermittent because of alcoholism. Julie has had to have a job for all her married life. She has three children, a 12 year old girl, an 11 year old boy and a 12 months old baby. The two older children help with the evening meal and the care of the baby. When I interviewed Julie she had just finished an enormous pile of ironing for the family and was preparing to travel 20 kilometres to work in a factory from 4 p.m. to 11 p.m. She says that she often gets home from work and finds she still has to wash the dishes from the evening meal. She feels tired and worn out and looks much older than her 35 years. She longs for the day when she can give up work. Her life centres around her husband and children, her employment is a physically exhausting necessity, bringing little enjoyment or satisfaction—it is an extra physical burden for her.

Employment for these mothers makes little difference to their home roles and self concepts, it does not provide them with economic independence and detracts from rather than adds to their satisfaction with life.

On the other hand the 5 (20%) ambivalent progressive mothers in this group are all full-time professional women whose jobs are important to them as a source of satisfaction and self-fulfilment. They have been able, due to the material resources available to them to pay for some child care and/or housecleaning tasks and in their own words have 'all the appliances' to help them in the home. In addition their own and their husband's more flexible attitudes to sex roles allows for more sharing of roles than is evident for working class employed mothers.

Typical of these mothers is Kathleen Brown who is a full-time teacher. She has a three year old daughter and took 4 months off from teaching when she was born. She enjoys her work, and her colleagues and superiors think that she is very good at it. Her ambition is to become a headmistress. Katherine believes that if the mother is happy, whether employed or not, then the husband and children will be too. She and her husband try to share housework and child care 50/50, although she says, in reality, it is 60/40 on her side. The first person home cooks dinner and if either is very busy at work the other takes more responsibility in the home. Katherine pays for family day-care, that is a local council approved 'at home' mother for day-care for her daughter. She feels she has the best of both worlds and looks forward to her future in both.

As other research has found (e.g., Harper and Richards, 1979:191), it is only in professional families that husbands such as Katherine's take any real share in household tasks and child care and then, as with this family, the balance is always in favour of the wife. Nevertheless it is this class difference for employed mothers that enables the middle class mother such as Katherine to pursue her career with enthusiasm and commitment, so that it becomes an important source of satisfaction in her life.

These nine mothers represent the extremes of the class differences in the employed sample and demonstrate that being employed can be very different for a working class mother than for a middle class mother. The rest of the employed mothers interviewed are ambivalent in their beliefs about motherhood, sex roles, etc. Some of this ambivalence can also be accounted for by the bias in this group of mothers towards middle class origins and strong market capacity. Some can also be attributed to the different frame of reference which entry into the market sector has given mothers. Within this frame of reference motherhood is reassessed.

The percentage of the Employed group of mothers who had professional/managerial fathers and mothers is closer to the middle class Nth Shore group than to the working class Mt Druitt group, although husband's occupations are not so biased (Tables App. 4.7, 4.9 and 4.11). The percentage of Employed mothers in professional/managerial occupations (Table App. 4.15) is also high, compared with other groups, 52% in these occupations and 48% in clerical/sales or manual occupations. The middle class backgrounds of the majority of these mothers has probably contributed to the ambivalence of their attitudes towards mothering and their present employment has certainly improved the material conditions of their mothering. None of these ambivalent mothers has a family income below $10 000 per year. The availability of material resources is evidenced by the fact that 16 (64%) employed mothers have their own car and 6 (24%) have access to the family car, and this has already been shown to alleviate some of the limitations of mothering.

Nevertheless not all of the ambivalents in this group are middle class. Across class, except for the 4 ideological traditional mothers already discussed, employment outside the home does appear to have a significant effect on the mother's attitudes to mothering and sex roles and most particularly on her own self-esteem. The entry into the work-force has given these mothers another framework within which to view themselves and their home roles.

**Effects of employment on ideologies of
motherhood and sex roles**

Most employed mothers have adapted the ideology of motherhood
to accommodate their own absence from their pre-school children
for periods during the day as was shown in the discussion of the
tenets of the ideology. Only 7 (28%) of these mothers believe that
mothers of pre-school children should not work outside the home
unless it is financially necessary, compared with 86% of Mt Druitt
and 72% of Nth Shore 'at home' mothers. A typical view of these
employed mothers on this question is as follows,

> I think if they can do it, it's fair enough. If you really look around you
> can find child-minding facilities and if the mother wants to work or needs
> to work she should be able to without too much criticism from the rest of
> the society.

In pragmatic day-to-day terms the mother's employment outside
the home does result in more flexible attitudes to sex roles in that
fathers partake more than other fathers in household tasks and
child care, although the responsibility remains with the mother, and
in fact, even when the mother is employed full-time she performs
the majority of the tasks herself. Fathers helped with bathing
children and putting them to bed, playing with them or entertaining
them, but did not assume responsibility for their care otherwise.
Help with housework remained largely at the level of doing anything
they were asked to do, but taking neither initiative nor responsibility. Exceptions were 6 respondents who said that husbands shared
50/50 when they were working full-time and 6 respondents who said
that fathers cooked meals on a regular basis. None of the 'at home'
Nth Shore or Mt Druitt respondents included these responses. At the
other extreme, whereas 32% of Mt Druitt and 40% of Nth Shore
mothers said that husbands did nothing, or very little, only 12% of
Employed mothers gave this response.

In terms of the day-to-day activities of Employed mothers there is
little variation in the basic household routines of these mothers compared with the other groups. Going out to work is apparently an
additional activity which precludes at home personal interests such
as reading, sewing, hobbies, music, etc. No employed mother mentioned these activities as part of her day, but the majority did include
feeding the family, caring for the children, housework, etc.

The mother's employment does have an additional effect on perception of the sex-based division of authority in that it is no longer
assumed by the majority of these mothers that the husband should

be the head of the house. Whereas 64% of 'at home' Nth Shore and 52% of 'at home' Mt Druitt mothers said that the husband should be the head of the house, only 20% of Employed mothers said this. A typical response is as follows,

> It should be team work, in some things a wife is better to make choices and in some a man is better, and it varies from marriage to marriage.

These mothers feel that because they are contributing economically to the family, their share in leadership and authority should increase. In terms of economic independence, in 40% of cases the wife's working has relieved her of dependence upon her husband financially—if he left her or she wanted to leave him she could support herself and her children. In 40% of cases the mother's employment has also given these women money which they can spend just as they want to, on themselves if they choose. For mothers such as Coral Searl, this economic independence is important to her own sense of identity and autonomy. Coral says,

> I didn't like feeling dependent, I hated it, that's one reason I kept working. Not that he actually ever did or said anything to make me feel like that, but I just hated the fact that he was bringing in all the money and I was just sitting there spending it.

Admittedly these are professional women whose salary enables them to contribute significantly to household finances and would be sufficient for self-support. However even mothers who earned a lot less and whose earnings could not make them totally economically independent had improved self-images because of their earning capacity and gave as one reason for working outside the home, the need for a lack of complete dependence upon their husbands.

Effects of employment on the material conditions of mothering

For the 60% of mothers whose employment neither gives them money which they can spend on themselves nor makes them independent of their husbands for economic support, it does nevertheless improve the material conditions of their mothering. The money these mothers earn is used to help pay off the mortgage on the house and to buy commodities for the family which could not be afforded on the husband's wage. These mothers feel that they are contributing to the family's welfare in this way. The pattern amongst working class mothers is to work for periods of time to achieve specific objectives such as a new washing machine or refrigerator, to buy the children's Christmas presents or to refurnish the lounge room, etc.

Amongst the middle class employed mothers the money they earn is used (apart from helping with mortgage repayments and household expenses) to improve the quality of life of their families in other ways. Children's schooling and cultural accomplishments, holidays, overseas travel, visiting distant relatives, eating out, the theatre, family outings, clothing for self and family are some of the items mentioned by these mothers as those purchased with their earnings. The Community Social Worker at Mt Druitt pointed out that for working class mothers at least this aspect of their contribution to the family is increasingly a part of their perception of 'good' motherhood, but must be reconciled with their belief that their 'place is in the home' while their children are young. The inability of the male wage to support a dependent wife and family is indicated here and evidently the ideology, while not suggesting any attenuation of the mother's total responsibility for child care is being adjusted to include the mother's economic contribution to the family's welfare.

For the mothers in the sample, across classes, the money they earn in the market sector contributes to and in most cases improves the material conditions in which they experience motherhood and for some middle class mothers it gives them the added resources necessary to transcend some of the limitations of motherhood.

Effects of employment on self-concepts and life-satisfactions

There is no doubt that earning some income in a cash-nexus society contributes to changes in self-image which, in the present research, is the most obvious difference between the Employed mothers interviewed and Nth Shore and Mt Druitt 'at home' mothers. However it is not the only contributing factor. As Rowbotham (1973:62–64) points out, the subordination of the family and women's domestic labour to the dominant system of capitalist commodity production results in a different set of values and form of consciousness for women at home than for men in the market place, the former being subordinate to and dependent upon the latter. When women enter the market place Rowbotham has suggested that their consciousness may be changed so that they become aware of their oppression in the domestic sphere of labour. Employed mothers in the sample did not have their consciousness raised to this level, although some Feminist employed mothers whose jobs put them in touch with other feminists and reinforced their feminist ideas were more aware of the limitations mothering has on political activity and of the lack of recognition of mothering as an important economic contribution to society. For example, Mary Tyler is a feminist doctor working in a Women's Health Centre, she says,

> Part of the whole process of having a child is that you become less active in whatever else you've been doing. Before I had Kim I was the sort of person who actively participated in feminist politics and who they rang up to get information on the media. And as part of the process of being pregnant and so on I've become much less confident and much less active or able to do these things. I feel as if I'm just moving back into a more active phase now . . . I worked up until the day he was born, two days a week. I was on maternity leave for 3 months, but I couldn't stand it so I went back. Yes, I do think working does make a difference. I think it's very important to have a recognised role in society. It's a pity that society doesn't recognise motherhood more as an important economic role in our society. Motherhood is recognised in other societies. In primitive societies it's a really important role and in China for example it's a much more important role than it is here.

The majority of Employed mothers did not reach Mary's level of awareness, nevertheless release from encapsulation within the domestic sphere and the woman's world of associated activities and entry into the market sector, did provide another frame of reference from which they could view their own position.

For many, this perspective, with its alternative sources of identity and satisfaction, has had a paradoxical effect. It has raised the mother's self-esteem and sense of autonomy while at the same time making her realise that, by comparison, in terms of long range goals, mothering is the most fulfilling part of her life. This is so across class and is also evident in the responses of many of the Feminist mothers when asked about their satisfactions with life. Nor can it be explained by the generally inferior positions of women vis-a-vis men in the work place or the gender identity associated with motherhood for women. In her study of professional fathers at home, Harper (1980) found that once men became involved in active parenting, they too felt this to be an important and long ranging source of satisfaction in their lives when compared with the values and satisfactions of the work place. No doubt if men participated more the status of mothering would be raised. In present society however, in terms of status or prestige, the individual's role in the market place has greater value than domestic roles. The following excerpts from the interviews give the mothers' own accounts of the effects of employment outside the home on their self-concepts and satisfactions with life.

Kristy Allen is a working class mother who describes the differences working outside the home has made to her self-confidence, ability to express her opinion and the notice taken of her by her family,

I didn't go to work until my little one was 5, and this is another part of being a Mum, I used to sit here—I did the work, the three were at school—and then it seemed so long till 3 o'clock.

My husband was away, and then they'd come in and take it all and then they'd be gone. Sometimes it'd quite upset me, I'd think they'd wronged me, they hadn't done it on purpose, but I'd think 'Gee whiz' you know, martyr would come out. I'd been sitting here all day waiting for them to come home and I felt that was wrong and they didn't appreciate me. I felt I was just a doormat. My husband didn't turn to me for any decisions at all, you were just told to do something and you did it and you didn't think for yourself at all. My brain didn't like that one little bit, there was nothing there, no incentive for anything. As fast as you'd cleaned up they all dirtied it and at any rate you get to the point once they're all at school—and I had a job in two hours and it scared me. I hadn't worked for ten years and you think 'Can I do it? Can I cope with it? There's a brain there, I'm not so bad after all'.

It was great, it got everyone into a routine, made beds, set table, etc. They didn't mind at all, it made them more independent, pulled them closer together.

I find that when talking to other people about various jobs, leaning towards engineering, it rounds you out. It benefitted my husband and I because I had things to discuss, not just the house and children and after so many years of patiently listening to him rave on and on, I could say 'Oh well this happened at work this week' and he would sit and listen to me for a change. The old doormat suddenly shook itself.

This mother had another child after starting work, but kept up her secretarial job three days a week after a brief period at home.

Marion Joy is a middle class mother who tells of the difference going out to work has made to her self-esteem,

Now that I've started work again, I've only been working for a term, I did casual work before that, but I feel as though I'm back getting my own life back together again. But I spent three years at home with very little money, I didn't even have my bus fare to Hornsby most of the time, it's very confining and frustrating . . .

Sylvia Barnes comes from a working class background and now owns her own hairdressing salon. She presents the paradox that many Employed and Feminist mothers express concerning the effect of employment on their self-concepts and satisfactions with life.

It's funny you know, since I've worked I've become more fulfilled. I felt that before I was working—I felt, you know 'What do I do? Muck around. I've got nothing to say what I am.' I was really lost.

When I first got married everything was fine. When you first have your baby that's fine and then there's a period of time when they're growing up when you feel 'Well who are you?' Really and truly it hit me and I felt very depressed and that, with all the family ties. But since I've got this now and I've got busy and I'm dealing with people and I'm handling the business and I'm doing the books and the banking and all this sort of thing and it's terrific. I've felt a complete woman doing that.

I think the men have the best life really, but I think 'best' as far as fulfilment, I think women have really. To see that child when it's growing. And I think it's a lovely feeling to give birth to a child and just to see them, and for the husband to be there with you and it's lovely. But I think you end up having a lot of fulfilment in life, more so than a man because a man's only got his work to fulfil him and we've got a lot more in life.

For the employed mothers, the most significant difference in their self-concepts from the 'at home' Mt Druitt and Nth Shore mothers is in their heightened sense of self-esteem once they entered the work-force. Whereas 44% of Mt Druitt and 52% of Nth Shore mothers felt that people would take more notice of them as a person and of their ideas and opinions if they were working, employed mothers had actually had this experience and 80% said that, in fact, people did, or that they felt better about themselves now they were working.

A Feminist employed mother says,

It does make a difference to the way I feel and the way I present myself, I think. I just am more assertive and more sure of myself when I'm working, because I value it. I'd hope it wouldn't make any difference—but it does to the way I feel.

A greater sense of autonomy for these mothers is evident from the fact that compared with the other groups interviewed, fewer Employed mothers felt that they were a 'cog in the machinery of life' (28% compared with 50% for Mt Druitt and 36% for Nth Shore mothers) or that they couldn't cope (56% compared with 72% and 64% for Mt Druitt and Nth Shore mothers respectively). These mothers, on the whole felt that they were in control of their situation as is evident in the following,

No, I'm not a cog, I'm doing what I want to do. I'm very self-sufficient now.

Across class then, in the present research, with the exception of some working class mothers whose job is an added physical burden for them, employment has given the majority of these mothers a sense of competence and control which many 'at home' mothers lack. 65% of Employed mothers felt that people respected them for their own individual achievements rather than for the fact that they were someone's 'Mum'. Although many said that at times they felt very tired with the demands of job and home and that they weren't doing either job as well as they'd like to, they still felt that ultimately they were in control and that by organising their lives they were able to cope with these demands.

The fact of being employed full-time or part-time did not appear to make a difference to the effect of employment on the mother's attitudes to mothering, sex roles and self-concepts. 60% of the group were employed full-time and 40% part-time for at least three days a week, the effects of employment crossed this division, getting out of the home and participating in the market sector and having independent access to money appear to be the salient factors.

Conclusions

Entry into the dominant sphere of commodity production for exchange in a society economically based in this sphere with its emphasis on achieved rather than ascribed status did bring about some change in consciousness for these mothers concerning themselves, their sex role ideology and the ideology of motherhood. Such changes occurred across class and across full-time/part-time categories of employment. Such consciousness did not take the form of awareness of oppression in the domestic sphere, although it did reveal some of the limitations of economic dependence. Mostly it took the form of an increased sense of self-worth and competence, autonomy and control, as opposed to a sense of powerlessness and inferiority. Paradoxically, the enduring nature of personal fulfilment experienced through mothering was highlighted by the added perspective of work-force participation. It also enabled some mothers to question the necessity for their constant attendance upon their pre-school children.

Two important reasons have been suggested for women's lack of consciousness or awareness of their oppression in the domestic sphere even when they actively participate in the market sector and make contact with others who share their oppression. Firstly, women in the family (the subordinate group) live in such close emotional interdependence with their male significant others (the superordinate group) that the separation of their interests is almost totally obscured (Cass, 1976:22). Secondly, Bell and Newby (1976:167) suggest that traditional forms of authority in the face-to-face situation of the family maintain a 'deferential dialectic' in the relationship between husband and wife which stabilises the structural differentiation of power in such a relationship, in spite of 'swinging the norms' of actual behaviour in the relationship. In quite subtle ways, deference to traditional authority stabilises legitimation of the husband's superior power and status in the wider society and in the family. This 'deferential dialectic' say Bell and Newby 'is likely to be a central inhibitor of the growth of consciousness among wives of their subordinate position'.

It could be conjectured then, that absence both of continuous face-to-face deferential encounter with the significant superordinate other and of close emotional reciprocity with him may lead to a change of consciousness of mothers concerning their oppression in the domestic sphere, or at least to a questioning of traditional ideas relating to motherhood and 'woman's place'. The following chapter looks at the effect of the rearing of children in a single parent, mother-headed family on the ideologies of motherhood and of sex roles and on the mother's self-concepts and life-satisfactions.

8   Single mothers

The most obvious difference between the never married, widowed, divorced or separated mothers interviewed for the research and the rest of the sample, is the absence of a male breadwinner in the structure of the family and the consequent lack of his income. In the present chapter the interaction of these factors with social class, employment/non-employment, contact with significant others, experience of motherhood, beliefs about motherhood and sex roles and self-concepts and life-satisfactions will be examined.

The material conditions of mothering for single mothers

Comparison of the family incomes of the group of Single mothers interviewed with those of the rest of the sample shows that across class their level of family income is lower. In fact 88% of these mothers have a family income below $10 000 per year (Table App. 4.19) and the majority of these are between $4000 and $5000 per year. The 12% with incomes about $10 000 per year are employed full-time and only one of these has an income above $15 000 per year. The generally low level of income of this group of mothers limits the material conditions of their mothering across class when compared with other mothers and to a large extent limits their participation in activities beyond the home. The limitations are felt by both middle and working class mothers.

For example, Betty Harwood is a middle class mother who works part-time as a relief pharmacist and receives maintenance for the children from her ex-husband, she retained a share in the family home and her own car after the divorce, she feels her life is monotonous, a nervously exhausting existence between work and home with no money for any extras such as a dinner out or the theatre or a concert which she used to enjoy. She says,

> It always comes back to money, I pay baby-sitters for when I work, but I can't afford to pay for baby-sitters when I'm going out and spending money for outings on top of that.

Sarah Butler is a middle class mother who describes her situation when her husband left,

> I had to make considerable adjustments, I wasn't working and wasn't receiving any social security. I was relying on my husband's alimony, that is, what money he would send us. Quite often I had no money, no bread, it was really quite desperate. Fortunately I had things like flour in the house, and I could make scones and this is what we'd have to eat. We ate lots of cheese and eggs.
>   It's not quite so bad now. Last year it was really quite difficult. I started cleaning houses and taking in ironing and doing all sorts of things at the beginning of this year, because I just didn't want to go through all that any more. But then of course this job came along so that was a real godsend.

She is now teaching three days a week and is able to manage because she has been able to retain the family home and a car, but has no money for any extras. She would very much like to finish her university degree, but cannot afford the cost of books, etc. at the present time.

Pip Brown is a working class mother with five children, who was existing on social services benefits assisted by a rebate in rent for the Housing Commission house in which they live. Recently her eldest daughter entered the work-force and is contributing $30 a week to housekeeping expenses which 'helps a lot' says Pip. Although she feels much better off than when she was dependent upon an unreliable husband, money is her biggest worry, she lives for her children and their friends, she has no contact with relatives and deliberately 'keeps to herself' feeling the stigma of her poverty and her divorced state.

She has no car or phone, her house is very sparsely furnished and in a state of disrepair. The President of Birthright through whom I contacted this respondent had recently negotiated for a second-hand refrigerator to be passed on to this family before the onset of the summer months. Pip insisted on paying $40 for it. In the following comment she compares her present position favourably with her married situation and emphasises the place of her children in her life.

> I'm coping better on my own. I go without so the kids can have, that's the way it should be. They went without for so long, they were walking around in rags. No one can look at my children—except for the little girl

who keeps throwing out all the clothes—I can say 'Well they're well dressed, nice clothes'.

I'm stupid with kids but I love them, and I shouldn't. I've got to learn to let them go. I go on the bus to have lunch with my eldest daughter every day—she works at Grace Bros.

In terms of absolute poverty, this respondent's experience is probably the most extreme I encountered in the course of the interviews, and demonstrates inter-class differences in the material conditions of mothering experienced by these mothers in spite of cross class similarities in income level. All the middle class mothers in this group (except one whose ex-husband had bought and furnished a town house for her) had retained the family home or lived at home with parents, had a car and were either employed or receiving maintenance. All the working class mothers (except one who was buying her home) were renting houses or flats. With three exceptions (who were employed full-time) they were existing on social security benefits. Nevertheless as the comments quoted above demonstrate, there is a sense of 'relative deprivation'[1] for each of these mothers when they compare their situation with those of two parent families around them. Compared with the homes of other respondents in similar areas the majority of these mothers whether middle or working class were living in homes which were in poor condition and poorly furnished, no income being available for repairs, painting or renewing furnishing. Compared with the activities available to other mothers in their area, lack of money and lack of a husband limited the options of these mothers severely and they felt their lives to be dull and monotonous, their life-satisfactions being narrowed to their relationships with their children, for the most part.

Middle class mothers who had been adequately provided for by a professional or managerial male in their marriage, compared their present situation with the life-style of their marriage and found it wanting. Having retained the family home, these mothers still lived in a middle class milieu and their significant reference groups were middle class people. Compared with their families, neighbours and relatives and the lives they had been able to live in a two parent family they felt improvished.

For many of the working class single mothers however whose husbands had been extremely unreliable breadwinners due to fluctuations in market requirements for secondary workers or to the husband's alcohol problem or ill-health, their present situation appeared to them to be a distinct improvement on their married situation, economically. The regular social security benefit over which they had complete control and a rebate on their rent enabled them to stretch their finances to an extent which had not been previously possible.

For example, one mother says,

> Life's better now. There were too many upsetting times when I was married, one upsetting thing after another. My husband was out of work most of the time and even when Robin was born. It's easier now because I've got an income coming in and you know where you are.

These mothers were reluctant to marry again as they feared that they would lack control over any allowance from a new husband and more generally would lose their independence.

Pip Brown expresses this feeling,

> I don't want to get married again. Maybe later on when the kids grow up I might meet someone I could say to 'come around Monday, Wednesday and Friday', sort of thing, but that'd be all.
>
> It's easier without a man around. I wouldn't want to get someone who drank a lot like my husband. He wouldn't work, he was an alcoholic.

Economic dependence in the marriage situation meant economic deprivation for these mothers. For many of the middle class mothers the reverse was the case, economic dependence meant economic support and absence of such support meant economic deprivation for them. However, amongst these middle class mothers economic support for some had entailed a high price in terms of personal freedom and development. In return for economic support they had given assent to personal oppression and subservience. For them, their single state had given them a new frame of reference within which to view their former oppression.

The effects of being single on mothers' self-concepts and life-satisfactions

Within the frame of reference which is free of the physical presence on a day-to-day, face-to-face basis of a male breadwinner with all that is entailed in terms of deference and demeanour (Bell and Newby, 1976:152–168), some middle class mothers have now become aware of the 'relative oppression' of their former situation. The effect has been to raise their self-esteem and sense of personal worth.

Renate Kettlewell describes such a situation.

> I think you've get to be a little bit firm in your stand. I know I wasn't firm enough in my stand and I took too much of the everyday jobs and chores and everything like that. I always did all the gardening and the lawn mowing and the majority of the painting work around, as well as

doing all the cooking, all the housework and I left him free to follow his hobbies. I thought that was really what he wanted to do and that was right, but actually it let us get further and further apart. Up until Betty was born I participated, I did a lot of sailing and we were actually champions in our type of boat. And as soon as Betty turned up he found it rather hard to accept that I couldn't be there all the time for the championships. I tried it a number of times. We always went out sailing every weekend, but I was feeding her up until nine months and I was on call every four hours to feed her and he found that hard to accept.

I think next time around I would have a husband who could see my point of view in the light that he has to take his share of the jobs too and maybe share in the kitchen things and maybe the outside things, but I'd rather like to do these things together and get them over and done and out of the way and do other activities as a family . . . .

There were times in the past couple of years of Betty's life when I would have liked time to myself, because a child is very demanding and it would have been lovely to have a day or so on my own, just away from that continual demand. Now that I can communicate with her I enjoy her company and I miss her when she is away from me, which is a lovely way to have it. But for those first two years it is hard to communicate, it's hard to find what the problems are if there are some. Nappies used to get me down. All her washing and all my husband's washing. It would have been nicer to have a husband who was a little more helpful, someone supportive rather than someone who expected a three course meal and the washing up done afterwards and then wonder why you went to bed at ten o'clock.

With business dinners there was a load of shopping to do and preparations and you have to have your children pretty happy around you and they know when something like that's going on and they sense the strain building up in you and there must be tensions. And particularly in this situation it was somebody who would help my husband get higher up the ladder and I was getting very fed up with that sort of thing and I really didn't want to see them. And I'd be rushing from the time I got up in the morning until I went to bed.

I think I gave in too much all the time. I should have just put my foot down and said '*Right*, you've got to do your bit or . . .' I didn't. I just did all these things and of course it welled up inside me, a very self-righteous feeling and a very indignant feeling. There was never any violence or anything, I'm not a violent sort of person and I guess things build up in me and I retreat more into myself as a result of that. And I found it rather hard to hold a conversation with these people that came. Probably I just rejected most of these people and didn't want much to do with them.

Life's just so different since then. Actually my husband's changed too, he's showing much more interest in Betty. He'd like to have Betty in Manilla with him for a while. I think it's important not to react against the situation. It's the usual story of going off with the secretary and I just let things ride. I was very miserable and very unhappy but I just didn't react to things and I think that this saved the situation, so that there was no hate or bitterness and I could look on very easily. And I realise he's done me a good turn by doing this and he feels his sense of obligation and duty to do the right thing by us financially, it's worked out very well . . .

I think now I just want to find myself a bit better really, it's a thing I'm going through. Other people seem to be noticing it a bit too, a bit of a change in me, just in my attitude. I think I'm becoming more relaxed and that's what I needed to do. I was a very tense sort of person, due to the situation I was living in with a very ambitious husband in a very high powered type of work and trying to entertain a couple of nights a week, business contacts who were not really friends and keeping Betty happy and keeping him happy and you know all of a sudden all of that's just dropped away.

I think I'm just finding myself now, finding I can relax and I can enjoy the company of other people and just be more loving and everything.

I have quoted this respondent at length because her position in her marriage is typical of the oppression of many of the middle class mothers I interviewed in the North Shore, and Single groups of mothers and of some of the Feminist mothers prior to their contact with notions of equal rights for women. The qualitative oppression of these mothers differs from that of their working class sisters and is obscured by the affluence of their circumstances, by the ideologies of motherhood and of 'equal but different sex roles' as well as by the 'rightful patriarchy' of the husband as breadwinner. For this mother and for other single mothers like her, the frame of reference of her single parenthood has enabled her to become aware of her former oppression and to begin to develop as a person in her own right. A North Shore mother in a very similar position to Renate realises that she is really only an appendage to her husband and not treated as a person in her own right, but she still enjoys her position and concludes that any frustrations she feels are only the result of her own temperament. She says,

The only men and women I come in contact with socially would be the people my husband does business with and they treat me quite respect-fully. I'm not taken out on equal footing, I'm just the wife of so and so who they do business with and they're all very charming and polite to me, so perhaps they treat me as an object, not even an object as an append-age. But I enjoy myself anyway and I usually have a good time and we become quite good friends of some of the people . . .

The only thing that really gets me down is when you're cranky with yourself and when you feel that you've been shortchanged. But when you boil it all down again, you're not really, it's just your temperament or whatever that was affecting you that day that makes you feel that way, your depression.

This mother keeps a thirty square home, built on three levels with polished wood floors in the main living areas in spotless condition, in case she has to entertain her husband's business associates. At weekends in summer she sits on the beach at Manly with her 4 year old while her husband and 12 and 13 year old sons sail. In winter they play football. On holidays at Surfers Paradise for three weeks each year she again sits on the beach with a book and the four year old while the older boys and her husband go fishing. Most of her acquaintances are in a similar position, and, having no other frame of reference her sense of personal oppression is minimal. A really happy day for her is when the family is all at home together 'pottering around, talking together, just so that you feel like a family'. Such a day was the Sunday before the interview she said, when it rained and sailing was off, everyone was at home and she spent the day helping her husband with his income tax return. In return for such subservience there are material rewards and the status attached to her husband's position and the prestigious home and the privilege of sending the children to 'the best private schools'; holidays at Surfers Paradise, etc. Such middle class oppression is inextricably linked with the economic support of the husband and the value in the day-to-day, face-to-face encounter that he places on his wife's homemaking, mothering and entertaining abilities. This mother was also conscious of the fact that she must keep her face, figure and clothes in the right shape to be a credit to her husband when she went out or even on holidays with him. When I arrived to do the interview, she was busy doing floor exercises from a glossy woman's magazine to be the right shape for the bikini she had bought to go on holidays. The homemaking skills, personal appearance and unpaid labour in the house are not so vital to the working class man's job or promotion as in these middle class families. As the comments made by Renate Kettlewell and Sarah Butler have shown the absence of such a breadwinner from the structure of the family has enabled them to achieve some awareness of their former oppressive position.

Nevertheless, this awareness remains very much at an individual level without contact with ideas which challenge traditional ideologies and an alternate reference group. Renate Kettlewell was looking for a man whose ideas on the division of labour in the home weren't as rigid as those of her former husband—at the time of the interview she had formed a liaison with such a man with a view to remarriage and already he was providing some economic support. Remarriage was, in fact, seen more often by the Single middle class mothers interviewed as a solution to their economic and social problems than by the Single working class mothers. For example,

Jill Danvers describes the socially dependent position of a single middle class woman in a male defined social milieu, the effect of male attention on her self-concepts and her desire to remarry. She says,

> I get depressed when a nice fellow doesn't ring when he says he's going to, and that amazes me, being in the position I was when I was a teenager, hoping someone will ring and if they don't you think, 'Oh, I wonder what I did wrong' or 'Why don't they do what they say?' But I guess that's just part of—I think a man in a situation of being divorced has a lot more opportunities for meeting people. I don't like to go to dances and things like that by myself, I don't do that, or to a wine bar—whereas a man can do that. It doesn't worry me to be an odd one out at dinner parties, but you don't get invited so often when you're divorced.
>
> I see myself primarily as a mother at the moment. Actually I went out with a fellow a couple of weeks ago and he really made me feel more like a woman than just a mother and it was really nice, because at this time in my life I tend to just see myself as a mother. And when someone takes me out and they do the whole thing with candlelight dinner and the wine and the nice music, I think 'Well, he's not seeing me just as a mother' and that sort of shocked me a bit and I thought, 'Right, I'll try and build that up a bit and come out of this mother thing', because the baby's getting bigger now and he'll be going to a minding centre a couple of days a week next year. Then the image will change a bit.
>
> I think marriage is still in. I don't think it's on the wane as a lot of people do. I think it's the ideal. I don't think people are meant to live alone, I think we're meant to have a partner to share things with and I would very much like to marry again.

Amy Friend is a working class single mother who left her husband six months ago, he was the typical Australian male she says, 'I'm the man and you're the woman' who pleased himself what he did and expected her to serve all his needs. She describes some of the differences in her self-concepts now that she has broken away from him, her determination to make a better life and her reservations about marrying again,

> At the moment I feel very satisfied because I've achieved a lot of things I didn't ever think I'd be able to do. And I think the biggest thing was leaving my husband. It was a hard thing to do because I'd been with him for 10 years, I was only 14 when I first met him and that's a decade of your life that you're throwing away and from 14 to 24 is the biggest part of your life really. That was probably the biggest thing I've ever done...
>
> It's been better because I'm not living in fear of what I'm going to cop tonight when he comes home from the club. And it's been a lot better for the kids too. Our marriage did have a bad effect on the kids...

Until six months ago I couldn't say 'No,' to anyone. If someone said 'go and cut your throat', I'd do it. But not now, I'm just sick of being walked on. I used to get walked on by everybody . . .

Now, if I think I'm right I'll push it. That's part of the new me that I'm trying to bring out. I don't want to push my old life away, but I was so weak before and now I'm different and I'm determined that there's a better life for me and the kids and I've got to be strong to make a better life . . .

I've got a thing at the moment that everything's positive and if something goes wrong I try and work another way around it. I've got a happiness now I never had before . . .

I don't think I'll ever marry again. I'd live with a guy, but I don't think I'd ever remarry. It'd depend on the sort of person he was and what he wanted.

Oppression for this working class mother included physical violence, subservience to her husband's needs and wishes as well as very meagre resources with which to perform her unpaid domestic duties of husband and child care. Separation for her has improved both her economic position and her sense of autonomy. During the August school holidays with her three children and another single mother with five children, she travelled 1500 miles around New South Wales in her friend's $130 Falcon station wagon with a double bed mattress in the back. They changed their own tyres and felt really independent and in charge of their own situation and 'had a really good time'. Contact with a Women's Refuge has also had an effect on the attitudes and self-concepts of these two single mothers.

Although many Single mothers expressed a new sense of self-X awareness and the freedom to develop as a person in their own right and an increase in their self-esteem once freed from face-to-face domination by a male in the hierarchical structure of the two parent family, this did not lead to freedom from the demands of mother-hood, or to an awareness of the constraints placed upon them by the ideology of motherhood. In fact, in the majority of cases it served to focus their attention on their children and the satisfactions association with motherhood. This is evidenced by the fact that every Single mother included in her main aim in life the successful raising of her children and/or their happiness. In addition, in the majority of cases the husband still had access to the children on frequent occasions and his view of her mothering or that of another significant male was important to the mother. For example, Denise Watt says,

My husband takes the children on Friday evening and drops them back on Sunday evening. When he drops them back he usually makes some comment about their behaviour and so on. He makes me feel 'Oh crikey'.

The approval of her mothering of a significant male or males in her milieu remained an important source of self-esteem for these mothers. Although 40% of the Single mothers interviewed said that they felt people respected them for what they are, for their individual characteristics, 44% said that people respected them as a mother. 76% said that they felt that they were coping well with motherhood and were 'good' mothers and 80% said that the children's fathers thought they were 'good' mothers. Many of these mothers gave as their primary identity 'mother' and as the following comment by a Feminist single mother shows, motherhood is an important source of satisfaction in their lives,

> There was a time when I would have said the man straight away (has the best life). I don't really think that that's necessarily the case. I think he might think he's having the best time, but in the long run probably she feels better about what she's put her time into. On a daily basis he has more satisfaction and less responsibility, but overall probably at the end of it she will feel that she has achieved more than he has. And that's because I think that people and especially children are more important than jobs. I certainly get more satisfaction from my children than from my job.

With the absence of the male breadwinner and support in her day-to-day mothering however, the tensions of this aspect of her life, in many cases, increased for the mother. Many Single mothers found the task of being both mother and father to their children extremely difficult especially with regard to the discipline of older children. The extra jobs of 'fathering' and/or employment apparently increases the tension of mothering. Concerning 'baby bashing' the percentages of the Single and the Employed mothers groups who gave instances of when they could have 'bashed' their children were higher than for the other groups in the sample (72% and 84% respectively, as against 60% for Mt Druitt and Nth Shore mothers and 32% for Feminist mothers). The effect of being a single parent for those mothers who were employed full-time increased the day-to-day activities and responsibilities of some mothers to a point where nothing else became important or possible in their lives than their responsibilities of breadwinner and mother. For this working class mother who is renting a private flat in an area where long day-care is only available privately at a price she could not pay, the day begins at 5 a.m. with ironing and it's activities do not cease until 8.30 to 9 p.m. She lists her daily activities as follows,

> Up at 5 a.m. Iron till 6 a.m. Shower. Wash some mornings. Do some housework. Make beds. Alan awake, turn T.V. on he sits and watches T.V. Make lunches. Get Mark up. Make breakfast. Make their beds. Get

things ready for school. Get them dressed, brush hair, clean teeth. Get ready for work.

Drive to mother's and drop children there until they go to Kindergarten at 9 a.m.

Drive to work, half an hour. Work from 9 to 5. Pick children up from mother's. Drive home, have a drink. Bath them one at a time and put their pyjamas on. Get tea on while they are in the bath. Have tea. Find out what's happening at school, sit down and watch T.V. with them until they go to bed at 8.30. Wash up, tidy up and go to bed about 9.30.

She says she doesn't have many happy moments in her life at the present time, it's just a matter of getting through each day. On Sundays she works from 6 a.m. to 5 p.m. with her father cleaning offices to help pay $10 a day for the children's Kindergarten. She would like to marry again 'and be a wife for a man and run around and do everything for a man; I'd never start again with children'; she says, although the only times she feels happy are 'when everything's quiet and we have a nice quiet little talk that turns out to be happy'.

In itself, being single does not necessarily cause a mother to question the ideology of motherhood, although it does provide an alternative structure to the nuclear family from which to view sex role ideology. The following section looks more specifically at the effects of single parenting on mother's beliefs about sex roles and motherhood.

Effects of single parenting on ideologies of sex roles and motherhood

In the structure of the one parent mother headed family where the woman performs on a day-to-day basis the formerly gender designated activities of 'instrumental leader' and 'expressive follower' (Parsons and Bales, 1955:10–12), some challenge is possible to the 'equal but different' ideology of sex roles. Only four mothers (16%) in the single group of mothers said that the husband should be the head of the household as compared with 20% of Employed mothers, 52% of Mt Druitt mothers and 64% of Nth Shore mothers. A typical response to the question 'Who do you think should be the head of the house, the husband or the wife?' by the single mothers interviewed is as follows,

I don't think there should be a little 'head of the house'. For my mother, my father was and probably that statement was true 20 years ago, because

the man was the breadwinner and the woman stayed at home. But everyone works now and everyone shares ideas so it shouldn't be one or the
other.

Implicit in these responses is some questioning of former beliefs
which accepted the husband's role of breadwinner and leader as the
natural, sex related division of authority in the home. The mothers,
with one exception, a never married teenager who lived with her
parents, had in fact become both the 'instrumental leader' and the
'expressive carer' in their own family structure and had assumed an
authority which may have formerly been the husband's prerogative.
Within this frame of reference designation of 'head of the house' as
an exclusively male preserve, legitimated by the breadwinning role,
no longer has meaning.

Such a structure does not, however, have a similar effect concerning the ideology of motherhood. The very fact that these mothers
and not the fathers have the children in their care is an indication
that the 'natural' propensity for women to nurture and care for
children has been accepted by those involved, such as the father, the
mother herself and in some cases (12 mothers interviewed were
divorced) by the law. 56% of the Single group of mothers may be
described as ideological traditionals, a higher percentage than in
any other group except the Mt Druitt group. An examination of
the distribution of ideal types in the Single group of mothers shows
that being single reacts with other factors such as social class, em-
ployment/non-employment and contact with significant others and
ideas which either reinforce or challenge the ideology to affect the
mother's experience of mothering and her beliefs about motherhood.

Of the 14 Single mothers interviewed who may be described as
ideological traditionals, eight have working class backgrounds.
Working class Single mothers who are ideological traditionals are
similar to the Mt Druitt mothers in that they left school with
minimal educational qualifications, married and for the most part
had their first child before they were 20 and then stayed at home to
care for their children. Only one of these mothers is in full-time
employment, the others are in receipt of social security benefits and
all believe that their place is in the home with their children. Single
parenting for them has reinforced their ties with their children and
emphasised for them that they need their children and that their
children need them. Hannah Waters is a widow (the only widow
interviewed), she expresses her beliefs about the investment she has
in her children. Other Single mothers implied on various occasions
what she has made explicit. She says,

I think you get so much from children. The more you put into a kiddy, the more you get out of them. I'd put them first all the time because I thought, when they grow up I'd look back and think I didn't give them enough time with this and that. There's always washing, there's always cleaning, there's always something to do, but with the kiddies you can never regain that. I do think you do gain a lot from them.

I could go to work, I do have qualifications, but I don't want to neglect them in any way and I want to give them as much time as possible.

For some of the middle class mothers being single has had a similar effect. For example, Denise Watts says,

The companionship of my children is very important to me because I don't have a husband at home. The companionship I get is terrific. They're 2 years and 4 years, a delightful age although they're little devils. The companionship is fantastic.

On the weekends that I don't have the children, then, I mope around. I enjoy having the time to myself, but the breakfast sessions—you just sit there, you've got no one to have breakfast with. So in a way that's made me closer to the boys because I like that companionship . . .

For other Single mothers this effect has been reinforced by daily contact with significant others who espouse traditional beliefs about motherhood and women's place. One unmarried teenager mother lives at home, her father is a clergyman and her responsibility for the care of her child and it's need of her, especially during the early years is emphasised at home; the God-given nature of motherhood and woman's place in the home is continually implied. Another mother who is very much involved in church activities and goes either to a play group or a Bible study at the church on three weekends says,

The people I mix with think mothers are mothers and stay in the home and look after children and that's how I think too.

For one ideological traditional Single mother with a middle class background who was in a situation very similar to Renate Kettlewell's, divorce meant a complete rejection of the middle class life-style and values which were associated with such a marriage. She moved into the Balmain area, but her significant reference group is not a feminist group but a counter culture which emphasises the naturalness of motherhood. For a while she lived in a co-operative household in a communal style of living which is based on 'natural' foods, 'natural' living, 'natural' childbirth, etc. Although she and a friend she introduced to the researcher were the only two mothers in the sample whose experience of mothering and beliefs about mother-hood took this particular form, they do represent a counter culture which is almost in opposition to the feminist counter culture.

154	*Ideology of motherhood*

For this mother awareness of her oppression in a traditional middle class marriage has led to commitment to ideological traditional ideas concerning motherhood. Breast feeding and the baby's needs are paramount and the mother's life and needs are fitted in around the baby. This mother does not go anywhere where her baby is not accepted, or that would interfere with the feeding of the baby. For the interview we sat on jute mats on the floor and drank herbal tea while the naked 12 months old baby crawled wherever she chose and drank from her mother's breast whenever she wanted to.

For some of the Feminist mothers interviewed the path to Feminism had led through such counter cultural communes. Once they became aware of their oppression within this system, they looked for an alternative.

With the exception of one working class mother, none of these Single ideological traditional mothers were employed full-time. All believed that mothers with pre-school children should not be employed outside the home, their place is in the home. For example, one of these mothers says,

> No way, no way, very strongly, no, I don't believe Mums should be working.

Exclusion from the work-force helps to encapsulate these mothers ideologically within the home and to limit contacts to others in a similar situation, and activities to those associated with this sphere.

On the other hand seven of the eight Single ambivalent mothers are employed part or full-time and the eighth is a full-time student who attends Art College every day. These mothers have modified their ideology to incorporate the activities and values of the world beyond the home. Only two of these mothers have working class backgrounds and they live in areas in which there is a mixture of middle and working class people and contact people in both classes. One of these mothers manages a T.A.B. agency where she earns close to $20 000 a year. She is buying her own home and has money available to pursue activities outside the home if she wishes. At the time of the interview she was arranging a street party for her neighbours for the following Saturday night. One of these neighbours is a Single mother (also interviewed) with a middle class background and the two share many activities. For example I arrived at 7 p.m. to do the interview, nobody was home and about 7.30 both of these respondents and their children arrived. They had been having their evening meal together at the second mother's house five doors away. Both of these mothers feel that although their children take up most of their time and energy outside working hours now, once they are a little more independent they will be able to pursue many more activities which interest them personally.

The importance of contact with alternative ideas and significant others who hold these ideas is emphasised when the backgrounds and situations of the three Single ambivalent progressive mothers are examined in conjunction with those of the ambivalent progressive Feminist mothers who are single. Although they are not at present actively associated with a feminist group so are not included in the Feminist sample, all of these mothers have had some contact with feminist ideas and significant others in their social milieu hold these views. Although it has been pointed out in a previous chapter that access to material resources enables middle class mothers to transcend some of the limitations of mothering, so that the majority of ambivalent and ambivalent progressive mothers in the sample have middle class backgrounds, three single working class mothers, one in the Single group and two in the Feminist group are ambivalent progressives. In a family situation free of a dominant male and with a supportive network of people with alternative ideas, material resources *per se* are not essential for some challenge to be made to the ideology of motherhood. Shared material resources within a female network or a co-operative household may of course, enable scarce resources to be utilised more effectively. These mothers have low market capacity, low educational qualifications and low incomes, two are below $5000 per year and the other is around $7000 per year.

Amy Friend is a working class mother living in the Mt Druitt area in a Housing Commission house. She has three children under 10 and the home is sparsely furnished with few conveniences. Six months ago she went to the Women's Refuge in Rooty Hill in a desperate attempt to get away from her husband who was drinking heavily and physically abusing her. Through the Refuge she was assisted to leave her husband and she and another single mother who lives in the next street, whom she met at the Refuge, spend their weekends helping at the Refuge, thus maintaining contact with a supportive group. Some of her attitudes to herself and her situation have already been presented in this chapter and show a marked difference from those of the majority of Mt Druitt mothers. The support they give to each other and that received from the Refuge, as well as the ideas presented there, enabled these two mothers to question the ideology and to go beyond its limitations to new life experiences.

Rosemary Hill is a Feminist single mother with a working class background living in a co-operative household with two other single feminist mothers and their children and two single men. She is 24, left school at 4th Form, was married at 18 and had her first child at 20 years of age. She is divorced and receives $70 a week as a supporting parent's benefit and $43 a fortnight for her cleaning job. She pays $32 a week rent and stretches her resources by buying second hand clothes and says,

> I've been doing a lot of shoplifting to keep the clothes up. If it weren't for that my daughter wouldn't have any clothes at all.

She rarely has any money to spend on herself. She says concerning her contact with feminist ideas,

> It's mainly the people I socialise with. I belong to a Feminist Drama Group, I'm starting up a Women's Theatre Group and I help with the Women's Press every Wednesday. In the social circle I mix with it's a life-style.
> It's something that had always meant a lot to me before there was any real Women's Movement. I was aware that I couldn't do a lot of things because I was female.
> I moved into a household that was into this. I seemed to get more and more involved as I became more aware. I go to conferences and read papers sometimes. It's made me realise the possibilities for change.

Daily contact on a face-to-face basis with other women and men in the household who are committed to feminist ideas (one woman is editor of a feminist journal) and participation in feminist activities have progressively raised her consciousness of her former oppression and enabled her to break away from the traditional ideas of her background. The feminist activities in which she is involved also extend her life experiences and satisfactions beyond those associated with her children. Material resources, formal educational qualifications and market capacity in this case are low. But sharing material, philosophical and educational resources with people of differing backgrounds in a co-operative household, buying food co-operatively for a number of such households and rostering cooking, cleaning and child care duties in a milieu which supports women's liberation has enabled this mother to expand her life beyond the traditional limitations of working class mothering.

Other single Feminist ambivalent progressive mothers lived in similar situations, although some of those with middle class backgrounds who were employed had higher incomes, and the convenience of a car of their own.

Single parenting for mothers tends to emphasise the need of these women for their children, thus reinforcing traditional ideas about motherhood, especially where material resources are scarce. However, employment outside the home, and more importantly, contact with alternative ideas on mothering and the support of significant others who hold these ideas can, in spite of scarce material resources, low market capacity and the added restraints of single parenting, make possible some questioning of the ideology of motherhood as well as life experiences and life-satisfactions not entirely centred on motherhood.

The evidence from interviews with single mothers demonstrates the complex interaction of factors which affect a mother's self-concepts and life-satisfactions as well as her beliefs about sex roles and motherhood. Social class, the material conditions of mothering, employment/non-employment of the mother and contact with the ideas of significant others interact with the absence of the male breadwinner from the structure of the family to reinforce or challenge traditional patterns of mothering behaviour and associated beliefs.

Throughout this analysis of the research data and especially in this chapter, the importance of contact with ideas and significant others who hold such ideas has emerged as a factor which helps to either reinforce traditional patterns of mothering or to allow some questioning of these patterns of mothering and some challenge to them. The following chapter sums up the effects of feminist ideas and feminist networks on the sample of mothers actively associated with feminist groups who were interviewed for the research.

Note

1   Runciman (1966:10–12) initiated the use of the term 'relative deprivation' in sociological literature to denote the sense of deprivation experienced when one's own situation is compared, not with some abstract or average level of living, but with that of a significant reference group which is 'better off' in some way. By 'reference group' Runciman means,

> The term . . . can be used not only to mean the group with which a person compares himself; it can also be used to mean either the group from which he derives his standards of comparison or the group from which the comparison is extended and to which he feels he belongs . . . the reference 'group' need not be a group at all; it may be a single person or even an abstract idea.

9 Feminist mothers

This chapter is specifically concerned with feminist mothers and attempts to draw together the data concerning these mothers which has been scattered throughout previous chapters. Feminist mothers have been purposively sampled in this research in order to see whether, in fact, women would think and act differently if their lives were not entirely constrained by the ideology of motherhood. In Lukes' view of power they provide the 'relevant counterfactual' (1974:41). That is, they demonstrate that individuals or groups can, and will within limits, think and act differently from the way they think and act under conditions of operative power when the conditions of such power are attenuated. Within Mannheim's view of utopia (1936:173–90), feminist mothers represent a group expressing some utopian ideas. That is, they are an ascendant group gaining access to sources of power in society which enable them to challenge existing structures and ideologies and to give voice to ideas which transcend the existing order but are unrealisable within it. Their ideas grow out of the aspirations of a particular strata of that society and express tendencies already present within the existing order and appropriate to the changing situation. In this chapter the structural position and material conditions of mothering of the feminist respondents are examined and the extent to which feminist beliefs and experiences of motherhood embody counterfactual and utopian ideas concerning motherhood is analysed.

The sampling of feminist mothers for the research sought out mothers who were actively associated with feminist groups. The 25 mothers who make up the Feminist Group sample consist of 8 women who are actively associated with Women's Electoral Lobby and 17 who are engaged in one or more of the following activities: teaching or studying women's study courses in a tertiary institution; participating in a consciousness raising group; medical care in a women's health centre; counselling in a rape crisis centre or an abortion centre; participating in a feminist based children's co-operative. The

Feminist group is not therefore homogeneous. Those women belonging to W.E.L. have differences in the details of their feminist charter from those women who have had associations with the Women's Liberation Movement (for a brief outline of the main differences see Note 1, Chapter 11). Those feminists living in nuclear family situations have different life-styles from those living in lesbian relationships or those in co-operative feminist households. Nevertheless there is sufficient agreement amongst the majority of the feminists interviewed, on the issues with which the research is concerned, for them to be treated as a group.

The mothers designated as ambivalent progressive ideal types in the other research sample groups (1 Nth Shore, 5 Employed and 3 Single) may also be considered as feminists due to their previous or present contact with feminist ideas and their inclusion of these ideas and beliefs in their own attitudes to motherhood. Percentages given in this chapter refer specifically to the 25 mothers in the Feminist group sample, but qualitative data refers to mothers in the total sample who voice some utopian ideas concerning motherhood.

Social class similarities and differences

By virtue of their father's occupation, their own educational and occupational position and, where married, their husband's educational and occupational position, the majority of the Feminist group mothers could be considered middle class. For example, 84% have fathers in professional/managerial or self-employed occupations (Table App. 4.9); 73% of married Feminist respondents have husbands in these occupations (Table App. 4.11) and 80% of these husbands have some tertiary qualifications (Table App. 4.13). 70% of Feminist respondents have been, or still are, in professional or managerial positions (Table App. 4.15), 64% have some tertiary qualifications (Table App. 4.17) and a further 12% are at present engaged in tertiary studies.

The expectations concerning individual achievement and equality of opportunity with males, associated with the middle class backgrounds, as well as the resources in terms of education and money provided by such a background, may be a necessary precursor for the assimilation of feminist ideas and the carrying out of some feminist practices. In any case, by virtue of their class position these women have had access to personal contacts, reading and group situations in which feminist ideas are incorporated or at least presented. The following excerpts from interviews illustrate how these women contacted and maintained feminist ideas or encountered significant others who held these ideas.

> I suppose I've basically been a feminist without knowing it for a number of years. I was the eldest and a daughter and I was treated more uni-sexually than as a girl, I was brought up to be independent and to want a career—rather than the 'nice little girl' image. But I think I've always had this idea that a woman should be independent and should have a career and it extended into feminist issues and finally joining the W.E.L. three years ago when I thought, 'I should be doing more than just agreeing with the ideology'.

> I've been involved in the women's movement since the new wave of it began. I've been really active in it for a long, long time. I did a large amount of work to set up the Women's Health Centre in Adelaide. And before that I was involved in lots of different areas. I used to run off pamphlets in the very early days and take part in demonstrations and campaigns against consumerism and mother's day and for the right to work and abortion. I didn't take an active part in child care issues, but I can see that's an area that is very necessary and which I do want to be active in. I was in a lesbian relationship for three years, so I was very active in the Gay women's movement. I'm working in a Women's Health Centre. I haven't been actively associated with Women's House for two years, but I'm feminist representative on the Board of Family Planning. I'm also involved in setting up a Women's Clinic for Aboriginal women. I'm not so outspoken on the media as I was. But it's just a matter of taking feminism into all aspects of existence, whatever you're doing making people aware of how their sexism's affecting what they're doing in any situation. It's just in everything I do.

Their middle class position has enabled these mothers to make and maintain contact with feminist ideas and activities in ways which are not open to the majority of working class women. Low educational levels, unskilled clerical and manual occupations, early marriage and child-bearing, coupled with few material resources confine most working class women to a circle of ideas and acquaintances which reinforce traditional ideas and limit questioning of already existing structures of society and the legitimation of these structures through ideology. Nevertheless three feminist mothers in the sample (2 in the Feminist Group and 1 Single mother) have working class backgrounds.

In these instances contact with feminist ideas (in one instance through a women's refuge and in two through joining co-operative households) and the support of a feminist network have enabled these women to break out of this circle. Contact with feminist ideas has altered the mother's attitudes to herself and her mothering. Along with these changes has gone a sharing of resources with other parents which has improved the resources available to these mothers compared with those available to the working class mothers in the Mt Druitt sample. The emphasis on co-operation in parenting, rather than competition and on sharing of resources rather than privatisation, in feminist utopian ideas, has enabled these working class mothers to make some challenge to the constrictions of traditional motherhood ideas and practices.

On the other hand two of the Feminist group of respondents who have middle class backgrounds and educational and occupational capacities which are middle class and who have active associations with feminists groups are severely restricted in their expression of utopian ideas concerning mothering. They have been designated as ambivalent, rather than ambivalent progressive with regard to ideal type. Strongly held views about the benefits of bonding the biological mother to her child and the necessity for her presence during the early years of the child's life derived from tertiary studies in psychology override certain feminist ideas for these mothers. In one instance the mother's personal responsibility for mothering is further reinforced by the husband who as a psychiatrist holds similar ideas and whose ambition to progress in his own career requires his wife to take almost complete responsibility for parenting. She describes her situation as follows,

> My involvement in the women's movement has corresponded with my child rearing and I find it very hard to do both. I fall asleep at night and I've gone to meetings and fallen asleep. I've got friends who do both. The quality of family life is very important to me. I really like the house to run, the meals to be there and the clothes to be clean and the children to have my personal attention. And it's very hard to do all these things and to be active on committees and things like that. So there I am a token supporter . . .
> My husband's a very important person in his job and it's very demanding and everything. I think I would quite like it if I had a wife to come home to at night. I'd quite like to have two beautiful children being very well brought up, to come home to at night, and to read to for half an hour or so. It's not an alternative open to me, but I'd quite like it. I think objectively my husband has the best life.

It is clear from these instances that middle class resources are insufficient on their own to generate utopian ideas. There must be a source of these ideas and possibly a supporting group or significant others who are supportive of utopian ideas of mothering in order that the ideas can endure and be translated, even in a limited way, into the experience of mothering. Structurally, however, it is more likely that middle class rather than working class women will be in a position to construct utopias concerning motherhood.

The material conditions of mothering for feminist mothers

Along with the middle class market capacity of the majority of Feminist mothers (and of their husbands for those in nuclear families), goes an income which provides sufficient economic resources for them to transcend some of the limitations of traditional motherhood. 40% of Feminist respondents have a family income above $20 000 per year compared with only 19% of the total sample who have incomes this high (Table App. 4.19). These women can afford goods and services which cut down on the time and energy they need to spend in mothering and household duties and they can also afford to spend money on activities outside the home. In addition their own questioning of the naturalness of these activities for women has to some degree freed them from emotional and psychological ties to these activities and the sense of feminine identity associated with them. Given middle class incomes and ideas which challenge the ideology of motherhood, these women have been able to think and act differently from mothers constrained by the ideology. All feminist mothers in the sample pursue activities in which they, as individuals apart from their families, are interested. Some are professionally employed, some are engaged in full-time or part-time study, some pursue artistic, musical, drama or craft activities and all are involved in varying degrees in the feminist activities outlined at the beginning of the chapter.

Nevertheless within the Feminist Group not all respondents have high incomes. 32% have incomes below $10 000 per year and for over half of these, income is below $5 000 per year. These mothers are single and exist on supporting parent's benefits, supplemented in some cases by Tertiary Education Allowances or Postgraduate Scholarships. Their utopian ideas concerning motherhood are enabled expression in co-operative feminist households with supporting feminist networks in which some child care is shared with other adults both in the household and in the children's co-operative in some instances. Group buying amongst these households, particularly of groceries and fruit and vegetables, shared accommodation and rent and shared facilities such as washing machines, and other household appliances as well as shared use of motor vehicles, has given these mothers resources which are not available to other single mothers, or to some mothers in nuclear family situations. The point is again emphasised that the change in the ideology has substituted co-operation for competition in parenting and shared use of material possessions rather than privatisation, thus making good use of scarce resources, and improving the material conditions of mothering for these single mothers. Some single mothers initially entered co-operative households out of sheer necessity to make ends meet and through living contact with other feminists came to espouse feminist ideas themselves. Within the structure of the co-operative household they are able to put some of these ideas into practice.

The material conditions of mothering for feminist mothers varies between middle class nuclear family situations where a relatively high income enables the mother to transcend some of the limitations of traditional mothering and housework patterns by buying help and investing money in other activities to co-operative households where low individual incomes, but shared resources, enable mothers to challenge traditional patterns for women. In both of these cases however, certain limitations to the implementation of counterfactual or utopian ideas are present.

The structure of the nuclear family requires that one or both parents go out to earn an income which will provide housing, household appliances, furniture, food, clothes, etc. and that one, or both parents be responsible for parenting. In all nuclear family situations except one, in which feminist mothers were involved, the husband, by virtue of his greater earning capacity, was the main breadwinner and the mother retained primary responsibility for child care and household tasks. Although, in most cases, the wife also was employed at least part-time and the husband was more involved in household tasks than other husbands in the sample, the implementation of utopia, as far as motherhood is concerned, is severely limited.

In co-operative households, especially where children formed close attachments to a number of adults from an early age, and where income resources were shared, there was a greater opportunity for shared parenting and housework and for all members to be involved in employment or other activities outside the home. Nevertheless the biological mother still retained primary responsibility for her own child. For example, where a child was sick or woke at night, it was always the biological mother who attended to it. In some respects mothers saw this situation as worse than the nuclear family situation because of the possibility of infecting or waking children who did not belong to them and the sense of responsibility and strain that this imposed on them. Thus the idea of the child belonging to its own mother and her primary responsibility for it, persists.

Effects of feminist ideas on ideologies of motherhood and sex roles

The data presented in Chapter 4 has indicated that most feminist mothers have challenged the ideology of motherhood in the following ways:

1   Feminist mothers tend to believe that motherhood is neither inevitable nor necessary for woman's fulfilment but that it does build character.
2   They stress that adults of both sexes are better parents if their own needs are being met and their own potentialities are being developed.
3   Woman's as against man's natural propensity for child care is challenged.
4   Feminist utopias suggest that responsibility for parenting should be shared with other adult carers, both male and female and that the community and the state should take more responsibility for the rearing of children.
5   If men participated more in parenting feminists suggest that its status would be raised and that structural changes should be made in wider society to facilitate this.

As previous discussion has shown, these utopian ideas are not completely realisable within the structure of present society. This is a basic characteristic of Mannheim's concept of utopia. But Mannheim (1936:187) also suggests that,

> it is a very essential feature of modern history that in the gradual organisation for collective action social classes become effective in transforming historical reality only when aspirations are embodied *in utopias appropriate to the changing situation*. (My emphasis)

In this respect the utopian ideas suggested by the majority of feminist mothers interviewed and summarised above are appropriate to the changing situation of present family life for two reasons. First, the increasing number of married women remaining in the work-force or re-entering it after marriage and the large numbers of these women with pre-school children precludes the individual and constant attention of the biological mother which the ideology suggests. The utopian idea of a number of adult primary care givers not confined to one sex, appears a more realistic expectation for parenting in the present and emerging conditions of Australian society. Second, the increasing rate of divorce with the removal of the physical presence of one parent and the traumatic emotional effects on the child whose primary care giver has been this parent would suggest a change in parenting to include a number of primary care givers, so that at least one or more remain with the child when separation of the parents occurs. Presumably a child will feel more secure if some of the adults for whom he/she has formed an attachment from an early age remain within his/her circle of relevant others.

The utopian ideas of motherhood outlined above and incorporated into the beliefs of feminist mothers suggest that when women are released from some conditions of operative male power, through absence of a face-to-face male authority in the home due to physical absence or attenuation of equal but different sex role ideology and/or through increased access to sources of power in the wider society, they will think and act differently with regard to motherhood. The primary thrust of the relevant counterfactual is that parenting will become a part, but not the whole, of woman's existence. Parenting shared with the father and/or other adults, both male and female, could make the experience more enjoyable, allow for the pursuit of other potentially rewarding activities and for the increase in the status of parenting activities. In this way women see their lives as being more rewarding and as giving them greater options when some of the constraints of the ideology of motherhood are removed from them

Effects of feminist ideas on self-concepts and life-satisfactions

Evidence has already been presented in previous chapters which demonstrates that mothers in the Feminist group have self-concepts and life-satisfactions which are not as tied to the traditional wife and mother roles as are those of the other mothers interviewed. This evidence is briefly summarised here.

Whereas from 84–100% of respondents in the other sample groups gave as their main aim in life 'to rear, educate and/or make children happy' 64% of Feminist respondents gave this response. 68% of Feminist mothers said their main aim was 'to grow, know themselves better, find self-fulfilment or satisfaction'; 24% of Nth Shore, Single and Employed mothers gave this response and only 4% of Mt Druitt mothers. Feminist mothers do not see their lives focussed entirely on their children, although their welfare is of importance to them. A typical feminist response to this question is as follows,

> To do with myself really. To get rid of the self-doubt or work out why it's there, and do something about it and get more into feeling I'm a good person. Working on myself and my own self-image.

Along with this focus go self-concepts which are not entirely associated with motherhood. 84% of respondents designated as ambivalent progressive ideal types included in their perception of their primary identity 'a person in their own right, an individual or 'me'' and only 28% included mother. In addition 56% of Feminist mothers felt that people respected them 'as a person, for what I am/for *me*' rather than for their performance of the motherhood role. Mothering is a part rather than the whole of their existence and it is important to them to be defined in terms of their own personality, character-istics and talents rather than in terms of a role. In this expression they are asserting their right to have some control over their life's course and the realisation of their individual potentialities rather than being confined by the expectations of behaviour associated with a particular role.

Although 88% of Feminist mothers said that at times they felt they couldn't cope, largely due to the activities they desired to under-take in addition to their mothering, on two other questions asso-ciated with a sense of powerlessness they showed less powerlessness than other mothers. No Feminist mother indicated that she felt pessimistic about the future, compared with 4% Nth Shore and 30% Mt Druitt mothers who did express pessimism. 24% of Feminist mothers said that sometimes at least they felt like a 'cog in the machinery of life' whereas 36% of Nth Shore and 50% of Mt Druitt mothers said this. Typical Feminist responses to these questions are as follows:

Rosy, I feel comfortable and optimistic about it (the future).

No, I don't think I am (a cog in the machinery of life). But I think that education and a profession and money have brought me the privilege not to be that. I aim to keep myself in that privileged position.

The majority of Feminist mothers feel that they have some control over their lives both present and future and that it is up to them to bring about changes that are necessary in their own lives and in the conditions of society. Some of their feminist activities are aimed at bringing about social changes which favour the position of women and improve the quality of women's lives.

Fewer Feminist mothers (40%) than Nth Shore or Mt Druitt mothers (80%) suggested that their satisfactions in life were asso-ciated with husband and/or children, although when questioned further many said that they felt in a long-term perspective their most meaningful activity was child-rearing. 68% of Feminist mothers associated their satisfactions in life with their own hobby, interest or activity outside the home as compared with 28% of Nth Shore and no Mt Druitt mothers. These results suggest that life-options and life-satisfactions of Feminist mothers go beyond those associated with the roles of wife and mother, and that given some kind of choice women will extend their activities beyond the confines of the family.

Conclusions

For the majority of feminist mothers in the research sample, the resources and interpersonal contacts provided by middle class backgrounds and educational and occupational opportunities, as well as middle class expectations, have placed these women in a structural position in which it is possible for them to challenge and transcend some aspects of the ideology of motherhood and the practices of motherhood prescribed by the ideology. Material conditions provided by middle class nuclear family situations or co-operative household sharing of resources, together with feminist utopian ideas concerning motherhood and sex roles has enabled feminist mothers to include in their lives activities and interests which are specifically related to their own needs as well as activities associated with parenting and household tasks. The incorporation of feminist ideas into the 'world view' of feminist mothers along with an increase in power vis-a-vis significant males in their milieu has enabled them to increase their autonomy and expand their self-concepts and life-satisfactions beyond those traditionally associated with wife/mother roles. One feminist mother expresses this idea in the following way,

> I think women's liberation is really people's liberation because they support the liberation of both sexes by just generally allowing people to be as they choose to be and to do what they choose to do without any of the preconceived ideas society tries to force upon them.

The feminist mothers in this research provide evidence that women can and will think and act in a way that comes closer to their own interests when operative male power is attenuated in their lives, that is they provide the relevant counterfactual in this particular piece of research. Feminist utopias of parenting constructed when such power is attenuated, although not completely realisable in present society, are adapted in some ways to changing conditions within that society, namely the increase in the number of married women with young children in the work-force and the high incidence of divorce. For this reason they may be expected to persist and facilitate changes in patterns of parenting, suited to emerging patterns of family living.

The following chapter examines the part played by networks of women in supporting feminist mothers in their challenges to the ideology of motherhood and alternatively those networks which help to entrap women within the ideology.

10 Networks of mothers

Analysis of the research data as presented in the foregoing chapters has repeatedly emphasised the importance of significant female others and networks of these others in reinforcing or challenging traditional ideas about motherhood. In this chapter analysis of data focusses more specifically on the networks of significant female others within which mothers' experience of mothering and beliefs about motherhood are embedded.

Domestic labour theorists have attempted to use the 'women as a class' concept as a rallying point for women's liberation both in overthrowing men as a class (Delphy, 1976; Kuhn, 1978) and in attacking the capitalist system (Seccombe, 1974: Harrison, 1973). Women, because of their common exploitation in the domestic sphere have been seen as a 'class-in-itself'. But because of the isolated and privatised nature of this work, domestic labour theorists claim they have been prevented from becoming a 'class-for-itself' with all that this Marxian term implies, concerning consciousness of oppression and solidarity in overthrowing such oppression. In contrast with these theorists, empirical studies of both middle and working class families have provided evidence of female solidarity especially amongst kin. The questions then arise, 'If such solidarity is present amongst domestic labourers, why is there little awareness amongst the majority of them of their common oppression?' and 'To what extent is such solidarity a protection against, or a force for resistance to male domination?' The present research suggests that ideology plays a part in suppressing such consciousness, in spite of solidarity.

Working class networks

The networks of the mothers interviewed in the Mt Druitt area are made up of kin, neighbours and friends and, for half of the sample, at least one formal mother's group. As Mt Druitt is a relatively new housing estate on the fringe of the metropolitan area and a considerable distance from the older working class areas in the inner city and industrial suburbs where families of origin live these categories do not overlap. Nevertheless, the *ideas* transmitted by the various members of the network do overlap, reinforcing traditional ideas about motherhood and assist in encapsulating these mothers within the ideology of motherhood.

For the majority of Mt Druitt mothers daily, face-to-face interaction with family of origin and the network of neighbours and friends associated with that family is excluded. Consequently the daily companionship, support and help with child rearing and household tasks which was available to women in more traditional working class areas is not available to these mothers. Distance from kin does not mean however lack of contact with kin. These mothers keep in contact with their own mothers by telephone (almost daily), visit at weekends when the family car is available and call on their own mothers or sisters during illness, childbirth and emergencies for child care and emotional or material support. Although the distance prohibits face-to-face interaction on a daily basis, contacts tend to increase in duration when they are made. For example, one Mt Druitt mother with her pre-school child travels by public transport to Coogee to spend two or three days a fortnight with her mother and sisters. On several occasions a respondent's mother was present during the interview having come to spend the day or a few days with her daughter and her family. Where the respondent's parents lived in the country, children would often be taken to visit for the school holidays. Through such contacts with her mother and often her sisters these working class mothers learn their job, and ideas and methods of child-rearing are transmitted and the ideology of motherhood is regenerated and reinforced.

The absence of kin from the day-to-day, face-to-face encounters of Mt Druitt mothers and the lack of viable transport for visiting kin during the week is a factor in their dependence on neighbours and female friends in the neighbourhood for more immediate support in their job. Although many mothers commented on the difference in the basis of kin and neighbour/friend relationships, in fact neighbours and friends do form a supporting network for the majority of Mt Druitt mothers. The ideal basis of kin relationships includes duty and love, and on this basis many mothers felt that they could call on their own mother at any time for help and support with their children whereas with neighbours reciprocity was all important.

Respondents also distinguished between neighbours and friends, in that neighbours were not chosen, but friends were, and that in some cases it was best not to get too close to neighbours. However for many respondents, selected neighbours had become close friends. Similarly, not all the people contacted through voluntary associations were friends, but those mothers within the group with whom they had established more particularistic primary ties became part of the support network and consequently were considered to be friends.

While the relationships between kin, neighbours and friends have different bases, all can form an important part of a mother's supportive network. For these Mt Druitt mothers neighbours and friends supplement kin relationships. Only four of the 50 Mt Druitt mothers interviewed said that they did not make contact with either neighbours or friends in the area during the week. These four mothers say they deliberately keep to themselves as they dislike gossip and prying. On the other hand 70% of Mt Druitt mothers interviewed have neighbours who are friends with whom they chat several times during the week and for the most part it is on a daily basis. These neighbours would be called on in a crisis for help and their job of mothering is a frequent topic of conversation between them.

Women in the same street share shopping and child care tasks and consider each other to be good friends. On several occasions at the end of the interview when I asked the mother if she could recommend another mother whom I might interview, she said 'Just a minute I'll call out to so and so next door'. A friendly 'drop in' type relationship between the two women was apparent and I would then go next door and interview the neighbour. For other interviews, a neighbour was present and looked after the children while the mother was being interviewed. At the end of one of these interviews two other neighbouring mothers came and a cup of tea was shared by all. These four mothers and one other form what they call their 'neighbourhood coffee club'. They meet in one another's homes with their children and talk about 'everything from politics to sex, to what's on special' and help each other with child-minding, shopping and shared equipment such as the child's swimming pool or swing. Few of these mothers kept in regular contact with their former girlfriends who now lived in other suburbs, instead their friends usually consisted of the wives of their husband's work 'mates' or soccer club members with whom they had formed a primary attachment and who also lived in Mt Druitt, and had pre-school children. Picnics and barbecues with these families formed an important part of their social life and here again the women shared the experiences of their job while the husbands shared their job, sporting or automobile interests.

In such informal groups mothers talked about children and the problems associated with babies and children, general topics, the house and household things, husbands and other people, family life and television. As one of these mothers say,

I think the main conversation of women when they've got young children is children. I think that's about all because they haven't really got many other interests.

An important source of friendship for mothers for whom neither kin nor neighbours supply a strong supportive network in Mt Druitt appears to be organised mothers' groups such as Play Groups. The Mt Druitt sample was divided into two equal halves with half of the mothers (25) belonging to such a group and the other half (25) not belonging to any formal mothers' group. Whereas 84% of the mothers who do not belong to a formal mothers group have friends and neighbours with whom they interact on a daily basis, only 56% of mothers who belong to formal groups have such a neighbourhood network. Whereas 40% of mothers who do not belong to a mothers' group see a female relative at least once a week, only 28% of mothers who belong to such a group have this contact. This suggests that the voluntary association is a source of support for the mother in her task, when kin and neighbourhood support is diminished. The data collected from each half of the Mt Druitt sample is compared in order to ascertain whether such groups of mothers reinforce the ideology of motherhood or enable mothers to make some challenge to such an ideology.

Seventeen mothers belong to Play Groups, three to a mothers' Activity Group and two to a Twins Club. The general aim of each of these groups is to help mothers cope with and adjust to mother-hood by putting them in touch with other mothers in a similar position.

Through discussions in these groups mothers receive support for the values and beliefs associated with motherhood and the 'ideal' mother towards which they are encouraged to aspire is presented and reinforced. There is very little room in such discussions for any questioning of the ideology of motherhood, rather its tenets are being regenerated by those present. Nor is there room for mothers to discuss any disenchantment with motherhood as the predominant occupation of mothers with young children.

The ideology of motherhood, accepted and regenerated by such groups effectively suppresses any form of consciousness raising. The paradox is that these mothers' groups give support to mothers in their job and provide a venue for female solidarity, but that this solidarity in fact reinforces and legitimates their subordinate posi-tion and ensures the standardisation of their domestic labour.

Typical responses to the question 'When you meet with other mothers in mothers' groups what do you talk about?' are,

We talk about how the kids are going at school, the boy's football and things like that.

We talk about husbands, kids and other people. You don't really want to talk about that, but you don't have anything else in common.

Mainly about children and how to cope with problems your kids do. For example, Mary's little boy bites.

Some respondents are quite critical of mothers' conversations. For example,

A subject I find continually boring, pregnancy—everybody talks about their pregnancy, the more gorier the better it is you know. There is not enough stimulating conversation. A lot of them are more interested in how Billy Joe did yesterday, the fact that he fell over and grazed his knee and so on. We talk about stupid things, it's the one thing I find restricting at times.

What we've been doing, where we're going, what we're going to do, the kiddies. I can't stand these women who say 'When I had so and so I had a terrible time.' I'm not one of those, when you've had your baby and the baby's three years old and they're still saying what sort of trouble they had.

However, in no case is there any suggestion of questioning women's place or the mother's role or the general position of women in our society.

To the outsider and even to some of the mothers themselves, as already shown, such talk appears rather trivial, but it is the very fabric of which the lives of these women are woven. Through such conversations the ideology of motherhood is reinforced, mothers urged to be at least as good as other mothers they know and to have children that will achieve and perform as a credit to good mothering. These mothers appear to be content with their present situation and determined to be the best mothers they can be and to have the best children it is possible to have. It is the striving after these ideals which dominates their conversation and when children do achieve, the bench marks are emphasised by the proud mother. Status and achievement in life for these mothers is largely determined by the achievements of their children and the element of competition between mothers concerning these achievements is implied by remarks such as 'Betty can count to ten and she is only two and a half' and the mother's accounts of their children's swimming and football success.

On the other hand if a mother is not fulfilling her role according to the ideology, she is criticised and sometimes ostracised by other mothers, as were two deserted wives in one play group whose children were held to be disobedient and noisy.

Within the mothers' groups I observed at Mt Druitt, the ideology of motherhood is reinforced, its principles reiterated, either implicitly or explicitly and its rewards in terms of children's achievements emphasised. General problems of children are discussed, such as health, educational or growth problems, but never critical problems such that the mother's failure to be a 'good' mother might be revealed. Competence in mothering is assumed, lack of competence is seen as an individual matter and mothers who exhibit incompetence are excluded from the solidarity of the group. Support is generally reserved for mothers who conform to the ideology and show by their efforts that they are striving after the ideal of the 'good' mother.

In answer to the question 'If you had a problem with one of your children (other than a medical problem) who would you turn to for help or advice?' only one mother suggested that a discussion at play group might help. In fact Mt Druitt mothers would prefer to take a serious problem with their children to a professional person rather than another mother. Nor would they discuss a serious personal problem in such a group, but prefer to try to sort it out themselves.

There is little difference in fact between organised mothers' groups and informal groups of mothers in the content of discussions. Both the formal and informal kin, neighbour and friendship groups in Mt Druitt support mothers in their traditional role of housewife/-wife/mother and act as mechanisms for transmission and recreation of the ideology of motherhood while offering them limited opportunity to improve their individual family relations and the conditions of their mothering. These findings suggest that in the organised and informal groups to which working class women belong there will not be any significant discussion of women's issues or structural oppression. Rather there is reinforcement of their motherhood role and of the ideals and satisfactions of motherhood as measured in achievement and growth of children. While existing social structures require a female orientated domestic labour force striving to achieve high quality in their nurturing and housekeeping tasks and such a force is legitimated by the ideology of motherhood which is accepted and regenerated by mothers themselves, it is doubtful whether female solidarity of this nature will be fruitful in bringing women to any consciousness of themselves as an oppressed and subordinate group. In any case within the symbiotic economic and psychological relationships of the working class nuclear family, any attempt to 'rock the ideological boat' would probably increase man-woman-child conflict to a point where the woman could not bear it, her identity would be challenged and her immediate life satisfactions diminished.

The overlapping nature of the life experiences and beliefs of the members of kin, neighbourhood and friendship networks and the limited nature of the choice Mt Druitt women have concerning the members of their networks, constitute Simmel's 'concentricity' of group affiliations, such 'concentricity' severely restricts the individuality of these persons, and according to Simmel prevents women from realising their solidarity of *interests* with other women. The groups to which they belong reinforce in concentric circles the same, norms, values, expectations and identities for women i.e., those associated with their home roles. Thus they act upon the individual rather than allowing the individual to join and form groups directed at achieving goals which seek to achieve the rights of women (Simmel, 1936:183–84).

Mt Druitt mothers by virtue of the fact that their choice of group affiliation is limited to 'concentric' type affiliations with kin, neighbours and friends who live in proximity to them and mother orientated groups, miss out on the enrichment of life and individual development that is possible for middle class and feminist mothers who have a greater choice of friends and groups to which they could belong. Members of female kin groups, neighbourhood and friendship groups as well as members of the mothers' groups and sporting groups to which they belong have similar experiences of life and beliefs about motherhood, so that group affiliation for them tends to confine rather than enrich their individual development.

For this reason, Amy Friend, (the single mother quoted in a previous chapter who had of her own volition sought out a Women's Refuge where the group to which she became affiliated, presented goals, interests and ideas which are not generally encountered by Mt Druitt mothers), stands out as not being as confined by her motherhood as are the majority of Mt Druitt mothers. She has a greater sense of her ability to act on her life circumstances and of her own individuality. Middle class mothers on the other hand have a greater choice in their group affiliation leading as Simmel (1936:141) suggests to greater ambiguity and less security in the conditions of their lives, but also to strengthening of individuality and integration and reinforcement of individual personality. The networks within which Nth Shore mothers carry out their mothering are now examined.

Middle class networks

Middle class Nth Shore mothers, like the working class mothers at Mt Druitt, keep in close contact with their own mothers and sisters and the intensity of such contact does not necessarily diminish with geographical distance. The majority of these mothers have their own car, so that if the respondent's mother lives in the Sydney area she is able to make frequent contact with her, and this she does on a weekly or fortnightly basis as well as telephoning her two or three times a week. If the respondent's mother lives in the country or interstate as did the mothers of a number of spiralist families interviewed, contact is maintained by letter and/or long distance telephone calls. In addition, a trip home for the respondent and her children or her mother visiting for a week or two at least once a year is common. Here again her own mother is the primary source of the respondent's information and experience concerning child-rearing. In fact a higher proportion of Nth Shore respondents than other respondents say that they are bringing up their children similarly to the way they were brought up (56% as against 33.67% for the whole of the sample). The respondent's mother or sister is called upon for baby-sitting, illness and child birth, one mother flying from as far away as Perth to be with her daughter for the birth of her second child and to care for the husband and first child while she was in hospital.

Nevertheless the mother-daughter relationship is a little different for these mothers than for the Mt Druitt mothers. Whereas the majority of Mt Druitt mothers felt that they could call on their mother at any time and that she would 'drop everything else' and give priority to her daughter's needs and those of her grandchildren, many Nth Shore mothers were conscious of the fact that their mothers had their own social networks and their own lives to lead. These mothers did not call on their own mothers for casual baby-sitting as they felt this was imposing on their already busy lives. For example, Ann Baker says,

> There's a bit of a gap in understanding between my mother and I. She doesn't 'drop everything' and come running, which is a selfish outlook I guess. She does care but then she has Dad to look after and a job and she lives at Cronulla so I can't say 'Mum, will you come up and look after the children, I'm fed up'. Richard's mother (they live in Brisbane), when they come down here twice a year, his mother thinks of no one else but me and looks after the children for me. Yet Mum's got her own life more, she's more an individual which I'm hoping to be and yet I don't like that side of her.

Even where the respondent's parents lived in the same or adjacent suburbs, or even in the same house (as did the parents of one respondent and the mother of one) the social networks of the two generations did not overlap. One of these respondents says of her mother,

> She came from South Australia too, with us and hasn't got enough to do here. She left her friends behind. It's very difficult for her too. She plays bridge but the group is breaking up for the summer. She gets lonely and depressed.

For many mothers in the Nth Shore sample there was considerable ambivalence in their attitudes to their own mothers, although they desired their help and support and at times needed them, they did not wish to be too dependent upon them, nor did they want their mothers to dominate them.

For the Nth Shore mothers in professional households female friends are an important source of social interaction as well as of help and support. These friends are drawn from a number of networks and go to make up possibly the most significant part of their loose-knit social network. Primary ties have been established and maintained with some of their former school or work friends and these friends are added to from women they meet through their children, neighbours and voluntary organisations. For example, Jean Lang says of her friendship network,

> I have made a lot of friends through kindergarten and around this area, there's a lot of young people moved in around here. Then there are people I used to work with that I'm still friendly with. For example, the person's place I'm going to for lunch today is a girl I used to teach years ago and a whole group of us still see each other and still meet. So it's usually people from a work context that I'm still friendly with and people from around this area who I play tennis with or something like that.
>
> Some of them I see every day and some I see once a month or once every two months. But the one's in terms of the child context, I'd see every second day picking up the children from kindergarten, etc.
>
> Also, everyone's very friendly around here and especially the girls up the street who have children around Charles' age. They are very good friends. We see each other every day or every second day, we're always helping each other out in one way or another.

Availability of their own transport and wider previous life experiences enable these women to keep in contact with a variety of female friends who form a loose-knit network thus putting the mother in touch quite often with a variety of ideas. Many Nth Shore mothers have friends from school or employment who are not married and/or who don't have children, thus bringing a different perspective into their network.

In addition, these mothers belong to a variety of groups which demonstrate their individual interests. Besides mothers' groups such as Play Groups and Nursing Mothers' Associations they participate in clubs and groups as diverse as the Apricot Poodle Dog Training Club, the Liberal Party, the Friends of the Australian Opera, the View Club, a Music Club, Church Fellowships and Bible Studies, a Marketing Group and Old Girls' Unions of their former schools. Several are doing part-time courses at universities which extend their web of group affiliations beyond that of mothers with pre-school children. Some with their husbands also belong to golf clubs and yachting clubs. Like the networks of Mt Druitt mothers those of Nth Shore mothers are loose-knit, in that the majority of members do not know each other. Unlike the Mt Druitt networks, the members of Nth Shore networks do not necessarily overlap in interest goals, life-experiences or ideologies. In Simmel's terms these women are enabled to experience and develop an individuality which is denied to Mt Druitt mothers. Access to money and a car of their own widens the choice of their group affiliations and of their friends and contributes to the ambiguity they feel about their motherhood role. The high priority given to friends by these mothers for support in their mothering and for themselves as individuals is demonstrated by the fact that 52% of these mothers would ask a female friend for help and advice if they had either a problem with their children or a personal problem, (compared with 10% and 15% respectively of Mt Druitt mothers who would turn to a friend in these situations).

Networks of friends observed amongst Nth Shore mothers were mainly association orientated with only one very strong neighbourhood network in evidence. The pattern of making friends through voluntary associations is particularly suited to spiralist families. The wives join associations such as Play Groups when they move into a new city and through the association make friends who then become a social group for other activities such as luncheons, tennis, dinner parties, and occasionally dances, so that often husbands are drawn into the network.

Although conversations of middle class mothers in informal groups are broader in scope than those of Mt Druitt mothers (68% of these mothers said that they talked about, entertainments, sports, travel, holidays, as against 6% of Mt Druitt mothers) the main topic of conversation is children and child related problems. For many of these women the mothers' group both formal and informal is seen as a means of learning expertise in the job. For them it becomes more of a 'professional association' than a 'trade union'. Mothering is seen by them as a profession with a body of knowledge and expertise to be acquired and improved by discussion with colleagues. Of course mothering can never be a 'career' in the sense that it offers possibility for promotion and a life-plan with predictable increases in responsibility, economic remuneration and status rewards (Bell, 1968: Ch 4.). For these mothers the self-conscious approximation of mothering to a 'career' or to their former profession is their way of resolving the conflicts they have between the ideological demands of motherhood and their own sense of individuality. It is also a means by which they see the quality of mothering being improved.

For example, a Nth Shore mother describes her group affiliation and discussion as follows,

> I go to Play Group when I know friends of mine will be there. We usually talk about child centred issues and occasionally personal issues, for example, 'we've got these horrible house guests who won't leave'. And that doesn't worry me at all. I regard the knowledge of childrearing and the expertise as just as demanding and everything else as a Social Work degree. I've structured my life as a mother much like a job. I go to meetings with my colleagueses and so on and in the structure it's not much different from working in a Social Work Agency and having regular case conferences, etc. I quite like it.

The networks of the middle class Nth Shore mothers in the sample, like those of the working class Mt Druitt mothers are loose-knit and based on kin, neighbourhood, friends and voluntary association contacts. For these mothers, however, greater resources in the form of life-experiences prior to marriage and motherhood as well as access to money and a car, enable them to have a greater diversity in group affiliations and a greater choice of maintaining contacts outside their own area. Members of their networks do not necessarily overlap in life-experiences or in beliefs about motherhood allowing for greater expression and development of individuality and resulting in some ambiguity of attitude to their motherhood role. Female networks for these mothers, as for the Mt Druitt mothers are an important source of support in their mothering and act as a mechanism for transmission of the ideology of motherhood while at the same time providing solidarity for improving the immediate conditions of their mothering. Within middle class female networks there is room for some questioning of the ideology of motherhood, but the general impact of the solidarity engendered by such networks is to improve the standards of individual mothering, rather than to make any challenge to women's 'natural' propensity for mothering or to the male dominated structures which enforce this view.

Feminist networks

For each of the mothers interviewed in the Feminist sample, significant others in her network hold utopian ideas concerning women's place and motherhood. The support of a close-knit network of like-minded women enables these mothers to make some challenge to the ideology of motherhood and the ideology of sex roles. Two such close-knit networks are evident in the sample of Feminist mothers. The first consists of five mothers who belong to the Northern Suburbs branch of the Women's Electoral Lobby (W.E.L.). The second is made up of feminist women living in the Balmain, Glebe, Annandale area, all of whom know each other and participate in various feminist activities from consciousness raising groups and women's study groups, to Women's Health Centres, marches, demonstrations and conferences.

Kin and immediate neighbours are not as important in the networks of these mothers as they are in the networks of Mt Druitt and Nth Shore mothers. Choice of friends and associates according to feminist ideals, once a woman becomes committed to these ideals, appears to be an important factor in the formation of these networks. In this way the effectiveness of the network as a support group for a way of life and ideas which are at variance with traditional suburban motherhood is ensured. The exercise of such choice and the orientation of the group towards individually held ideas and goals, in Simmel's terms, provides a milieu for the development of individual potential which is important in the feminist framework.

In addition Mannheim points out that once one becomes aware of a factor which has dominated one's life, it is removed from the realm of unconscious motivation into the realm of the 'controllable, calculable and objectified'. He says (1936:169),

> Choice and decision are thereby not eliminated, on the contrary, motives which previously dominated us become subject to our domination; we are more and more thrown back upon our true selves and, whereas formerly we were the servants of necessity, we now find it possible to unite consciously with forces with which we are in thorough agreement.

Awareness of male domination and of some of its ramifications and ideological aspects has enabled these mothers to choose to 'unite consciously' with forces with which they 'are in thorough agreement' and to consciously eliminate some sources of ideological propagation. Feminist mothers as a result are less constrained by their motherhood than the women in the other groups interviewed. Nevertheless they are constrained in a different way by the strongly held norms of their own networks.

For a number of Feminist respondents living in the Balmain, Glebe, Annandale area, a deliberate break has been made with the life-style, norms and values of their middle class families of origin. Kin for these women do not therefore play the important part in their networks that they do for other mothers. Other feminist mothers are preferred as models for motherhood and child-rearing to their own mothers. Only one Feminist mother would ask her own mother for help and advice concerning a problem with her children, whereas 72% would ask a woman friend, whom many identified as another feminist. Nevertheless in some instances, especially amongst the single Feminist respondents, their own mothers still give considerable help with child care on a regular basis, for example, in spite of differences in attitudes to child care and family life-style one respondent's mother takes both her pre-school children once a month for the weekend 'to give me a break', she said. For another whose mother lives in the next street, daily child care is available when she needs it. In one instance the respondent's mother is herself a committed feminist and the mother-daughter relationship remains strong and supportive, in spite of the fact that her mother lives interstate. Sisters too remain an important part of the network only if they also subscribe to feminist ideas, otherwise the relationship attenuates. For example, this feminist respondent emphasises that friends are more important to her than sisters,

> I don't have very much in common with my sisters now. I usually see them when I go home about once a month. But my sisters are not as important to me as my friends.

Nor do immediate neighbours form a significant part of the networks of these mothers, unless they support feminist ideas. One of the W.E.L. mothers lives in a conventional suburban street and while she maintains cordial relations with her neighbours, one of these referred to her as 'our resident feminist' clearly indicating to me that she is different and to be kept at a distance. She herself says of her relationship with her neighbours,

> As everybody knows I'm the 'local feminist' around here. But I do make attempts to widen the scope of conversation all the time, sort of consciousness raising is a very important thing.

Through W.E.L. she has formed a network of like minded women in the Northern Suburbs whom she contacts frequently by telephone or car.

For the most part the inner city Feminists did not know their immediate neighbours but chose those in their neighbourhood or beyond as close friends who held ideas and lived life-styles similar to their own. For example Mary Tyler says of her neighbours,

> No, I don't see my neighbours at all. I wouldn't have that much in common with them. It's very difficult being neighbourly because a lot of my values are in conflict with suburban Australia.

The proximity of a number of other feminists in the inner city area studied enables Feminist mothers to choose and contact a supportive group of feminist women, as does the availability in this area of feminist voluntary associations and feminist orientated groups. In this way a close-knit network of like-minded women is built up who are able to challenge some existing ideas and practices concerning motherhood.

Amongst the five W.E.L. mothers there existed a conscious, supportive sisterhood relationship which facilitated discussion of motherhood at a different level from that of the Mt Druitt and Nth Shore groups described previously. One of these women, Katherine Harlow, describes the difference being in the women's movement has made to her perspective on mothering,

> Being in the women's movement has helped me get through these last few years. You meet so many terribly supportive friends, it makes all the difference. Because I find it terribly difficult to get along with a lot of other mothers. I know I'm not—I don't have anything in common with them. So this is why the women in the women's movement are so very important to me, because they sort of spoke about things that worried me. I mean you always feel guilty about saying 'I *hate* being at home, I *hate* having the kids, I *hate* never being able to go into an art gallery and have five minutes to look at the pictures. I *hate* not being able to go into the library and spend as long as I like without someone saying, 'I've chosen my books, I want to go home now'.
>
> It's those things you are able to discuss with other women. I *hate* not having my own income, I *hate* being dependent upon someone else for everything I buy. And it's just the personal freedom that is so restricted.

Women who belonged to consciousness raising groups told of the discussions they had in these groups. Topics included, relationships with husband, the division of labour in the home, relationship, with their own mother, relationships with children and labour both inside and outside the home. The tenor of these discussions is illustrated in the discussion of division of labour in the home described by one respondent. Over a period of four weeks the members of the group kept a diary of the number of actual hours per day they spent in child care and household activities. For no mother was it less than four hours per day, all the mothers in the group had at least one pre-school child and all were employed outside the home at least part-time. For the majority of the women this discussion resulted in discussions concerning the division of labour in the home with their husbands and in some redistribution of tasks. Only one mother in the group, she said, came into such conflict with her husband over the issue that she did not pursue it. It is evident that in these discussions there is room for questioning the status quo, at least at the individual level of women's oppression, although they do not necessarily entail an outright challenge to the male dominated structures of society.

In informal discussions with other mothers, feminist mothers are more likely than the other groups of mothers interviewed to discuss the mother's own position in the home. 44% of these mothers said that they discussed the hassles of being a mother/housewife; some single mothers (24%) were the only other mothers to include such a mother centred topic. 44% of Feminist mothers also included the position of women, sex roles and women's liberation as topics of discussion in their informal groups. Two Employed mothers were the only other respondents to include these topics. Mary Tyler describes her informal discussions with other mothers,

> Nearly all the mothers I know are feminists and so we talk about what we're doing, what struggles we're involved in and what we're working on. And the other thing we talk a lot about is other women and how they're surviving and who's in trouble and how relationships are going and how we can help. Real women's business.

Exclusion of kin and neighbours who do not see the world from a feminist perspective from the significant others in one's network and both the freedom to choose and the availability of feminist friends are characteristic of the networks of the Feminist mothers in the sample.

The same is true of the voluntary associations to which they belong; groups which strongly support traditional ideas concerning women, such as church groups are avoided and feminist groups are preferred. Some Feminist mothers did belong to Play Groups, but only associated with those in the Play Group who were also committed to feminist values and, like the 'career mothers' already quoted they regarded these associations as an arena for gaining expertise in the job of mothering, not as a charter for their lives. The voluntary associations which form a significant part of the networks of these mothers include the following: Women's Electoral Lobby, Parents and Citizens Associations, Play Groups, Friends of the Earth, Women's Resource Centre, Rape Crisis Centre, Abortion Clinic, Women's Health Centre, Children's Co-operative, Women's Committee of Ethnic Communities Council, Family Planning Association,

Feminist Drama Group, Women's Press Collective, the Labour Party and Alcoholics Anonymous.

It is interesting to note here that no Feminist mother interviewed belonged to a church group. Those who had had close associations with church groups during their upbringing now saw them as restrictive and oppressive for women. Whereas for 28% of Nth Shore mothers their church affiliation was an important part of their lives, no Feminist respondent considered religion to be of importance in her life.

A comparison of the following comments by two respondents on sex roles shows how group affiliation can act as a mechanism for transmission of ideologies or utopias of motherhood and sex roles. The first mother is a Nth Shore mother whose traditional church affiliation has priority in her life, the second a Feminist mother brought up in a 'straight down the line orthodox, Protestant indoctrination' which she sees now as oppressive; affiliation with a consciousness raising group has priority for her.

> For various reasons I think God has made a man physically and mentally different to a woman to be able to be the best at his particular job and that is to be the 'go getter', the earner, the wage earner, the competitor, the protector of his dominion, his home. And he's got the strength, the drive, the ambition and the make up suited for this. And the woman's role is to be the helpmate of the husband, to be the homemaker for him and his children. She's been given abilities that he hasn't got, that are more suitable to this job. I think if you try to reverse the roles or change them there's trouble and it's not really as good.

> I'm really opposed to any one single person having to stay home and look after the house and the kids. I think that the whole role of 'housewife', say someone who looks after the *house*, even after the kids go to school, should be abolished. I don't know what else can be done, but for either a man or a woman to spend all their labour on the maintenance of the house I consider to be regrettable and the sort of absurd situation that can only happen in a highly restrictive culture. But I don't see that there'd be any problem in a man looking after the kids and relating to them. Except that I feel that anybody alone looking after their children is at risk in a way. They're bound to suffer some sense of isolation, loss of identity or loneliness. I think men tend to think, 'That'd be fantastic, I'd love to do that, I could do that plus'. Ideally I think both people could be involved both at home and in the workplace.

By eliminating significant others who hold ideas which morally legitimate both the ideology of sex roles and the ideology of motherhood from their networks Feminist mothers leave the way open for alternative ideas. By selecting friends who form a close-knit, female feminist network with the occasional inclusion of sympathetic males, these mothers have been able to carry out their mothering in a sub-culture with strong norms and values concerning women's rights, women's place and parenting rather than mothering. One Feminist mother describes her female network thus,

> I meet a lot of women. It's like being part of a sub-culture. I know masses of feminist women. And I know hardly any men, unless they are husbands of women I know first and are sympathetic to women's issues.

Their close-knit support group encloses these women within an alternative sub-culture which supports them in their attempts to transcend some of the limitations of conventional motherhood, but at the same time brings to bear on them a strong set of alternative norms which can also restrict personal behaviour to patterns accept-able in this milieu. For example, two Feminist mothers were pregnant at the time of the interviews, one with a second child and one with a third. Because neither had planned their pregnancies, the feminist network to which they belonged expected them to have abortions. Both decided not to and felt sanctioned by the group in various subtle ways because of this. One lesbian Feminist described her situation as a 'feminist ghetto which does not have an awful lot of contact with the outside world'.

Choice of Feminist oriented networks of group affiliations and friends, and elimination of significant others and groups which adhere strongly to traditional ideologies of sex roles and of mother-hood, provides Feminist mothers with a close-knit network of sup-portive others who have utopian ideas concerning motherhood and women's place. Solidarity amongst these women not only supports them in their mothering (single mothers in feminist households share child care, housework, cooking, shopping, laundry, etc.) but enables them to challenge some of the traditional ideas concerning the 'natural' propensity for women to bear and rear children and to perform the associated household tasks. Feminist men are drawn into this circle too, but as previous chapters have shown, there is still a gap in the assumption of total responsibility for children and household tasks, even between feminist men and women. In feminist nuclear families, contrary to Bott's hypothesis (1971:217), 'joint conjugal role relationships' are supported by a close-knit network of female friends, who endeavour to incorporate husbands more and more into shared roles at home. In some instances, as for the members of the consciousness raising group quoted here, female solidarity has been partially successful in doing this. It is suggested then that ideas can have a part to play in changing the hierarchical organisation of the nuclear family predicated on gender, but that further changes in the male dominated structure of the wider society are necessary before feminist utopias can become a reality. Feminist mothers experience their mothering within a close-knit network of friends who endorse feminist ideas and who help and support each other, materially and emotionally. A conscious attempt is made by them to eliminate some of the competition between women and some of the inequality of life-chances and life-options between men and women.

Conclusions

Within the networks of mothers described in this chapter significant individuals who possess both charismatic and institutional authority act as caretakers of the ideology or as agents for change. The final chapter of data analysis looks at the ideas being propagated by these influential individuals as a source of mystification or of revelation concerning motherhood.

11 Caretakers of the ideology and agents for change

Caretakers and agitators as foci in networks of mothers

The body of this book has been concerned firstly with legitimation given to existing male-female power relationships, both within the family and in wider society by the ideology of motherhood which emphasises women's 'natural' propensity for child care and related household tasks. Secondly, it has been concerned with contemporary challenges to this particular legitimation associated with some changes in women's power vis-a-vis men and ideas arising from the women's movement in the late 1960s. In the previous chapter networks of mothers have been shown to be an effective vehicle for transmission of the ideologies which legitimate women's position and for those utopias which challenge women's subordination. Within these networks key figures stand out as promulgators of conservative or radical ideas which they transmit through the networks available to them. Those who reinforce traditional ideas on motherhood and women's position are termed in this chapter 'caretakers' of the ideology and those who transmit feminist utopias 'agents' or 'agitators' for change.

The term 'caretaker' is used here to refer to those in official and semi-official positions who take care that the ideology of motherhood is rationally regenerated and communicated within networks of young mothers, so perpetuating the status quo of male-female power relationships. The terms 'agent' and 'agitator' refer to those middle class people, also in official or semi-official positions, who both disseminate and embody perspectives on motherhood which are at variance with the ideology, challenging and demystifying it. Caretakers represent the 'prevailing and intellectual order and experience that structure of relationships of which they are the bearers' while agitators represent 'the groups driven into opposition to the present order' who are 'oriented towards the first stirrings of the social order for which they are striving and which is being realised through them'

(Mannheim, 1936:173–90). In this chapter the ideas of caretakers and agitators concerning women's domestic labour are discussed.

Women's domestic labour as viewed by caretakers and agitators

Examination of the female networks of the Mt Druitt respondents revealed a concentric network of women with similar life-experiences and similar ideas on motherhood, thus enclosing the mother within a milieu of ideologically orientated significant others. Into these networks are introduced certain middle class 'external' caretakers (Bryson and Thompson, 1972:11) whose own life-experiences, life-styles and values differ quite markedly from those of the Mt Druitt mothers who are their clients. These caretakers are aware of the variance between their own lives and those of the mothers with whom they deal professionally and to a certain degree they attempt to adapt their ideas to the Mt Druitt situation. As will be seen in the following discussion, the rational, scientific, professional aspects of the ideology which are transmitted through them from male, middle class upholders of the status quo are continually intermixed with a certain perception of the experience of motherhood as it is lived by Mt Druitt mothers. Consequently the ideology is regenerated in a form acceptable and viable in a working class situation.

The Nth Shore mothers whom I have designated caretakers of the ideology, on the other hand, are 'internal' caretakers (Bryson and Thompson, 1972:11) who come from a similar situation and share the values of those to whom they offer assistance and ideological legitimation. They draw less on rational, scientific backing for their ideas than do the Mt Druitt caretakers but more on their own ideological interpretation of experiences they have had as a mother and those of mothers and children with whom they have had contact.

The agitators for change draw both on their personal experiences as mothers (the personal is political in the women's movement) and on their theoretical awareness of the oppressed position of women in contemporary society in attacking the status quo and in opening the way for a new order of existence.

The crucial issues will now be discussed concerning women's domestic labour as they appear firstly to caretakers then to agitators.

The ideal of motherhood: the 'good' mother versus the 'employed' mother

In a book by Burton White entitled *The First Three Years of Life* (1975) the author (a contemporary authority on early childhood

education) gives the following advice to mothers of 12–14 month old
children (1975:147–48).

> If a woman takes a full-time job during phase V of the child's life, she
> obviously has less to do with this early learning process. If she leaves
> someone in the home whose primary job is to take care of the house, then
> the child is going to be shortchanged. If, on the other hand, she leaves
> someone whose job is defined so as to emphasise interactions with the
> child, the child has a better chance. But whether the child will profit as
> much from this kind of experience as he would from his own mother is an
> open question.
> My feeling is that if a mother is aware of the importance of what is
> going on in a child's development at this point, she will be likely to stay
> home at least part of the day,
>   or for phase VI (14 months–2 years approx.) (1975:254)
> It is my considered opinion that attending just about any day-care
> institution full-time is unlikely to be as beneficial to the child's early
> educational development as his own home during the first three years.
> The author of the book bases his statements on: (1975:xiii)
> The most sustained (expensive) scientific study of the role of experience
> in the development of human abilities in the first years of life conducted
> to date.

These ideas have obviously been incorporated in the ideology of
motherhood as expressed by the mothers at Mt Druitt and are directly
referred to quite frequently by the caretakers. The ideology implied
in the book and expounded by such caretakers has the formal,
rational backing of scientific knowledge as the basis of its authority
and this is invoked by the caretakers. For example, one of the caretakers, following the above author, summarises her ideas concerning
a 'good' mother in the following way:

1   a *designer* who allows the child to explore his/her surroundings and
     designs the house so that there is a place in the house so that children
     can happily and safely explore and experiment;
2   a *responder* who responds immediately to the child, fulfilling its needs
     as far as is practicable at the time; and
3   an *authority* who sets limits that the child understands but which are
     not so restrictive that they prevent exploration.

Such a mother she believes will be a 'comfortable' mother and will
have a happy relationship with her children.
    In contrast to this child centred approach with accent on the
qualities and responsibility of the individual woman and total acceptance of the assumption that 'parenting' means mothering, one of the
agitators adopts a more critical approach to the position of mothers
in society and shows an awarenes of restrictions placed on individual

development for women due to their responsibility for parenting and the mystification which surrounds motherhood in our society. This agitator makes the following points concerning a 'good' mother:

1   Society's idea of a 'good' mother is one who does not have any needs or desires of her own but is there to provide services for both her husband and her children. She finds satisfaction in providing for the fulfilment of other people. She is there to support them emotionally and physically so that her husband and eventually her children can pursue careers and be a success in life.

2   Such a view she sees as hypocritical because, on the one hand women are applauded for such services, but on the other there is the subtle implication that they are stupid because that is all they do and this role effectively debars them from all the decision-making levels of society.

3   Her own ideas include substituting parenting for mothering; role sharing; parenting as only one aspect of life for both mothers and fathers and giving quality to children's lives, but not necessarily quantity.

Domestic labour in the view of the caretakers of the ideology is the rightful prerogative of women whose children are their primary concern, at least until they are of school age. Elaborate and expensive research into the early childhood years is used as scientific backing to encourage mothers to focus attention on the best methods of child care and the need for mothers to stay close to their children during these years. In the view of the agents for change, domestic labour, especially child care is seen as a servicing mechanism in the production of future labourers. The relegation of this responsibility to women is seen as an effective way of debarring women from positions of power in the decision-making bodies of society, which are the perogative of males who have been freed from domestic labour. Women's responsibility for parenting is also seen to effectively stultify her individual development and career advancement. In the 'new order' agitators see men and women sharing responsibility for parenting the children they bear and earning the income to support them. For her, domestic labour is the rightful responsibility of men and women alike, and a place in the work-force the right and privilege of both sexes. For agitators then, 'employed mother' is not in contravention of 'good mother'.

For example, one agitator comments on mothers of pre-school children working outside the home,

> Obviously I think it's all right as I do it. I think everyone should be able to work outside the home if she wants to. Obviously I think child care should be men's and women's responsibility equally and I think there should be much more child care. There should be child care on the job for

both men and women and obviously I believe in all that. We're a million miles away from all that.

There is a recognition here that her ideas are as yet utopian, in that they cannot be brought to reality in the present social order, but there is also a strong challenge to the existing order of male-female stereotypes and roles. On the question of mothers of pre-school children working outside the home, not surprisingly, the caretakers of the ideology are more equivocal. Says one,

> I think that there are problems in it always, if the kid is going to be minded by someone else. But if we can overcome these problems from the child's angle, like continuity of care, same value system, same surroundings sort of thing and I suppose I can add to that make sure that it's a stimulating environment, and substitute care is doing the things that White says we should do, tons of things to play with, etc. that'll be O.K. for the kid, but I think the other major problem about it is the jealousy between mother and substitute carer. So I don't really have a firm answer. It's got dangers in it, also there are dangers if kids are cared for by their own mothers. If we're aware of the dangers that's O.K. we can do something about it.

Another caretaker emphasised that there was a very strong feeling amongst the mothers in her area that if children were to be minded it should be by someone who has a family of her own and who in their eyes has shown herself to be a successful mother. She herself endorsed this view by compiling a list of mothers who were willing to look after other people's children, their reasons, what they wanted to charge and other information so that she could put mothers who wanted to work in touch with 'child-minders', and they could choose one who suited their own requirements. She also felt that there were pressures on the mothers to work to provide a better home materially, but that the mothers themselves felt strongly that they ought to be, and wanted to be at home.

Mannheim (1936:187) claims that 'utopias can only challenge the existing order when they embody currents already present in society which are appropriate to the changing situation.' The feminist agitators who challenge traditional ideas concerning 'good' motherhood and emphasise instead the involvement of men in parenting, the quality of care rather than quantity, the desirability of the child having contact with a greater number of adults than its biological parents and the fulfilment of the needs of the mother herself are, in fact, embodying aspirations in utopias 'appropriate to the changing situation'. In view of the increasing number of married women in the work-force and the number of these women who have children under school age, the fact of the 'employed mother' is evidence of a changing situation which feminist ideas on motherhood can more readily cope with than traditional ideas concerning the 'good' mother.' Feminist utopias then, which reconcile 'good' motherhood with 'employed' motherhood are challenging the ideology at a point which is extremely appropriate to the changing situation.

Once the idea that fathers can participate in child care just as effectively as mothers gains ground, the mystification of motherhood is revealed as an ideological support for the male-female division of labour in the home and the inequalities associated with rigid sex role definitions.

The division of labour in the home: rigid or flexible sex roles

Mt Druitt caretakers maintain that the fairly rigid division of labour in the home at Mt Druitt and the corresponding sex role stereotypes are functional for the Mt Druitt situation. Like other upholders of traditional ideologies, they do not perceive domestic labour as 'work' in the same sense that the man's labour in the market place is perceived as work. The man's long journey to his employment and his physical fatigue entitle him to rest and to be waited on when he returns home. What the mother with young children does at home all day is not perceived as 'work', so she is not entitled to such treatment. The superiority of the male role and masculine identity associated with the provider role and, on the other hand, femaleness associated with child care are also suggested.

They probably don't play as big a part here as say a father in a middle class area or a trendy type area. There's a few reasons for that. One is that people here feel happier that way at the moment. That's to do with the sex roles I think—father the breadwinner, mother the caretaker.

I think there's an expectation about the father's role is to bring home the 'dough' and to be around at weekends too, to take the kids to sport and watch them play footy, etc. I think the reason that they don't take more part in child-rearing is not only because of an expectation, but a second thing, there's not much time, there's such a long distance to work and they're so tired by the time they get home that they do just want to sit down by the telly with a tinny. There is a third element coming and that is unemployment, there are a lot more fathers at home, so some of them do play a much greater role within their families, but on the other hand—a lot of mothers tell me they don't and that does cause trouble because the mothers think that because they're there they should, even if their expectation and role expectation is different. But you see the fathers feel really awful about playing the role, that puts their ego down further, they've not only not got a job but 'Why should I do this namby pamby stuff of changing nappies?'

A Nth Shore caretaker of the ideology also sees the division of labour in the home, with the woman as nurturer and carer and the man as provider and protector as 'natural' and reverse sex roles as not quite normal. She says,

> I know two or three couples who are reversing their roles. It does seem to be working, but I have the feeling that there might be something lacking in each marriage.
>
> In one, I think her husband probably has homosexual tendencies and they've come to terms with it in this way, which is super for them. He is absolutely marvellous with the children, you could not fault him. I really take my hat off to him, but I think there is that problem for them.
>
> The other couple, I think she has the greater earning capacity than he has. And I think since they've accepted that and they're getting on together as best they can, well good luck to them.
>
> Personally, I wouldn't like it, obviously because I'm so very maternal and I don't want anyone else to be doing my mothering for me.

The agitators, on the other hand, see rigid sex roles as very limiting for both men and women. One commends as follows,

> I now have the realisation that my husband is as much trapped by the system as I am. I think you realise this through the women's movement. I went into it in a self-centred way. I mean I went into it because I suddenly realised there I was in the house with a three month old baby and 'My God, whatever am I going to do with the rest of my life?' And that led me to Women's Lib. But having been in the women's movement for four years now, I see that Adrian is as much trapped as I am and that we have to be talking about changing society to improve the quality of life of *all* people such as ourselves.

Feminist utopias see more flexible sex roles and a sharing of home and employment roles as liberating experiences for both men and women and that modern technology and work conditions could make this feasible. It is the man who will have to overcome greater normative opposition; in our society it still is 'definitely strange for a man to stay at home and look after children'. One of the agitators makes this following observation,

> If it's a couple's decision to reverse roles I see no reason why it shouldn't work. But they're going to have to be very stable people, they're going to have to be very sure of what they're doing and they're going to have to be very self-confident because—I don't think she will get a lot, but he's going to have terrible problems being the only fella in the supermarket, people are going to look at him when he wheels the pram along the road and he's going to have remarks made. His manhood will be questioned more, because he's doing, at this stage he's doing the more daring thing. It's not so strange for a woman to go to work, but it's definitely strange for a man to stay at home and look after children.

The actions of men who do stay at home constitute a threat to the ideology of motherhood and the division of labour in the home and sex role prescriptions based on this ideology. If men can successfully 'mother' there is no ideological backing for female responsibility for domestic labour.

The high or low status of motherhood

In circumstances such as exist at Mt Druitt where there are no other alternatives for women, the caretakers feel that mothers are respected at least by other mothers and possibly by teenagers.

> They're certainly not looked down on. They are all mothers you know. So they are all in the same boat and all sharing a place in society and I think a lot of teenagers look up to the parenting role. I think I'd be right in saying that most of them, they certainly don't look down to them, I don't know about looking up to, because they all just feel 'Right we're in this together'. That's their job of work.

The North Shore caretakers also feel that in their milieu mothers are not looked down on,

> There are lots of reports that society looks down on mothers but I must confess that I've never been in a situation where I've found anyone that has. I think people are rather too busy to be looking down on mothers or up to mothers. I think if a child is very badly behaved in public you can't really blame people for being aggravated by it. I've never found that anyone's looked down on me because I'm a mother. I think they probably have for other reasons, but not because I'm a mother.

Promulgators of utopia, on the other hand are more likely to see the domestic labour of women in relation to the economic value that is placed on such labour and the double standards evident in wider society towards motherhood.

> It's pretty obvious that mothers are looked down on in our society. There's all that stuff about motherhood's wonderful, bla, bla, bla, but it doesn't mean anything in practical terms. I mean I do it myself, I catch myself saying 'my mother only looked after kids, *but*' and all that. It's just really hard for us to escape from that, because we've accepted the inferior position allocated to mothers.
>
> The family day-care wage is an indication of what looking after children merits. They're paid 70 cents an hour under that scheme where children are looked after in the home. They're only paid 70 cents an hour, that's slave labour and I think that's an indication of the worth that's put on it.

This agitator also sees the low status of both mothers and children reflected in the lack of public provisions for them,

I can't understand why the world is so anti-kids when in a sense it's so pro-kids. I mean the ideology's so much for kids and yet it really isn't set up for them at all and so you just feel that you're struggling around. You go to Market Town and there are people with three kids hanging off them trying to do the shopping and there's no where to leave them. It just makes me really angry. I never understood it before, I went around with my eyes at this level and you just never saw these things. And now that I've had experience you just see it all the time.

When men become involved in tasks which have previously been given low status because they are performed by women, the status is raised. The ideology of motherhood has already stressed the importance of the first years of the child's life, but motherhood has had low status because it is performed solely by women. In the feminist utopia, men and women will both be constrained/benefitted by daily and close association with children, women's potentialities will cease to be confined and limited by children (Curthoys, 1976:3) and the status of domestic labour will be raised.

Baby-bashing as deviant behaviour or as an expression of oppression

Mt Druitt caretakers acknowledged the great difficulties mothers have in admitting that they abuse their children and that they need help in this area. They expressed concern for the child and sympathy for the mother and where cases came to their notice they tried to put the mother in touch with someone who would help them. They see themselves as resource people who can link the mother with problems to those who will give them support in their mothering. For example,

A lot of mums I know really well now, on a friendly basis as well as professionally . . . Recently three mothers who were actually physically abusing kids, and in many ways it was actually bad because they said 'Look I feel terrible about this, but I know you well enough to tell you' and in that way it was good, they weren't afraid of telling me. But on the other hand, it does make it difficult because they're telling you and they don't want anyone else to know, but of course—prevention and social responsibility, you know—you can't keep that sort of information to yourself.

A lot of them saw that film with Jacky Weaver and they all identified. Fifteen mothers in that group and they all said, 'This is exactly how we feel and we've all shaken a baby or shoved a baby in a cot and said "Look I've just got to go away"', and they all identified very strongly. It helped a lot because they realised the professionals knew.

They might talk a lot about the behaviour of a child without actually saying 'Look I've actually bashed this child' and it might be physical, it might be emotional, which is so much more prevalent, and so the sort of referral I'd do is contact the Poly Clinic or someone in the Child Health team to say 'Look, this is happening, could I put this mother in touch?' and then I'd let the mother make the contact, like open the doors and the mother she's got to make the phone call.

Although caretakers expressed concern for the mother, the remedy was seen to be support, especially emotional support for the mothering role, to return the mother to being a 'good' mother, her behaviour is treated as deviant, reinforcing the norms of 'good' motherhood. This impression was supported by one Mt Druitt mother who admitted times of wanting to strangle her children and of asking the doctor for help, she said, 'If I don't get some relief from those kids, I'll either kill them or desert them'. His answer was to give her some valium to calm her down, so that she could cope with them. 'What I really needed' she said, 'was a complete break from them'.

Sadness for the mother and concern for the child, but the deviance of the behaviour, especially outside the nuclear family is also expressed by Nth Shore caretakers. For example,

I feel very sad about it. I come across it a lot in my fostering work and it's almost inevitable that the baby-basher has not had good mothering herself. They usually do it because they aren't aware of what they're doing, despite the fact that people think that they are. I feel profound sadness about anyone who feels it necessary to beat a baby. I often wonder perhaps if we as responsibile citizens aren't pushing these girls into battering their babies more than they used to. I'm not convinced yet that it's a good idea to give unmarried mothers pensions which enable them to keep their babies. I think it works out at first but more and more babies seem to be going into foster care or institutional situations later. I think perhaps if we made it a little more difficult for these 15–16 year olds to make the decision to keep their babies then I think we'd have less battered children.

I feel sadness for the mother and concern for the child. I come across these girls who are living in one room who don't maybe realise that babies cry a lot, especially if they're not fed properly, etc.

It's really quite foreign to me. I have not ever been in the situation where I've felt like it.

Agitators on the other hand identify with the mothers and see the situation as one imposed on today's mothers by the structure of the circumstances within which they carry out their domestic labour. They say,

Oh there but for the grace of God go I—I'd say. I'm sure if most mothers are honest they'd say the same, that there comes a time in your life when you could have bashed your baby. Whether you gritted your teeth and went away and did something and shut the door so that you don't do it, the possibility is still there. I can understand it, yes. It shows you that the stresses—

that being at home alone with two or three children or a baby is a very stressful situation. When it goes on I should say it's due to a stressful situation seven days a week, 52 weeks per year.

Another caretaker puts the case more forcefully. She sees baby-bashing as a phenomenon of women's oppression through their responsibility for privatised domestic labour in a capitalist society. She says,

> I blame it on the state, because I think if people and child care and there was a more supportive framework—I think it's a social problem that has to do with the fact that the society we live in cuts people off into little privatised boxes and doesn't provide child care, doesn't provide social facilities because it's a capitalist system that's based on private enterprise and profit.
>
> So that means that you can choose between 54 brands of tooth paste, but as far as child care goes, you can't get any, so you take what you can get. So I just see it as a phenemenon which cannot be put down to people's individual faults, but just something where people get pushed beyond their limits because of the society in which they're living.
>
> I quite understand it. Also if men had the responsibility for child care I'm sure more facilities would be provided.

Caretakers of the ideology see baby-bashing and other problems that young mothers have as deviations from 'normal' motherhood and their function as one of support for traditional mothering and help in adaptation to the role. Feminist agitators, on the other hand, question the structures which place women in a situation where their children can become the recipients of the results of female oppression in the family. Problems that mothers have are more likely to be seen as symptoms of societal pressures placed on women in a male dominated society. In the one view female solidarity is used to support traditional motherhood and family models, in the other to question the place of women in contemporary society.

Female solidarity as a means of adapting to motherhood or as a force for change

Mt Druitt caretakers demonstrate their belief in the function of mothers' groups and networks of mothers in helping women to adapt to motherhood. For example, one caretaker says,

> My feeling is that if parents are put together they'll give each other wisdom, our role is to give them new information for them to digest and to see if it will fit into their value system and maybe it's O.K. it makes common sense.

Another says,

> Something I find, even with putting the scale outside the door—they'll all sit out there and they're all helping each other so much and sharing all their problems and their confidence is just growing and growing and growing so just even the contact at the clinic is actually making them happier in what they are doing. And if there's a mum who is not at all happy, the baby's crying all the time or she really doesn't know what to do and there's nobody to turn to, the mothers just help so much. The ones who have 2 or 3 are much happier in their role and just help the new Mums so much.
>
> Mothers who are happy in their role or felt quite happy to go and visit a new mum, they were just going around with information on the area, the mums with new babies had just come to the area and so didn't know a thing about it. They were just going from door to door and saying 'Oh I believe you've had a new baby', that was the way in and 'If you want to, come along to a coffee morning or a group, etc'. And the friendships which have sprung up are just incredible.

Nth Shore caretakers also see mothers' groups such the Nursing Mothers' Association as support groups for mothers in their task and as agents for disseminating information on breast feeding and the best ways of caring for children.

On the other hand agitators see their involvement in women's groups as politically orientated action. One of the agitators who belongs to W.E.L. sees her involvement in this group as a means of agitating for more child care services. She is concerned with the Children's Services Committee for W.E.L. which is involved in political action with this end in view.

Another agitator describes her involvement in the women's movement as follows,

> I've been involved with the women's movement for about six years. I sort of got involved with it through reading and through talking with friends who were more involved and then the penny started to drop. The first major thing I did was to put on a women's study course at my university. That was a kind of baptism by fire, I am just realising what was involved in trying to put on a course like that. That was my initiation into politics and into being a public person, having to stand up and make those speeches to 1000 people and to go on T.V. It was dreadful, but it was really good and achieved a lot, I think.
>
> Last year I was still involved in a group that was trying to organise around the Year of the Child and trying to mobilise against possible right wing attacks using the International Year of the Child sort of route to do it. Especially the Right to Life and Anti- Abortion and all that.

Female solidarity is seen by these agitators politically as an action group for reform or revoluation which will bring about a better world for women[1]. They perceive their women's groups as a means of changing society to benefit the needs of women, rather than as a means of adapting women to their predetermined role in society.

Conclusions

Caretakers of the ideology of motherhood accept domestic labour as the preserve of women and perpetuate the existing structure of male-female relationships, legitimating women's relegation to and responsibility for the domestic sphere by an emphasis on the biological mother as the primary caretaker for her children during the early years. For these caretakers sex roles are fairly rigidly defined and appear as functional both for individual members of the family as well as for society as a whole, with little adaptation even when the mother is also employed outside the home. Motherhood is idealised and its importance for the future of society emphasised, but its low status and exclusion from the decision-making arenas of society are not questioned. Women who do not cope well with motherhood such as 'baby-bashers' are considered deviant and female solidarity is seen as a means of assisting women to adapt to their role as mothers.

Agents for change, on the other hand, postulate alternative forms of 'mothering' including group caring and male parenting. Women's responsibility for domestic labour based on her 'natural' propensity for parenting is exploded as an ideological support for male-female power relationships and privatised child care in a capitalist patriarchal society. Sex role rigidity is also exposed as an ideological support for male freedom from primary parenting responsibility. The inability of some women to 'cope' with the demands of motherhood is seen as a result of structural pressures placed upon them in the privatised nuclear or single parent family. Female solidarity is seen as a means to reform or change society in the interests of the female half of the population. Such ideas remain 'utopian' in that they emerge from the needs of the present order but transcend that order and as yet are not totally realisable within that order.

Note

1   Cora Baldock (1978:139) points out the difference between W.E.L. and the Women's Liberation Movement. The main emphasis of W.E.L. is on reform through existing political channels and on educating women

through discussion and public debate. The Women's Liberation Movement challenges the very bases on which society proceeds and attempts to develop alternative structures which will provide a liberating environment for women and children, in this way the changes suggested are 'revolutionary' rather than reformist. Both groups are represented in this chapter. Differences in their approaches are obvious in the excerpts quoted, but in order to contrast these utopian views with those of the caretakers of the ideology, these differences have not been emphasised.

12   Conclusions

Having listened to and observed the 150 mothers whose lived experiences of motherhood are recorded in this book, I am convinced that amongst these mothers there is a set of ideas and beliefs which centres their time and energy day by day on the nurture of their children and on the care of the surroundings in which this nurturance takes place.

For the majority there is assent to the belief that the biological mother is the rightful person to take primary responsibility for such nurture and care and that this preogative is 'natural' and 'inevitable' for women. That such beliefs circumscribe the lives of mothers in our society, limiting their life-options, autonomy, self-concepts and activities outside the home has been amply demonstrated by the lives of the women discussed in this book. For those women who have, in some way, modified the ideology to allow themselves time to pursue other activities such as paid employment, study, cultural, political or social activities, these activities are achieved in addition to their mothering and do not to any degree diminish the primary place of mothering in their lives. For most of the women, in fact, a certain amount of satisfaction accrues from their mothering. Nevertheless the questions which remain to be answered in this concluding chapter are:

1   Whose interests are being served by the ideology of motherhood?
2   What material and power infrastructures enable such an ideology to be generated and perpetuated in Australian society?
3   What possibilities are there for change?

Whose interests are being served?

First, woman's lack of ownership of the means of production and lack of top level positions in bureaucratic structures together with her lack of power in the intellectual, psychic, political and religious

200

spheres of society are legitimated and obfuscated by the ideology of motherhood. Women remain in relatively powerless positions and power relationships based on gender are perpetuated and exacerbated. Male definitions of culture, values, achievement, status, prestige, equality of opportunity and distribution of material resources, which generally serve male interests, are those which predominate. For example, status and prestige are accorded to achievement in the market place, sporting and political arenas in which most women are disadvantaged by their parenting responsibilities, if they have not been completely excluded by them.

Second, in addition to, or as a consequence of lack of access to male defined sources of power, women lack autonomy to define their own interests as against those which benefit males and have accepted as their own the interests, desires, wants and satisfactions which have been prescribed for them. Conflict over 'who minds the baby' is thus averted and women continue to accept the burden of parenting as legitimately theirs. The use of the voluntary labour of women for child-rearing in a privatised setting thus absolves private enterprise, the state and the local community from financial responsibility for the care of future workers and future citizens.

Third, women's secondary position on the market sector, her confinement to low paid, gender-specific or part-time work and/or her exclusion from this sphere in times of economic recession are also justified by the ideology. Fourth, the ideology justifies the exemption of individual men in families across classes from major responsibility for child care and household tasks, so that they can pursue economic and status interests in the wider society, while they are provided with consistent physical and emotional support for achievement in those areas.

It can be seen then that the interests of both capital and patriarchy at the macro and micro levels of society are being served by an ideology which posits the 'natural' and 'inevitable' responsibility of women for child care.

What infrastructures support the ideology?

Fundamentally at the macro-social level, the capitalist nature of Australian society provides the bourgeois male with power resulting from ownership of the means of production to have ideas and values which serve the interests of capital accepted as consensual beliefs which are in the interests of all members of society.

As well, partly as the result of this power, but also as a result of the patriarchal nature of Australian society, where being male provides a power of its own relative to being female, men hold decision-making positions in all the major institutions of the society. Through control of the media, health and welfare services, as well as the institutions of the church, the state, education, medicine and the law, males can control the flow of ideas and values which serve their interests at the expense of the interests of women. It becomes almost impossible then, for women to imagine any other life for themselves, than that which has been reinforced for them through these institutions of our society. As the suggestions given by the mothers in this research have shown, they can imagine their lives being improved by better facilities in public places and alternative temporary child care, but everything they have ever experienced from birth onwards reinforces the view that the biological mother is the best and rightful caregiver for her children. They see this as 'natural and unchangeable' and, in many cases, value it as 'divinely ordained and beneficial'. These perceptions, in conjunction with the inability to imagine an alternative way of life, according to Lukes (1874:24) evidence the most 'insidious' use of power in our society.

In the microcosm of the family, the power base of the wider society is also in evidence. First, the property relations between men and women and the social relations which are these property relations in action, give the male power and autonomy vis-a-vis the female. The male wage earned by the labourer, or the salary earned in exchange for qualifications and expertise, or the ownership of property in the means of production, gives the male in the family in all classes, the material basis for male supremacy within the family. Thus the family itself is in a unique position for the generation and perpetuation of an ideology which serves the interests of the male and maintains relationships of domination and subordination not confined to the expression of class interests but extended to the interests of all males across classes, (Kuhn, 1971:53).

Second, gender itself within the family gives the man power and autonomy vis-a-vis the woman in that family. The supposed physical superiority of the male, his lack of 'time-out' for child-bearing, his generally higher level of education and greater age than that of this wife have given men in the family greater power based on male status in our society. On this basis, within the family, an ideology can be perpetuated which frees men from the demands of young children and provides them with unpaid household services. As Bell and Newby (1971:167) have pointed out, the power of the 'first' and the power of the 'purse' which belong to males, together with daily interpersonal acts of deference and demeanour on the part of women inhibit the 'growth of consciousness among wives of their subordinate position in the family'.

The research reported in this book has shown that some shift in the material and power infrastructures which support the ideology is a necessary condition for any challenge to be made to the status quo. Whether such a shift is a sufficient condition for change will be discussed in the following section.

What possibilities are there for change?

The findings of the research suggest that it is only those women who have been able to increase their material and status based sources of power, vis-a-vis the males in their immediate milieu who have been able to transcend some of the limitations of the ideology in their daily lives. It is only those women who have been able to align ideas concerning freedom, equality and justice for women with such a power base who have been able to challenge the ideology to any extent and to consider alternative utopian ideas.

For example, the study has shown that:

1   Entry into the dominant sphere of commodity production for exchange in a society economically based in this sphere, with its emphasis on achieved rather than ascribed status did bring about some change in consciousness for employed mothers. Such consciousness revealed the limitations of economic dependence and rigid sex role definitions with the underlying assumptions concerning equal but different roles. For mothers with middle class market capacity, employment provided the economic resources which enabled them to transcend some of the restrictions of mothering and enabled them to question the necessity for their constant attendance upon their young children.

2   Although absence of a dominant male from the family structure generally lowered the family income of single mothers relative to others in their own social milieu, it increased the sense of autonomy and sense of competence of the mothers concerned. The double role of provider/ protector and parent/carer within the family, also enabled these mothers to challenge the concept of equal but different sex roles. Many of these mothers became aware of their relative oppression within the marriage structure. Although single parenthood served to focus the mother's attention and satisfaction in life on her children and her relationship with them, the change in the structure of the family increased the mother's sense of self-worth, competence and control as opposed to a sense of inferiority and powerlessness.

3   It was only those women who had access to material resources such as middle class market capacity, money, housing, technology and transport, or who had been able to pool scarce material resources such as housing, transport, household appliances and domestic labour, who were able to transcend some of the limitations placed upon them by

the ideology and to pursue their own interests within and outside the family.

4   It was only those women who, in addition to the above material conditions of their mothering, had direct contact with feminist ideas and a supportive network of other feminists, who were able to demystify and challenge the ideology to any extent and to construct alternative utopias. The role of ideas aligned with material resources has been shown in this research to be of crucial importance for change, even though access to these ideas and networks generally required middle class material resources.

The research findings support Weber's claim that, although material interests play an important part in governing human behaviour, ideas are crucial in determining the direction of action associated with such interests, (Gerth and Mills, 1948:63).

In view of the above findings, possibilities for gradual change appear to rest on the ability of women in Australian society to gain a greater share of material and status resources through increased education, continuation in the work-force after marriage and the birth of children, control of contraception and abortion, enlightened solidarity and redistribution of the division of labour in the home. However, any appreciable difference to be made to the subjective experience of mothering in present society would require also an enormous redistribution of resources across classes and in favour of women. Child care facilities and shortened more flexible hours of labour, especially in working class jobs for men and women, without loss of wages, as well as schemes which will encourage men to participate in parenting without economic loss or diminution of status are immediate necessities. Continued and more widespread dissemination of the ideas of freedom, equality and justice for women is also vital. Even where men are unemployed and the economic balance of the family is upset or reversed, there is little change in the division of labour unless there is a corresponding change in male perceptions of child care and housework, as the working class families in the study indicated.

For more pervasive and lasting changes, there is a need for a rebalancing of productive power, institutional power and gender power in favour of women. For this, I believe female solidarity across classes but using the material resources of independent middle class women would be necessary. Such solidarity would have as its aim, not only a concerted attack on male dominated capitalism and on male bureaucratic structures, but also on the male hierarchical structure of all the major institutions in our society including the state, law, education, medicine, the church, health and welfare services and the traditional family. An attack such as this may effectively challenge the ideology of motherhood which, in present Australian society, reinforces a division of labour along sex lines both within and without the family so that women remain in a subordinate, dependent and oppressed position vis-a-vis the majority of men. It may also enable utopias of motherhood, or rather parenthood, to be realised.

Bibliography

Acker, J. (1973) 'Women and Social Stratification: A Case of Intellectual Sexism' *American Journal of Sociology* 78, 4, pp. 936–54.

Adler, D.L. (1965) 'Matriduxy in the Australian Family' pp. 149–55 in A. F. Davies and S. Encel eds. *Australian Society, A Sociological Introduction* Melbourne: Cheshire.

Ainsworth, M. (1973) 'The Development of Infant-Mother Attachment' pp. 1–94 in B. Caldwell and H. Ricciuti eds *Review of Child Development Research 3*.

Allen, S. et al. eds (1974) *Conditions of Illusion* Leeds: Feminist Books.

Allen, S. and Barker, D.L. (1976) *Sexual Division and Society: Process and Change* London: Tavistock.

Althusser, L. (1977) *Lenin and Philosophy and Other Essays* London: Unwin. (2nd edn; translated from the French by Ben Brewster).

Australian Bureau of Statistics (1976) *Census of Population and Housing*.

Bahr, S.J. (1975) 'Effects on Power and Division of Labour in the Family' pp. 167–85 in L. W. Hoffman and F. I. Nye, *Working Mothers* San Francisco: Jossey Bass.

Baldock, C. (1978) *Australia and Social Change Theory* Sydney: Ian Novak.

Barnett, L.D. and MacDonald, R.H. (1976) 'A Study of the Membership of the National Organisation for Non-Parents' *Social Biology* 23, 4 (Winter): pp. 297–310.

Battle-Sister, A. (1971) 'Conjectures on the Female Culture Question' *Journal of Marriage and the Family* 33, 3 (August): pp. 411–43.

Bell, C. (1968) *Middle Class Families* London: Routledge and Kegan Paul.

Bell, C. and Encel, S. (1978) *Inside the Whale* Sydney: Pergamon.

Bell, C. and Newby, H. (1971) *Community Studies* London: Allen and Unwin.

Bell, C. and Newby, H. (1976) 'Husbands and Wives: the Dynamics of the Differential Dialect' pp. 152–68 in D. L. Barker and S. Allen, *Dependence and Exploitation in Work and Marriage* London: Longman.

Bell, D. (1962) *The End of Ideology* N.Y.: Collier.

Bell, N.W. and Vogel, E.F. (1968) *A Modern Introduction to the Family* N.Y.: The Free Press (rev. edn.).

Bell, R.R. (1963) *Marriage and Family Interaction* Homewood, Illinois: The Dorsey Press.

206

Bell, R.R. (1975) 'Significant Roles Among a Sample of Australian Women' *The Australian and New Zealand Journal of Sociology* 11, 1 (February): pp. 2-11.
Benston, M. (1972) 'The Political Economy of Women's Liberation' pp. 110-28 in N. Glazer Malbin and H. Youngelson Waehrer eds. *Women in a Man-Made World* Chicago: Rand McNally.
Berger, P. and Kellner, H. (1970) 'Marriage and the Construction of Reality' pp. 50-72 in H. P. Dreitzel ed. *Recent Sociology No. 2* N.Y.: Macmillan.
Bernard, J. (1972) *The Future of Marriage* Harmondsworth, Middlesex, England: Penguin.
Bernard, J. (1974) *The Future of Motherhood* N.Y.: The Dial Press.
Bernard, J. (1975) *Women, Wives, Mothers* Chicago: Aldine.
Blaikie, N.W.H. (1977) 'The Meaning and Measurement of Occupational Prestige' *The Australian and New Zealand Journal of Sociology* 13, 2: pp. 102-15.
Blood, R.O. and Hamblin, R.L. (1958) 'The Effect of the Wife's Employment on the Family Power Structure' *Social Forces*, 36: pp. 347-52.
Blood, R.O. (1963) 'The Husband-Wife Relationship' pp. 282-305 in F. I. Nye and L. W. Hoffman eds. *The Employed Mother in America* Chicago: Rand McNally.
Blood, R.O. and Hamblin, R.L. (1968) 'The Effects of the Wife's Employment on the Family Power Structure' pp. 182-87 in N. W. Bell and E. F. Vogel eds. *A Modern Introduction to the Family* N.Y.: The Free Press (rev. edn.).
Blood, R.O. and Wolfe, D.M. (1960) *Husbands and Wives* N.Y.: The Free Press.
Borrie, W.D. et al. (1978) *Population and Australia: Recent Demographic Trends and Their Implications* Canberra: Australian Government Publishing Service.
Bott, E. (1968a) 'Conjugal Roles and Social Networks' pp. 248-57 in N. W. Bell and E. F. Vogel eds. *A Modern Introduction to the Family* N.Y.: The Free Press (rev. edn.).
Bott, E. (1968b) 'Norms and Ideology—The Normal Family' pp. 435-52 in N. W. Bell and E. F. Vogel eds. *A Modern Introduction to the Family* N.Y.: The Free Press (rev. edn.).
Bott, E. (1971) *Family and Social Network* London: Tavistock (2nd edn.).
Bowlby, J.A. (1958) 'The Nature of the Child's Tie to His Mother' *International Journal of Psycho-Analysis* 39: pp. 350-73.
Bowlby, J.A. (1969) *Attachment* N.Y.: Basic Books.
Bowlby, J.A. (1971) *Attachment and Loss* Harmondsworth, Middlesex, England: Penguin.
Bryson, L. et al. (1965) 'Working Mothers and Family Life' Pilot Study, University of Melbourne.
Bryson, L. and Thompson, F. (1972) *An Australian Newtown* Nth Melbourne: Kibble.
Bryson, L. (1974) 'Men's Work and Women's Work: Occupation and Family Orientation' *Search* 5, 7 (July): pp. 295-99.

Bryson, L. (1975) 'Husband and Wife Interaction in the Australian Family: A Critical Review of the Literature' pp. 213–23 in Jan Mercer ed. *The Other Half* Blackburn, Victoria: Dominion Press for Penguin.

Bunch, C. (1978) 'Lesbians in Revolt' pp. 135–39 in A. M. Jaggar and P. R. Struhl eds. *Feminist Frameworks* N.Y.: McGraw Hill.

Burgess, E.W. (1926) 'The Family as a Unity of Interacting Personalities' *The Family*, 7: pp. 3–9.

Burns, A. and Goodnow, J. (1979) *Children and Families in Australia* Sydney: George Allen and Unwin.

Burton, C. (1979) 'Women-Marriage in Africa: A Critical Study for Sex-Role Theory' *The Australian and New Zealand Journal of Sociology* 15, 2 (July): pp. 65–71.

Cartwright, A. and Jeffries, M. (1958) 'Married Women Who Work: Their Own and Their Children's Health' *British Journal of Preventative Medicine* 12, 4 (Oct.): pp. 159–71.

Cass, B. (1976) 'The Australian Woman's Home is Her Factory (or Cottage Industry)' Paper delivered at S.A.A.N.Z. Conference La Trobe University, August.

Cass, B. (1977) 'Family' pp. 138–75 in A. F. Davies et al. eds. *Australian Society* Melbourne: Longman Cheshire (3rd edn.).

Cass, B. (1978) 'A Critical Evaluation of the Concept of Consumption in Urban Sociology'. Paper delivered at S.A.A.N.Z. Conference, Brisbane, May.

Cass, B. (1980) 'The Changing Nature of Dependence and the Concept of 'Family Policy': Some Interconnections' Paper delivered at a Conference on 'Poverty, Income Maintenance and Welfare in Australia in the 1980's' organised by the Institute of Applied Economic and Social Research 11–12 July, University of Melbourne.

Cass, B., and Resler, H. (1978) 'Some Thoughts on Reading Norman Blaikie's "The Meaning and Measurement of Occupational Prestige"' *The Australian and New Zealand Journal of Sociology* 14, 1 (February): pp. 78–81.

Chodorow, N. (1978) *The Reproduction of Mothering* Los Angeles, California: University of California Press.

Cohen, G. (1977) 'Absentee Husbands in Spiralist Families' *Journal of Marriage and the Family* 39, 3 (August): pp. 595–613.

Colliver, A.S. (1974) 'The Socio-economic Aspects of Family Life' pp. 47–65 in J. Krupinski and A. Stoller *The Family in Australia* Sydney: Pergamon.

Connell, R.W. (1974) 'You Can't Tell Them Apart Nowadays Can You?' *Search* 5, 12 (Jan–Feb): pp. 282–85.

Connell, R.W. (1979) 'The Concept of Role and What to do With It' *The Australian and New Zealand Journal of Sociology* 15, 3 (November): pp. 7–17.

Coser, L. (1977) 'George Simmel's Neglected Contribution to the Sociology of Women' *Signs* 2, 4 (Summer): pp. 868–77.

Curthoys, A. (1976) 'Men and Childcare in the Feminist Utopia' *Refractory Girl*, 10 (March): pp. 3–5.

Cutright, P. and Polonko, K. (1977) 'Areal Structure and Rates of Child-lessness Among American Wives' *Social Biology* 24, 1 (Spring): pp. 52–61.

Davidoff, L. et al. (1976) 'Landscape with Figures: Home and Community in English Society' pp. 139–75 in J. Mitchell and A. Oakley eds. *The Rights and Wrongs of Women* Harmondsworth, Middlesex, England: Penguin.

Davis, J.R. and Spearritt, P. (1974) *Sydney at the Census: 1971* Canberra: Urban Research Unit of the Australian National University.

Delphy, C. (1976) *The Main Enemy* London: Women's Research and Resource Centre Publications.

Dennis, N. et al. (1956) *Coal is Our Life* London: Tavistock.

Department of Labour and National Service (1968) *Women in the Work Force No. 5* October, 'Children of Working Mothers' Melbourne: Women's Bureau.

Dowick, S. and Grundberg, S. (1980) *Why Children?* Ringwood, Victoria: Penguin.

Eisenstein, Z. (1977) 'Constructing a Theory of Capitalist Patriarchy and Socialist Feminism' *The Insurgent Sociologist* 7, 3 (Summer): pp. 3–17.

Engels, F. (1942) *The Origin of the Family, Private Property and the State.* N.Y.: International Publishers.

Engels, F. (1968) 'The Transformation of the Family' pp. 45–47 in N. W. Bell and E. F. Vogel eds. *A Modern Introduction to the Family* N.Y.: The Free Press (rev. edn.).

English, B. (1973) 'Notes on a Conceptual Framework for the Study of the Australian Family' pp. 11–24 in *The Australian Family, Bulletin 1* December. Sydney: Family Research Unit, School of Social Work, University of N.S.W.

English, B. et al. (1978) *Families in Australia—A Profile* Sydney: Family Research Unit, University of N.S.W.

Fallding, H. (1957) 'Inside the Australian Family' pp. 54–81 in A. P. Elkin ed. *Marriage and the Family in Australia* Sydney: Angus and Robertson.

Fallding, H. (1961) 'A Cardinal Role' *Human Relations* 14, 4 (November): pp. 329–49.

Feld, S. (1963) 'Feelings of Adjustment' in F. I. Nye and I. W. Hoffman eds. *The Employed Mother in America* Chicago: Rand McNally.

Feree, M. (1976a) 'The Confused American Housewife' *Psychology Today* 10, 4: pp. 76–80.

Feree, M. (1976b) 'Working Class Jobs: Housework and Paid Work as Sources of Satisfaction' *Social Problems* 23 (April): pp. 431–41.

Firestone, S. (1970) *The Dialectic of Sex. The Case for the Feminist Revolution* London: Jonathan Cape.

Frankenberg, F. (1976) 'In the Production of Their Lives' pp. 23–48 in S. Allen and D. L. Barker eds. *Sexual Divisions and Society: Process and Change* London: Tavistock.

Freeman, J. (1975) *The Politics of Women's Liberation* N.Y. David McKay.

Friedan, B. (1963) *The Feminine Mystique* London: Victor Gollancz.

Game, A. and Pringle, R. (1979) 'Sexuality and the Suburban Dream' *The*

210   Ideology of motherhood

Australian and New Zealand Journal of Sociology 15, 2 (July): pp. 4–15.

Gardiner, J. (1976) 'Political Economy of Domestic Labour in Capitalist Society' pp. 109–20 in D. L. Barker and S. Allen eds. *Dependence and Exploitation in Work and Marriage* London: Longman.

Gavron, H. (1966) *The Captive Wife* Harmondsworth, Middlesex, England: Penguin.

Geiger, H.K. (1968) 'The Fate of the Family in Soviet Russia: 1917–1944' pp. 48–67 in N. W. Bell and E. F. Vogel, *A Modern Introduction to the Family* N.Y.: The Free Press (rev. edn.).

Gerth, H.H. and Mills, C.W. (1948) *From Weber: Essays in Sociology* N.Y.: Routledge and Kegan Paul.

Giddens, A. (1973) *The Class Structure of the Advanced Societies* London: Hutchinson.

Glueck, E. and Glueck, S. (1957) 'Working Mothers and Delinquency' *Mental Hygiene*, 41, 1, p. 3.

Goffman, E. (1963) *Stigma: Notes on the Management of Spoiled Identity* Harmondsworth, Middlesex, England: Penguin.

Goldthorpe, J.H. et al. (1971) *The Affluent Worker. Volume 3* Cambridge: Cambridge University Press.

Goode, W.J. (1963) *World Revolutions and Family Patterns* N.Y.: The Free Press.

Goode, W.J. (1968) 'Pressures to Remarry—Institutionalised Patterns Affecting the Divorced' pp. 331–41 in N. W. Bell and E. F. Vogel, *A Modern Introduction to the Family* N.Y.: The Free Press (rev. edn.).

Grabiner, V.E. and Cooper, L.B. (1973) 'Towards a Theoretical Orientation for Understanding Sexism' *The Insurgent Sociologist* 4, 1 (Fall): pp. 3–14.

Gray, A. (1979) 'The Working Class Family as an Economic Unit' pp. 186–231 in C. C. Harris et al. eds. *The Sociology of the Family: New Directions for Britain* Keele, Staffordshire: University of Keele.

Harper, J. (1980) *Fathers at Home* Blackburn, Victoria: Dominion Press for Penguin.

Harper, J. and Richards, L. (1979) *Mothers and Working Mothers* Nth Blackburn, Victoria: The Dominion Press for Penguin.

Harris, C.C. (1969) *The Family* London: George Allen and Unwin.

Harris, C.C. et al. eds. (1979) *The Sociology of the Family: New Directions for Britain* Keele Staffordshire: University of Keele.

Harrison, J. (1973) 'The Political Economy of Housework' *Bulletin of the Conference of Socialist Economists* 4 (Winter): pp. 135–51.

Heer, D.M. (1964) 'Dominance and the Working Wife' pp. 115–23 in W. J. Goode ed. *Readings on the Family and Society* New Jersey: Prentice Hall.

Herbst, P.G. (1954) 'Family Living—Patterns of Interaction' pp. 164–79 in O. A. Oeser and S. B. Hammond eds. *Social Structure and Personality in a City* London: Routledge and Kegan Paul.

Hill, R. and Hansen, D.A. (1963) 'The Identification of Conceptual Frameworks Utilised in Family Study' pp. 494–507 in M. B. Sussman ed. *Sourcebook in Marriage and the Family* Boston: Houghton Mifflin (2nd edn.).

Hoffman, L.W. (1960) 'Effects of the Employment of Mothers on Parental

Power Relations and the Division of Household Tasks' *Journal of Marriage and Family Living* 12, 1 (Feb.): pp. 27–35.

Hoffman, L.W. (1975) 'Effects on Child' pp. 126–66 in L. W. Hoffman and F. I. Nye, *Working Mothers* San Francisco: Jossey-Bass.

Hoffman, L.W. and Nye, F.I. (1975) *Working Mothers* San Francisco. Jossey-Bass.

Huber, J. (1976) 'Review Essay—Sociology' *Signs* 1, 3 (Spring): pp. 695–97.

Jaggar, A.M. and Struhl, P.R. eds. (1978) *Feminist Frameworks* N.Y.: McGraw-Hill.

James, K. (1979a) 'The Home: A Private or Public Place? Class, Status and the Actions of Women' *The Australian and New Zealand Journal of Sociology* 15, 1 (March): pp. 36–42.

James, K. (1979b) 'Kin, Friends and Neighbours: Bilateral Kinship, Class and Status in Two Parishes in Rural Devon, England' unpublished paper.

Kagan, J. (1969) 'Continuity of Cognitive Development During the First Year' *Merrill-Palmer Quarterly* 15: pp. 101–19.

Kelly, E. (1974) 'Sociological Aspects of Family Life' pp. 18–30 in J. Krupinski and A. Stoller eds. *The Family in Australia* Sydney: Pergamon.

Kelly-Gadol, J. (1975–76) Book Review of Sheila Rowbotham's 'Women's Consciousness, Man's World' *Science and Society*, 39: pp. 471–74.

Kelly-Gadol, J. (1976) 'The Social Relation of the Sexes: Methodological Implications of Women's History' *Signs*, 1, 4: pp. 809–923.

Kingston, B. (1975) *My Wife, My Daughter and Poor Mary Ann* West Melbourne: Nelson.

Klein, J. (1965) *Samples from English Cultures, Volume II* London: Routledge and Kegan Paul.

Komarovsky, M. (1962) *Blue-Collar Marriage* N.Y.: Vintage Books, Random House.

Krupinski, J. and Stoller, A. eds. (1974) *The Family in Australia* Sydney: Pergamon.

Kuhn, A. (1978) 'Structures of Patriarchy and Capital in the Family' pp. 42–67 in A. Kuhn and A. Wolpe eds. *Feminism and Materialism* London: Routledge and Kegan Paul.

Land, H. (1980) 'The Boundaries Between the State and the Family' pp. 141–57 in C. C. Harris et al. eds. *The Sociology of the Family: New Directions for Britain* Keele, Staffordshire: University of Keele.

La Rossa, R. (1977) *Conflict and Power in Marriage (Expecting the First Child)* Beverley Hills: Sage.

Laudicina, E.V. (1973) 'Towards New Forms of Liberation: A Mildly Utopian Proposal' *Social Theory and Practice* 2, 3 (Spring): pp. 275–88.

Lawrence, R.J. (1972) 'Social Welfare and Urban Growth' pp. 100–28 in R. S. Parker and P. N. Troy eds. *The Politics of Urban Growth* Canberra: Australian National University Press.

Lefebvre, H. (1968) *The Sociology of Marx.* London: Allen Lane, the Penguin Press.

Littlejohn, J. (1963) *Westrigg* London: Routledge and Kegan Paul.

Lofland, L. (1975) 'The Thereness of Women: A Selective Review of Urban

Sociology' pp. 144–70 in M. Millman and R. Moss Kanter eds., *Another Voice* N.Y.: Anchor Books.

Lopata, H.Z. (1966–67) 'The Life-Cycle of the Social Role of the Housewife' *Sociology and Social Research* 51 (October) pp. 5–22.

Lopata, H.Z. (1971) *Occupation Housewife* N.Y.: Oxford University Press.

Lukes, S. (1973) *Individualism* Oxford: Basil Blackwell.

Lukes, S. (1974) *Power: A Radical View* London: Macmillan.

Lukes, S. (1977) *Essays in Social Theory* London: Macmillan.

Lynd, R.S. and Lynd, H.M. (1937) *Middletown in Transition* N.Y.: Harcourt Brace.

McCaughey, J. et al. (1977) *Who Cares?* Melbourne: Sun Books.

McGregor, C. (1975) 'What Counter Culture?' pp. 15–17 in M. Smith and D. Crossley eds. *The Way Out* Lansdowne Press.

McKinley, R. (1964) *Social Class and Family Life* N.Y.: The Free Press.

Mannheim, K. (1936) *Ideology and Utopia* London: Routledge and Kegan Paul.

Marsden, D. (1969) *Mothers Alone* London: Allen Lane.

Martin, J.I. (1957) 'Marriage and the Family and Class' pp. 25–53 in A. P. Elkin ed. *Marriage and the Family in Australia* Sydney: Angus and Robertson.

Martin, J.I. (1967) 'Extended Kinship Ties: An Adelaide Study' *The Australian and New Zealand Journal of Sociology*, 3 (April): pp. 44–63.

Marx, K. (1947) *The German Ideology* N.Y. International Publishers.

Marx, K. and Engels, F. (1970) *The German Ideology, Part One* Edited with an Introduction by C. J. Arthur. N.Y.: International Publishers.

Mason, K.D. et al. (1976) 'Change in U.S. Sex Role Attitudes 1964–1974' *American Sociological Review* 41, 1 (August): pp. 574–96.

Mead, M. (1962) *Male and Female: A Study of the Sexes in a Changing World* Harmondsworth, Middlesex, England: Penguin.

Mead, M. (1973) 'Marriage and the Family' Monday Conference, Australian Broadcasting Commission, June 4.

Mercer, J. ed. (1975) *The Other Half* Blackburn, Victoria: Penguin Books.

Millet, K. (1971) *Sexual Politics* London: Abacus.

Mitchell, J. (1971) *Women's Estate* Harmondsworth, Middlesex, England: Penguin.

Molyneux, M. (1979) 'Beyond the Housework Debate' *New Left Review* 116 (July–August): pp. 3–27.

Moore, T. (1963) 'Effects on the Children' pp. 105–24 in Yudkin and H. Holme eds. *Working Mothers and Their Children* London: Michael Joseph.

Morgan, D.H.J. (1975) *Social Theory and the Family* London: Routledge and Kegan Paul.

Morgan, D.H.J. (1980) 'New Directions in Family Research and Theory' pp. 3–18 in C. C. Harris et al. eds. *The Sociology of the Family: New Directions for Britain* Keele, Staffordshire: University of Keele.

Moss, H.A. (1967) 'Sex, Age and State as Determinants of Mother-Infant Interaction' *Merrill-Palmer Quarterly*, 13: pp. 19–36.

Movius, M. (1976) 'Voluntary Childlessness—the Ultimate Liberation' *The Family Coordinator* 25, 1: pp. 57–63.

Myrdal, A. and Klein, V. (1956) *Women's Two Roles (Home and Work)* London: Routledge and Kegan Paul.

Newson, J. and Newson, E. (1968) *Four Years Old in an Urban Community* London: George Allen and Unwin.

Nye, F.I. and Berado, E.M. (1963) *The Employed Mother in America* Chicago: Rand McNally.

Nye, F.I. and Berado, E.M. (1966) *Emerging Conceptual Frameworks in Family Analysis* N.Y.: Macmillan.

Oakley, A. (1974a) *Housewife* Harmondsworth, Middlesex, England: Penguin.

Oakley, A. (1974b) *The Sociology of Housework* London: Martin Robertson.

Oakley, A. (1979) *Becoming a Mother* Oxford: Martin Robertson.

O'Leary, V.E. and Depner, C.E. (1976) 'Alternative Gender Roles Among Women: Masculine, Feminine, Androgenous' *Intellect* 104, 313, 5 (January): pp. 313–15.

Osmond, M.W. and Martin, P.Y. (1978) 'A Contingency Model of Marital Organisation in Low Income Families' *Journal of Marriage and the Family* 40, 2: pp. 315–29.

Oxley, H.G. (1978) *Mateship in Local Organisation* Brisbane: University of Queensland Press (2nd edn.).

Parsons, T.P. (1954) *Essays in Sociological Theory* N.Y.: The Free Press.

Parsons, T. and Bales, R.F. (1955) *Family: Socialisation and Interaction Process* London: Routledge and Kegan Paul.

Paloma, M.P. and Garland, T.N. (1971) 'The Married Professional Woman: A Study in the Tolerance of Domestication' *Journal of Marriage and the Family* (August): pp. 531–40.

Rainwater, L. et al. (1959) *Workingman's Wife. Her Personality, World and Life Style* N.Y.: Oceana.

Rapoport, R. and Rapoport, R. (1972) 'The Dual Career Family: A Variant Pattern and Social Change' pp. 216–44 in C. Safilios Rothschild ed. *Toward a Sociology of Women* Lexington/Massachusetts/Toronto: Xerox.

Rapoport, R. et al. (1977) *Fathers, Mothers and Others* St. Lucia: University of Queensland Press.

Reed, E. (1978) 'Women: Caste; Class or Oppressed Sex?' pp. 119–29 in A. M. Jaggar and P. R. Struhl eds. *Feminist Frameworks* N.Y.: McGraw Hill.

Richards, L. (1978) *Having Families* Ringwood, Victoria: Penguin.

Rodman, H. (1965) 'Talcott Parsons' View of a Changing American Family' pp. 281–83 in H. Rodman ed. *Marriage, Family and Society* N.Y.: Random House.

Rossi, A. (1972) 'Sex Equality: The Beginnings of Ideology' pp. 344–53 in C. Safilios-Rothschild ed. *Towards a Sociology of Women* Lexington/Massachusetts/Toronto: Xerox.

Rowbotham, S. (1973) *Woman's Consciousness, Man's World* Harmondsworth, Middlesex, England: Penguin.

214   *Ideology of motherhood*

Rowe, G.P. (1966) 'Developmental Conceptual Framework to the Study of the Family' pp. 199–222 in F. I. Nye and F. M. Berado *Emerging Conceptual Frameworks in Family Analysis* N.Y.: Macmillan.

Rowse, T. (1978) *Australian Liberalism and National Character* Malmsbury, Vic.: Kibble Books.

Rozaldo, M.Z. and Lamphere, L. eds. (1974) *Woman, Culture and Society* California: Stanford University Press.

Rubenstein, D. (1977) *How the Russian Revolution Failed Women* Somerville, Massachusetts: New England Free Press.

Runciman, W.G. (1966) *Relative Deprivation and Social Justice* London: Routledge and Kegan Paul.

Rushton, P. (1980) 'Marxism, Domestic Labour and the Capitalist Economy: A Note on Recent Discussions' pp. 32–48 in C. C. Harris et al. eds. *The Sociology of the Family: New Directions for Britain* Keele, Staffordshire: University of Keele.

Russell, G. (1979) 'Fathers! Incompetent or Reluctant Parents?' *The Australian and New Zealand Journal of Sociology* 15, 1 (March): pp. 57–65.

Russell, G. (1980) 'Fathers as Caregivers' *Australian Journal of Sex, Marriage and Family* 1, 3: pp. 101–10.

Ruzicka, L.T. and Caldwell, J.C. (1977) *The End of the Demographic Transition in Australia* Canberra: Australian National University.

Safilios-Rothschild, C. (1967) 'A Comparison of Power Structure and Marital Satisfaction in Urban Greek and French Families' *Journal of Marriage and the Family* 29: pp. 345–52.

Safilios-Rothschild, C. (1969) 'Family Sociology or Wive's Family Sociology? A Cross-Cultural Examination of Decision Making' *Journal of Marriage and the Family* 31 (May): pp. 291–302.

Safilios-Rothschild, C. (1970) 'A Study of Family Power Structure: A Review 1960–1969' *Journal of Marriage and the Family* 32, 4: pp. 539–52.

Sandercock, L. (1975) *Cities for Sale* Melbourne: Melbourne University Press.

Schvaneveldt, J.D. (1966) 'The Interactional Framework in the Study of the Family' pp. 97–129 in F. I. Nye and F. M. Berardo *Emerging Conceptual Frameworks in Family Analysis* N.Y.: Macmillan.

Scott, H. (1976) *Women and Socialism* London: Allison and Busby.

Seccombe, W. (1974) 'The Housewife and Her Labour Under Capitalism' *New Left Review*, 83: pp. 3–24.

Seeley, J. et al. (1956) *Crestwood Heights* Toronto: University of Toronto Press.

Sharp, L.J. and Nye, F.I. (1963) 'Maternal Mental Health' pp. 309–19 in F. I. Nye and L. W. Hoffman *The Employed Mother in America* Chicago: Rand McNally.

Shaver, S. (1977) 'The Caretaker Network' pp. 165–290 in J. McCaughey et al. *Who Cares?* Melbourne: Sun Books.

Simmell, G. (1936) *Conflict. The Web of Group Affiliations* N.Y.: The Free Press (Translated by Reinhard Bendix.)

Sinclair, G. (1979) *I Only Work Here* Sydney: Holt, Rinehart and Winston.

Smith, P. (1978) 'Domestic Labour and Marx's Theory of Value' pp. 198–219 in A. Kuhn and A. Wolpe eds. *Feminism and Materialism*. London: Routledge and Kegan Paul.

Spitz, R.A. (1945) 'Hospitalisation: An Inquiry into the Genesis of Psychiatric Conditions in Early Childhood' *Psycho Analytic Studies of the Child* 1: pp. 53–74.

Sprey, J. (1969) 'The Family as a System in Conflict' *Journal of Marriage and the Family* (November): pp. 699–708.

Stilwell, F.J.B. and Hardwick, J.M. (1973) 'Social Inequality in Australian Cities' *The Australian Quarterly* 45, 4 (December): pp. 18–36.

Stilwell, J.B. (1980) *Economic Crisis, Cities and Regions* Sydney: Pergamon.

Stivens, M. (1978) 'Women and Their Kin: Kin, Class and Solidarity in a Middle Class Suburb of Sydney, Australia' pp. 157–84 in P. Caplan and J. M. Bujra eds. *Women United, Women Divided* London: Tavistock.

Stoller, A. (1974) 'Posing the Problem' pp. 1–4 in J. Krupinski and A. Stoller *The Family in Australia* Sydney: Pergamon.

Stretton, H. (1970) *Ideas for Australian Cities* Adelaide: The Griffin Press.

Stryker, S. (1966) 'Symbolic Interaction as an Approach to Family Research' pp. 24–32 in B. Farber ed. *Kinship and Family Organisation* N.Y.: John Wiley.

Summers, A. (1975) *Damned Whores and God's Police* Blackburn, Victoria: The Dominion Press for Penguin.

Theorson, G. and Theorson, A. (1969) *A Modern Dictionary of Sociology* N.Y.: Thomas Y. Crowell.

Turner, R. (1970) *Family Interaction* N.Y.: John Wiley.

Veevers, J.E. (1973) 'Voluntary Childless Wives: An Exploratory Study' *Sociology and Social Research* 57, 3 (April): pp. 356–66.

Warner, W.L. et al. (1949) *Social Class in America* Chicago: Science Research Associates Inc.

Wearing, B. (1976) 'The Loss of the Motherhood Role in the Middle-Life Period of Women' Unpublished Litt.B. Thesis, University of New England, Armidale, N.S.W.

Weber, M. (1947) *The Theory of Social and Economic Organisation* Glencoe: The Free Press (Translated by A.M. Anderson and T. Parsons.)

Weber, M. (1949) *The Methodology of the Social Sciences* N.Y.: The Free Press. (Translated and edited by E. A. Shils and H. A. Finch.)

White, B. (1975) *The First Three Years of Life* Englewood Cliffs, New Jersey: Prentice Hall.

Wild, R. (1974) *Bradstow* Sydney: Angus and Robertson.

Wild, R. (1978) *Social Stratification in Australia* Sydney: George Allen and Unwin.

Williams, C. (1976) 'Working Class Women in an Australian Mining Town' *Hecate*, 2, 1: pp. 7–21.

Williams, C. (1981) *Open Cut* Sydney: Allen and Unwin.

Women's Bureau Department of Employment and Youth Affairs. (1979) *Facts on Women at Work in Australia in 1978* Canberra: Australian Government Publishing Service.

Wright, J.D. (1978) '"Are Working Women Really More Satisfied".

Evidence From Several National Surveys' *Journal of Marriage and the Family* 40, 1 (May): pp. 301–13.
Young, M. and Willmott, P. (1957) *Family & Kinship in East London* Harmondsworth, Middlesex, England: Penguin.
Young, M. and Willmott, P. (1973) *The Symmetrical Family* London: Routledge and Kegan Paul.
Zelditch, M. (1955) 'Role Differentiation in the Nuclear Family' pp. 345–54 in T. Parsons and R. F. Bales *Family: Socialisation and Interaction Process* N.Y.: The Free Press.

Appendix 1

The operationalisation of social class

Giddens (1973:97) points out that Marx' abstract dichotomous model of class in which the bourgeoisie are those who possess and accumulate capital while the proletariat are the mass of propertyless workers who sell their labour power to the former, has theoretical and explanatory power but is not easy to reconcile at the empirical level with the complicated structure of actual forms of society. Giddens develops an empirical scheme which uses the Marxian dichotomy between capital and wage labour as a point of departure but includes the Weberian notion of 'marketable skill' as a means of differentiating between the propertylessness of the Marxian scheme.

The term 'market capacity' is used by Giddens (1973:103) to refer to 'all forms of relevant attributes which individuals may bring to the bargaining encounter' of the market place. Giddens proceeds to develop a scheme whereby the 'economic' relationships of the Marxian and Weberian schemes are translated into 'the structuration of class relationships' which include non-economic social structures. He distinguishes between 'mediate' and 'proximate' structuration. Mediate structuration depends on the degree to which mobility closure exists in relation to any specified form of market capacity. Giddens (1973:107) claims,

> There are three sorts of market capacity which can be said to be normally of importance in this respect: ownership of property in the means of production; possession of educational or technical qualifications; and possession of manual labour-power. Insofar as it is the case that these tend to be tied to closed patterns of inter and intra-generational mobility this yields the foundation of a *basic three class system* in capitalist society: an 'upper', 'middle' and 'lower' or 'working' class.

Proximate structuration can reinforce the above class structuration or can fragment class relationships. Giddens gives three sources of proximate structuration in capitalist societies: the division of labour within the productive enterprise; the authority relationships within the enterprise; and the influence of distributive groupings. The division of labour due to industrial technique he sees as creating a decisive separation between the conditions of labour of manual and non-manual workers in physically separated areas. This division

217

is reinforced by the authority system. 'Insofar as the administrative workers participate in the framing or merely in the enforcement of authoritative commands, they tend to be separated from manual workers who are subject to those commands' (Giddens, 1973:108). In addition 'distributive groupings', that is, those relationships involving common patterns of the consumption of economic goods (regardless of whether individuals make any conscious evaluation of their prestige relative to others) tend to reinforce the typical separations between forms of market capacity. The most significant distributive groupings in this respect are those formed through the tendency towards neighbourhood segregation. Such a tendency is not normally based only on differentials in income, but also upon such factors as access to housing mortgages, etc.

Giddens concludes that the conditions of the sources of mediate and proximate structuration as he distinguishes them, create a threefold class structure which is generic to capitalist society.

In applying Giddens' scheme to Australian conditions Wild (1978:174–75) shows that in spite of increasing complexity due to proliferation of the middle class propertyless white-collar employee, reduction of the independent middle class, expansion of the professions, increasing power of the state and bureaucratic rationalisation of production and administration, the three class system is still basic to Australian social organisation.

Wild describes an upper class, a middle class and a working class. The middle class he identifies as propertyless (i.e., lacking income—producing property), non-manual or white-collar workers whose market capacity arises from educational and technical qualifications. Qualifications and expertise thus characterise the middle class who are separated from the working class along the manual/non-manual cleavage. The working class he identifies as propertyless manual workers whose market capacity arises from their ability to sell their labour in the market place in return for wages.

For this particular research, in principle, Giddens' and Wild's three class structuration of society based on the Weberian concept of market capacity is adopted. The boundary between the middle and working class is defined by qualifications and expertise on the one hand and labour power on the other. However, it is recognised that white-collar workers are not automatically part of the middle class, their position depending on Giddens' proximate structuration as evidenced by conditions of work, relations of authority and distributive groupings. In order to incorporate Giddens' notion of proximate, as well as mediate structuration of class and his emphasis on class as a social group, residential area, rather than husband's occupation, has been chosen as the indice of family social class for the two parent families of the research. Two areas have been chosen, one predominantly middle class, the other working class. In the middle class area husband's market capacity depends on managerial and professional qualifications and expertise or ownership of a small business (both Wild and Giddens include the petit bourgeoisie in the middle class due to income, authority and conditions of work which are closer to those of the managers and professionals than to those of large scale owners of property in the means of production). In addition, such market capacity has enabled the family to obtain a mortgage on high cost housing and to achieve patterns of consumption and life-style which have much in common. In the working class area, husband's market capacity depends on skilled or unskilled manual labour or minimally skilled clerical and sales labour. Such market capacity has enabled the family only to rent accommodation or to obtain mortgages on low cost Housing Commission or private houses. Consumption patterns and life-style in this area are very different from those of the middle class area.

In common with previous male devisers of class schemes, both Wild and Giddens see women until liberated from the family as largely 'peripheral to the class system' (Giddens, 1973:288), 'the underclass of the white-collar sector' (Giddens, 1973:288; Wild, 1978:174), and so continue to subsume the position of women under male class categories, thus obscuring their own unique position in the class structuration of society. The husband's market capacity does not entirely explain social class influence on mothers in two parent families and is even less relevant for mother-headed families. An attempt has been made, therefore, in addition to the family's class position to view the mother in the family, whether two parent or one parent, as having her own unique position in the class structuration of society, based on her own social class background and present market capacity.

Appendix 2
Methodology

Pilot and group interviews and testing the interview schedule

For the purposes of developing an interview schedule, eight unstructured pilot interviews were carried out in March 1977, six in a middle class residential area and two in a working class area. As the interviews progressed, open-ended questions were formulated and added to, in order to build up a series of questions which would tap the ideology of motherhood. So that greater perspective could be gained, with the possibility of a variety of viewpoints and interaction other than that between interviewer and respondent, a number of small group interviews were also conducted. Four were in a middle class residential area and two in a working class residential area. Five to ten mothers were present and groups included play groups, neighbourhood groups and a tennis club.

Using the questions found to be most useful for probing the ideology of motherhood from the above interviews an interview schedule was drawn up. The schedule also sought to gather information concerning the mother's ideas on sex roles, her social contacts and networks, background information, her self-concepts and her general satisfactions with life. Open-ended questions were used in the schedule, some taken from the group and individual interviews conducted, some adapted from schedules used by previous researchers such as Hannah Gavron (1966:160–64) and Ann Oakley (1974:208–19) and some are questions which I had found helpful in my previous research (Wearing, 1976) with older mothers.

The interview schedule was tested with mothers of differing educational level and social class backgrounds to make sure the questions could be comprehended by a variety of respondents. One middle class mother with education at undergraduate level, one middle class mother with School Certificate plus secretarial training and three working class mothers with educational level below School Certificate were interviewed to test the schedule. The interview schedule revised after these interviews was the one adopted for the research. Details of this schedule are given in the doctoral thesis entitled 'The Ideology of Motherhood' upon which the material in this book is based.

The sample

A preliminary examination of the occupational maps in Davis and Spearrit (1974: maps 1 and 2) revealed that the Upper North Shore has a high concentration of male professional, technical, administrative, executive and managerial workers, whereas Mt Druitt has a high concentration of male workers in semi and unskilled manual occupations. Mt Druitt has the added characteristic for the purposes of the research of being one of the few working class areas in the Sydney Metropolitan area which does not have a high concentration of non-Australian born migrants. Discussions with initial contacts in each area revealed that differences in housing costs and the availability of rented accommodation are marked differences in the areas as are consumption patterns and styles of life. In recent years private developers have built tracts of private housing in some Mt Druitt suburbs and these command a higher price than the Housing Commission houses previously built. Nevertheless clerical and sales people attracted to these houses have weaker market capacity than white-collar workers in the Upper North Shore area in terms of qualifications and expertise, job security and access to housing mortgages, etc. Mt Druitt, as far as social class of the family is concerned represents a working class residential area and the Upper North Shore a middle class area.

For a detailed description of the two areas chosen to represent social class in the research see Appendix 3.

The social class of the mothers with whom the research is concerned however is not entirely dependent upon husband's market capacity and this is especially so for the single and employed mothers in the sample. Nor can it be defined exclusively by residential area, in spite of the foregoing arguments. The woman's own social class background according to parents' market capacity and her own present market capacity is therefore taken into consideration in analysis of data as well as the general social class position of the family according to residential area.

A randon sample was not possible in the Mt Druitt area where interviewing commenced in August 1977. Due to the number of other surveys already conducted in the area, the high incidence of door-to-door salespeople and the general distrust of the 'door-knocker', key informants suggested that the rate of refusal would be very high unless recommendation of the researcher was made to the interviewee by a person known and trusted by her. The snowball technique was therefore adopted and maintained for the whole of the sample. Initial introductions into the areas studied were given by trusted personnel in the areas such as social workers, community health personnel, leaders of mother's groups and a clergyman. Each mother interviewed was then asked if she could recommend other mothers who might be interviewed. Using this technique no direct refusals were experienced by the researcher.

In some cases identification of the researcher with 'official' personnel produced responses which were thought or known to be acceptable to that person and health workers tended to suggest mothers they judged to be 'good' mothers. However as socially acceptable attitudes rather than behaviour were being sought, these biases helped to build up a picture of what constitutes acceptable motherhood in that particular milieu. For example, in the Mt Druitt area mothers who belonged to the Emerton Community Centre Play Groups stressed explicitly that motherhood is a very demanding and difficult job while also being very important and worthwhile. In this they followed the precepts of the Community Social Worker who led the groups. This aspect of the ideology was found however to be implicitly suggested by the majority of mothers in the area, so that it helped to build up a picture of the acceptable social definition of the job in that milieu.

In the main mothers tended to suggest other mothers similar to themselves, so that mothers with different views could have been excluded from the sample and no claim is made that the sample is random. Strictly speaking the results of the research apply only to the 150 mothers interviewed.

Interviews were carried out between August 1977 and May 1979. Where possible interviews were conducted in the home so that mothers were in familiar surroundings. In most cases the child or children were present and in some cases a neighbour, friend, husband or mother was also in the house and contributed to the interview. Interactions between those present were observed and notes made of information given both before and after the taped interviews. All interviews except two were taped; these two respondents felt threatened by the tape and expressed a preference for notes being taken. All interviews have been replayed in full and all important information (including relevant digressions) transcribed. Some editing, for example of redundant phrases such as 'you know', 'sort of' has been carried out in the transcription. Interviews lasted from three-quarters of an hour to four hours, the average interview being one and a half hours.

The research

Initially the research set out on an exploratory basis to seek to discover the tenets of the ideology of motherhood as held by Australian-born mothers in two parent families in suburban settings which varied in terms of social class. After analysis of the first 50 interviews and development of the concepts of ideology and utopia, the propositions of the research were formulated and more specific groups of mothers included.

The final sample of 150 respondents has been made up in the following way:

1   Seventy-five mothers not employed outside the home, living in a two parent relationship. Fifty of these live in a working class area and twenty-five live in a middle class area (Mt Druitt and Upper North Shore respectively).
2   Twenty-five mothers living in a two parent relationship, employed on at least three days per week outside the home. These mothers are drawn from a cross section of social classes. Many were suggested by the respondents in group 1 and live in Mt. Druitt or the Upper North Shore, or in nearby suburbs.

3   Twenty-five mothers bringing up their children in a one parent family, that is the mother has never been married or is separated, divorced or widowed. These mothers are also drawn from a cross section of social classes. Most of them are friends of groups 1 and 2 but some were contacted through social workers at Mt Druitt and a clergyman and social workers in the Hornsby area which covers parts of the Upper North Shore as well as other middle class areas.

4   Twenty-five mothers who are actively associated with a feminist group. Previous contacts yielded only one feminist respondent, the publicity officer for Women's Electoral Lobby in the Hornsby area. She was the means of contacting four other W.E.L. members who also live in the northern suburbs. An introduction into the inner city areas of Glebe, Balmain, Leichhardt and Annandale by a student in a women's study course proved to be fruitful. A network of feminist mothers was found in this area with extensions to Hunter's Hill and North Sydney. These respondents were engaged in teaching, studying women's study courses, belonged to a consciousness raising group, a feminist based children's co-operative or worked in a women's refuge. The physical surroundings of the inner-city area of Glebe, Balmain, Leichhardt and Annandale are very different from either the Upper North Shore or Mt Druitt and a different life-style is evident here, due to recent class changes in the area. For a description of this area, see Appendix 3.

All interviews were carried out by the researcher herself. This has ensured consistency in interviewing and interpretation and avoided misinterpretation of the questions, nevertheless it also has certain disadvantages. As Hannah Gavron (1966:159) points out the main disadvantage of the interviewer who is also the author of the research is that the very expectations which led to the formulation of the research may determine some of the responses given. In circumstances such as these she suggests it is probably best to employ non-directive techniques. In this particular research open-ended questions and a flexible interview schedule have attempted to at least partially overcome this difficulty. In addition biases due to the researcher's own background and experience can be compounded when she is author, interviewer, analyser and interpreter. My own middle class background was at times a disadvantage. However the fact that I have five children appeared to be a positive factor in establishing rapport at the beginning of the interview, mothers related to me as a mother, rather than as a sociologist.

The non-random nature of the sample allows neither the use of probability statistics, nor the extrapolation of results to a universe wider than that of the sample obtained. Nevertheless there is no reason to believe that the suburban mothers interviewed are not representative of the particular groups which have been selected for the study and respondent's views are treated as illustrative of, for example, 'single mothers', 'employed mothers', etc. The advantages of the sampling method used for the research are in the low cost, the low rate of refusals, the trust and rapport established by recommendation by a friend or respected community worker and the evidence of female networks through which ideas are transmitted.

Within the sample the variety and depth of responses gives a dimension to the research which is felt to be important in understanding the tenets of the ideology of motherhood as held by suburban mothers and the effect such an ideology has on their lives. Such reports are regarded as vital evidence in research which is aimed at discovering how a particular ideology functions for its subjects.

Appendix 3

Description of residential areas relevant to the research

In a detailed statistical analysis of the Local Government Areas (L.G.As) of the Sydney Metropolitan Area, Stilwell and Hardwick (1973:21) using the 1966 census statistics show that the 'standard of living' indices represented by the average weekly rents of dwellings, ratio of white-collar to blue-collar workers, percentage of employers in the work-force, percentage of resident population with tertiary education, average number of persons per vehicle and the average number of persons per room of private dwellings, correlated highly within L.G.As and were also highly associated with perceived social status of the areas studied.

Although there are some changes since the 1966 census was taken, especially in the central area, Leichhardt in particular (which will be discussed presently), the pattern of social polarisation has remained. Some areas such as the far western area are consistently below average on a wide range of 'standard of living' indices, and other areas such as the northern and eastern suburbs are consistently above average. For example, in the two areas chosen to represent different social classes for the present research, that is, Mt Druitt which is part of the Blacktown L.G.A., a working class area and the Upper North Shore which is part of the Kuring-gai L.G.A., a middle class area, the figures calculated from the 1976 census reinforce those given by Stilwell and Hardwick (1973:22–23) using the 1966 census statistics.

Whereas the average number of persons per room in Blacktown L.G.A. in 1966 was 0.82 and Kuring-gai 0.55, in 1976 it was 0.70 and 0.48 respectively. In 1966 the average weekly rents for Blacktown L.G.A. were $9.76, for Kuring-gai $17.97; in 1976 the medians were $26.53 and $53.58 respectively and $28.52 for Australia. The percentage of employers in the work-force in Blacktown L.G.A. in 1966 was 2.60, in Kuring-gai 9.30; in 1976 the percentages were 1.66 and 7.40 respectively and 4.89 for Australia. In 1966 the percentage of the resident population with tertiary educational qualifications was 1.73 for Blacktown L.G.A. and 19.56 for Kuring-gai; in 1976 it was 1.68 and 19.66 respectively, and 6.03 for Australia. Another indice which Stilwell and Hardwick did not use but which is significant in the present context and which further demonstrates the discrepancy between living standard and more specifically 'market capacity' between Blacktown and Kuring-gai

225

residents is monthly mortgage repayments. In Blacktown L.G.A. in 1976 the median was $78.93, in Kuring-gai it was $144.26 and in Australia as a whole it was $98.15.

When the 'facilities of so-called 'collective consumption'' (Cass, 1978:2) provided by both the public and private sectors are examined in the two areas chosen to represent class differences in the research, further evidence is produced for social inequality between them. In Mt Druitt there is a lack of good roads, railway services and other public transport, tertiary educational institutions, hospitals, libraries, green spaces set aside for public recreation and playing fields normally provided by the public sector and of shopping centres, movie theatres, recreation centres, cafes and restaurants, normally provided by the private sector. On the Upper North Shore these facilities are easily accessible to the majority of residents.

Bettina Cass (1978:4) emphasises the particular relevance of spatial social class differentiation for women. She says,

The growth of suburbanisation in Australian cities like Sydney and Melbourne, did not only lead to spatial social class segregation, through the unequal distribution of desirable land and housing, the unequal distribution of housing in proximity to employment, and the unequal distribution of transport, health and educational facilities. It also gave an augmented spatial dimension to sex segregation: not only were women and their children relegated to their housing space . . . but the localities in which their housing space was situated became sex-segregated. In 'dormitory suburbs,' as they are so inappropriately (and masculinely) termed, men sleep, but women do the housework, take care of children, shop, oil the wheels of sociability by establishing new friendship networks, run the Mothers' Clubs and the school canteens, go to play groups, and sometimes bemoan their lack of employment opportunities.

For the present research then, the choice of residential area as an indice of social class appears to be particularly appropriate for non-employed mothers with pre-school children; the major part of their day being spent in their own locality and this is the area within which they experience their mothering.

The physical differences in the two areas chosen for the research are marked, and, not surprisingly in view of the foregoing discussion so are the life-styles. Mt Druitt lies on the outer western fringe of the Sydney Metropolitan area (see Figure App. 3.1). It is 30 miles from the city and is linked by a 60–65 minute rail or road journey. It covers 2800 acres with a rapidly increasing population (approximately 49 361, 1976 census). Development as a housing estate was commenced by the State Housing Commission in September 1965 and the first tender was completed in April 1966. At the time of the interviews dwellings totalled 11 362 of which 9800 had been built by the Housing Commission.[1]

The upper North Shore extends along the northern railway line from Roseville to Wahroonga (see Figure App. 3.1) and includes some of Sydney's old and stately homes as well as modern dwellings, many of which are architect designed. The boundaries of the area and hence the population are less well defined than the Mt Druitt area. The journey to the city by road or rail takes from 20–40 minutes from Roseville or Wahroonga respectively. Blocks of land are large with houses set well back, many being screened from the street and each other by trees and gardens. Streets are wide and tree lined. The Kuring-gai National Park borders these suburbs. The majority of houses are privately owned and owner occupied. Young marrieds who live in the area are either renovating older homes, or building new homes which encroach on the surrounding bush. Some of these young marrieds have grown up in the area, others have moved from the eastern suburbs or other northern suburbs and many are from interstate, the wives of spiralists. The cost and style of housing is one of the marked differences between the two areas, and is linked to the husband's market capacity and the type of housing loans, mortgages, etc. available to him.

Leichhardt local government area

Data from the 1966 census used by Stilwell and Hardwick (1973:22–23) showed the Leichhardt L.G.A. to be similar according to their 'standards of living' indices to Blacktown L.G.A. For example, the average number of persons per room was 0.82 for Blacktown L.G.A. and 0.67 for Leichhardt; average weekly rents $9.76 and $8.74 respectively; 2.60% of people in the work-force were employers in Blacktown L.G.A. and 2.03% in Leichhardt; 1.73% of residents had a tertiary education in Blacktown L.G.A. and 1.48% in Leichhardt. Data from the 1976 census shows however the following changes in Leichhardt L.G.A. compared with Blacktown. In 1976 the median weekly rent in Blacktown L.G.A. was $26.53, in Leichhardt $31.11; median monthly mortgage repayments in Blacktown L.G.A. were $78.93 and in Leichhardt $164.32. Percentage of employers in the work-force in Blacktown was 1.66% and in Leichhardt 3.06%. Percentage of residents with some tertiary qualification in Blacktown was 1.68% and in Leichhardt 8.07%. The entry of middle class professional people into the area is suggested by these figures.

The move of inner-city working class residents to areas like Mt. Druitt has been accompanied by the movement into inner-city areas by middle class professional and managerial people who are willing to pay for the privilege of access to the facilities of the city and of shortened travelling time to and from work. This 'gentrification' (Sandercock, 1975), has been accompanied by a change in the quality of housing, land and housing costs and life-styles in the area. This does not mean however that North Shore life-styles for example have been directly transposed to Leichhardt L.G.A. The area remains a mixture of older working class people, students and single parent families sharing housing and the middle class people who are moving in, some of whom are consciously attempting alternative life-styles guided by a variety of contemporary views on issues as diversified as conservation and feminism. The wife as well as the husband in the middle class families often has a professional job in the city, so that the young 'at home' mother of the two parent family is not a common feature here.

Appendix 3

Figure 3.1 Sydney Metropolitan area showing residential areas significant for this research

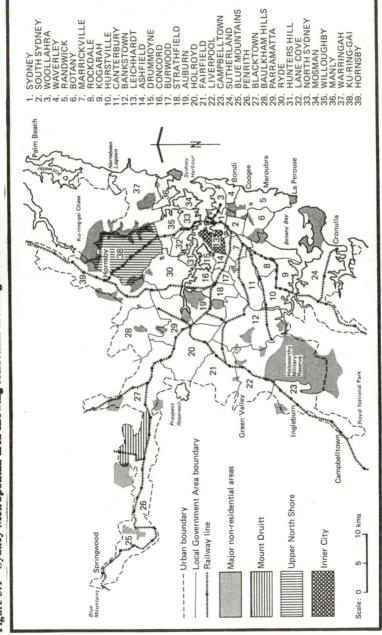

Legend:
- – – – – Urban boundary
- ——— Local Government Area boundary
- ++++++ Railway line

- Major non-residential areas
- Mount Druitt
- Upper North Shore
- Inner City

Scale: 0   5   10 kms

1. SYDNEY
2. SOUTH SYDNEY
3. WOOLLAHRA
4. WAVERLEY
5. RANDWICK
6. BOTANY
7. MARRICKVILLE
8. ROCKDALE
9. KOGARAH
10. HURSTVILLE
11. CANTERBURY
12. BANKSTOWN
13. LEICHHARDT
14. ASHFIELD
15. DRUMMOYNE
16. CONCORD
17. BURWOOD
18. STRATHFIELD
19. AUBURN
20. HOLROYD
21. FAIRFIELD
22. LIVERPOOL
23. CAMPBELLTOWN
24. SUTHERLAND
25. BLUE MOUNTAINS
26. PENRITH
27. BLACKTOWN
28. BAULKHAM HILLS
29. PARRAMATTA
30. RYDE
31. HUNTERS HILL
32. LANE COVE
33. NORTH SYDNEY
34. MOSMAN
35. WILLOUGHBY
36. MANLY
37. WARRINGAH
38. KU-RING-GAI
39. HORNSBY

Note Figures given here were obtained from the Bureau of Census and Statistics, Sydney, 1976: *Preliminary Characteristics, Summary Data*, and by telephone from the N.S.W. Housing Commission Head Office, Research Department on 25/1/78.

Appendix 4

Background tables

Table App. 4.1 Respondent's age by group

Group	Age		
	16–29 years No. (%)	30+ years No. (%)	Total No. (%)
Mt Druitt	34 (68)	16 (32)	50 (100)
Nth Shore	5 (20)	20 (80)	25 (100)
Single	9 (36)	16 (64)	25 (100)
Employed	8 (32)	17 (68)	25 (100)
Feminist	10 (40)	15 (60)	25 (100)
Total	66 (44)	84 (56)	150 (100)

Table App. 4.2 Respondent's age by ideal type

Ideal type	Age		
	16–29 years No. (%)	30+ years No. (%)	Total No. (%)
Ideological traditional	39 (54.17)	33 (45.83)	72 (100)
Ambivalent	13 (28.26)	33 (71.74)	46 (100)
Ambivalent progressive	14 (43.75)	18 (56.25)	32 (100)
Total	66 (44.00)	84 (56.00)	150 (100)

229

Table App. 4.3   Respondent's age at marriage by group

Group	Age at marriage[a]		
	16–24 years No. (%)	25+ years No. (%)	Total No. (%)
Mt Druitt	48 (96.00)	2 (4.00)	50 (100)
Nth Shore	19 (76.00)	6 (24.00)	25 (100)
Single	19 (86.36)	3 (13.64)	22 (100)[b]
Employed	22 (88)	3 (12.00)	25 (100)
Feminist	14 (70.00)	6 (30.00)	20 (100)[b]
Total	122 (85.92)	20 (14.08)	142 (100)

Notes: [a] Where respondent has been married more than once, age at first marriage is given.
[b] Three Single and five Feminist mothers have never married.

Table App. 4.4   Respondent's age at marriage by ideal type

Ideal type	Age at marriage		
	16–24 years No. (%)	25+ years No. (%)	Total No. (%)
Ideological traditional	65 (92.86)	5 (7.14)	70 (100)
Ambivalent	35 (79.55)	9 (20.45)	44 (100)
Ambivalent progressive	22 (78.57)	6 (21.43)	28 (100)
Total	122 (85.92)	20 (14.08)	142 (100)

Table App. 4.5   Age at birth of first child by group

Group	Age at birth of first child		
	16–24 years No. (%)	25+ years No. (%)	Total No. (%)
Mt Druitt	45 (90)	5 (10)	50 (100)
Nth Shore	10 (40)	15 (60)	25 (100)
Single	16 (64)	9 (36)	25 (100)
Employed	16 (64)	9 (36)	25 (100)
Feminist	11 (44)	14 (56)	25 (100)
Total	98 (65.33)	52 (34.67)	150 (100)

Table App. 4.6 Age at birth of first child by ideal type

Ideal type	Age at birth of first child		
	16–24 years No. (%)	25+ years No. (%)	Total No. (%)
Ideological traditional	61 (84.72)	11 (15.27)	72 (100)
Ambivalent	20 (43.47)	26 (56.52)	46 (100)
Ambivalent progressive	17 (53.13)	15 (46.87)	32 (100)
Total	98 (65.33)	52 (34.66)	150 (100)

Table App. 4.7 Respondent's mother's occupation by group

Group	Occupation			
	Managerial Professional Self-Employed	Clerical Sales	Skilled Unskilled Manual	Total
	No. (%)	No. (%)	No. (%)	No. (%)
Mt Druitt	3 (6.82)	14 (31.82)	27 (61.36)	44 (100)[a]
Nth Shore	4 (20.00)	15 (75.00)	1 (5.00)	20 (100)[a]
Single	3 (13.63)	10 (45.45)	9 (40.91)	22 (100)[a]
Employed	4 (23.53)	7 (41.18)	6 (35.29)	17 (100)[a]
Feminist	4 (16.00)	19 (76.00)	2 (8.00)	25 (100)
Total	18 (14.06)	65 (50.78)	45 (35.16)	128 (100)

Note: [a] Don't know and never employed have been omitted.

Table App. 4.8 Respondent's mother's occupation by ideal type

Ideal type	Occupation			
	Managerial Professional Self-Employed	Clerical Sales	Skilled Unskilled Manual	Total
	No. (%)	No. (%)	No. (%)	No. (%)
Ideological traditional	4 (6.45)	22 (35.48)	36 (58.06)	62 (100)[a]
Ambivalent	11 (29.73)	20 (54.05)	6 (16.21)	37 (100)[a]
Ambivalent progressive	3 (10.34)	23 (79.31)	3 (10.34)	29 (100)[a]
Total	18 (14.06)	65 (50.78)	45 (35.16)	128 (100)

Note: [a] Don't know and never employed have been omitted.

Table App. 4.9   Respondent's father's occupation by group

Group	Occupation			
	Managerial Professional Self-Employed	Clerical Sales	Skilled Unskilled Manual	Total
	No. (%)	No. (%)	No. (%)	No. (%)
Mt Druitt	1 (2.17)	7 (15.22)	38 (82.61)	46 (100)[a]
Nth Shore	20 (83.33)	2 (8.33)	2 (8.33)	24 (100)[a]
Single	8 (33.33)	5 (20.83)	11 (45.83)	24 (100)[a]
Employed	13 (52.00)	3 (12.00)	9 (36.00)	25 (100)[a]
Feminist	21 (84.00)	2 (8.00)	2 (8.00)	25 (100)
Total	63 (43.75)	19 (13.19)	62 (43.05)	144 (100)[a]

Note: [a] Don't know have been omitted.

Table App. 4.10   Respondent's father's occupation by ideal type

Ideal type	Occupation			
	Managerial Professional Self-Employed	Clerical Sales	Skilled Unskilled Manual	Total
	No. (%)	No. (%)	No. (%)	No. (%)
Ideological traditional	14 (21.21)	5 (7.58)	47 (71.2)	66 (100)[a]
Ambivalent	24 (52.17)	12 (26.09)	10 (21.74)	46 (100)
Ambivalent progressive	25 (78.13)	2 (6.25)	5 (15.62)	32 (100)
Total	63 (43.75)	19 (13.19)	62 (43.06)	144 (100)

Note: [a] Don't know have been omitted.

Table App. 4.11 Respondent's husband's occupation by group

Group	Managerial Professional Self-Employed	Clerical Sales	Unskilled Manual	Total
	No. (%)	No. (%)	No. (%)	No. (%)
Mt Druitt	3 (6.00)	14 (28.00)	33 (66.00)	50 (100)
Nth Shore	21 (84.00)	2 (8.00)	2 (8.00)	25 (100)
Employed	13 (32.00)	6 (24.00)	6 (24.00)	25 (100)
Feminist	11 (73.33)	3 (20.00)	1 (6.67)	15 (100)[a]
Total	48 (41.74)	25 (21.74)	42 (36.52)	115 (100)[a]

Notes: [a] Ten Feminist mothers are single.
[b] One husband is unemployed, one on worker's compensation; their usual occupation is indicated.
[c] One Nth Shore husband had a stroke which left him speechless and paralysed on one side. He is now a laboratory assistant, was formerly an electronics engineer.

Table App. 4.12 Respondent's husband's occupation by ideal type

Ideal type	Managerial Professional Self-Employed	Clerical Sales	Skilled Unskilled Manual	Total
	No. (%)	No. (%)	No. (%)	No. (%)
Ideological traditional	10 (17.24)	12 (20.69)	36 (62.07)	58 (100)
Ambivalent	25 (67.57)	7 (18.92)	5 (13.51)	37 (100)
Ambivalent progressive	13 (65.00)	6 (30.00)	1 (5.00)	20 (100)
Total	48 (41.74)	25 (21.74)	42 (36.52)	115 (100)

Table App. 4.13   Respondent's husband's educational level by group

Group	Educational level			
	High School completed + tertiary qualification[b]	High School completed	High School incomplete	Total
	No. (%)	No. (%)	No. (%)	No. (%)
Mt Druitt	5 (10)	2 (4)	43 (86)	50 (100)
Nth Shore	19 (76)	2 (8)	4 (16)	25 (100)
Employed	8 (32)	3 (12)	9 (36)	25 (100)
Feminist	12 (80)	2 (13.33)	1 (6.67)	15 (100)[a]
Total	49 (42.61)	9 (7.82)	57 (49.57)	115 (100)[a]

Notes: [a] Ten Feminist mothers are single.
[b] Tertiary qualification = bachelor's degree, higher degree or tertiary diploma.

Table App. 4.14   Respondent's husband's educational level by ideal type

Ideal type	Educational level			
	High School completed + tertiary qualification	High School completed	High School incomplete	Total
	No. (%)	No. (%)	No. (%)	No. (%)
Ideological traditional	11 (18.96)	1 (1.72)	46 (79.31)	58 (100)
Ambivalent	23 (62.16)	5 (15.00)	9 (4.06)	37 (100)
Ambivalent progressive	15 (75.00)	3 (15.00)	2 (10.00)	20 (100)
Total	49 (42.61)	9 (7.82)	57 (49.57)	115 (100)

Table App. 4.15 Respondent's occupation by group

Group	Occupation			
	Professional Managerial Self-Employed	Clerical Sales	Skilled Unskilled Manual	Total
	No. (%)	No. (%)	No. (%)	No. (%)
Mt Druitt	5 (10.00)	34 (68.00)	11 (22.00)	50 (100)
Nth Shore	12 (48.00)	13 (52.00)	0 (0.00)	25 (100)
Single	4 (17.39)	11 (47.83)	8 (34.78)	23 (100)[a]
Employed	13 (52.00)	7 (28.00)	5 (20.00)	25 (100)
Feminist	14 (70.00)	5 (25.00)	1 (5.00)	20 (100)[a]
Total	48 (33.57)	70 (48.95)	25 (17.48)	143 (100)[a]

Notes: [a] Never employed omitted.
[b] If respondent is employed at present this occupation is given, otherwise occupation before marriage or birth of children is given.

Table App. 4.16 Respondent's occupation by ideal type

Ideal type	Occupation			
	Professional Managerial Self-Employed	Clerical Sales	Skilled Unskilled Manual	Total
	No. (%)	No. (%)	No. (%)	No. (%)
Ideological traditional	8 (25.35)	43 (60.56)	20 (28.17)	71 (100)[a]
Ambivalent	22 (50.00)	18 (40.91)	4 (9.09)	44 (100)[a]
Ambivalent progressive	18 (64.29)	9 (32.14)	1 (3.57)	28 (100)[a]
Total	48 (33.57)	70 (48.95)	25 (17.48)	143 (100)[a]

Note: [a] Never employed omitted.

Table App. 4.17   Respondent's educational level by group

Group	Educational level			
	High School completed + tertiary qualification	High School completed	High School incomplete	Total
	No. (%)	No. (%)	No. (%)	No. (%)
Mt Druitt	3 (6.00)	5 (10.00)	42 (84.00)	50 (100)
Nth Shore	10 (40.00)	6 (24.00)	9 (36.00)	25 (100)
Single	3 (12.00)	7 (28.00)	15 (60.00)	25 (100)
Employed	11 (44.00)	2 (8.00)	12 (48.00)	25 (100)
Feminist	16 (64.00)	6 (24.00)	3 (12.00)	25 (100)
Total	43 (28.67)	26 (17.33)	81 (54.00)	150 (100)

Table App. 4.18   Respondent's educational level by ideal type

Ideal type	Educational level			
	High School completed + tertiary qualification	High School completed	High School incomplete	Total
	No. (%)	No. (%)	No. (%)	No. (%)
Ideological traditional	5 (6.94)	9 (12.50)	58 (80.55)	72 (100)
Ambivalent	20 (43.48)	9 (25.00)	17 (36.96)	46 (100)
Ambivalent progressive	18 (56.25)	8 (25.00)	6 (18.75)	32 (100)
Total	43 (28.87)	26 (17.33)	81 (54.00)	150 (100)

Table App. 4.19 Family income by group

Group	Income in $1000's			
	$20 000+	$10-20 000	$0-10 000	Total
	No. (%)	No. (%)	No. (%)	No. (%)
Mt Druitt	0 (0.00)	19 (38.00)	31 (62.00)	50 (100)
Nth Shore	11 (44.00)	13 (52.00)	1 (4.00)[b]	25 (100)
Single	0 (0.00)	3 (12.00)	22 (88.00)	25 (100)
Employed	8 (32.00)	15 (60.00)	2 (8.00)	25 (100)
Feminist	10 (40.00)	7 (28.00)	8 (32.00)	25 (100)
Total	29 (19.33)	57 (38.00)	64 (42.67)	150 (100)

Notes: [a] Income is per annum before tax.
[b] Husband had a stroke, he was an electronics engineer and is now a laboratory assistant, he can't read, write or speak.

Table App. 4.20 Family income by ideal type

Ideal type	Income in $1000's			
	$20 000+	$10-20 000	$0-10 000	Total
	No. (%)	No. (%)	No. (%)	No. (%)
Ideological traditional	2 (2.78)	25 (34.72)	45 (62.50)	72 (100)
Ambivalent	13 (28.26)	23 (50.00)	10 (21.74)	46 (100)
Ambivalent progressive	14 (43.75)	9 (28.12)	9 (28.12)	32 (100)
Total	29 (19.33)	57 (38.00)	64 (42.67)	150 (100)

Index

238

theory of women's position, 18–20,
204
White, Burton, 187–88
Wild, Ronald Arthur, 35, Appendix 1
Williams, Claire, 30, 34
Willmott, Peter, 34
Women's Electoral Lobby, 39, 97, 128,
158–60, 179–81, 197–99
Women's Liberation, 86, 88, 90,
158–59, 167, 179, 192, 198–99
as voluntary childlessness, 27, 30
women's
movement, 27, 78, 80, 86, 88, 97,
156, 197–98

refuges, 97, 149, 155, 160, 174
subordinate position, 16, 20, 40,
70–71, 140, 145–50, 173–74,
195–96, 202–3
Marxian view, 16–18
Weberian view, 18–20
working class
family studies, 34
mothers, 100–29, 168–74,
Appendix 1

Young, Michael, 34
young children need their mother's
constant care view, 60–67